Microsoft Excel
For Beginners

By Web Wise Seniors, Inc.
The Computer Training Specialists

TM

Web Wise Seniors, Inc.
305 Woodstock Rd.
Eastlake, Ohio 44095
www.WebWiseSeniors.com

©Copyright 2008 Web Wise Seniors, Inc.

Copyright

Trademarks

Limits of Liability/Disclaimer or Warranty

Sales Inquiries

For sales inquiries and special prices for bulk quantities, please call toll free (866) 232-7032.

Introduction

"The best computer class I have ever taken!" and "I never knew that computers could be explained so well!" are comments heard frequently from Web Wise Senior students. Since 2000, Web Wise Seniors has successfully taught thousands of beginning computer users. Now, the same teaching methods successful in Web Wise Seniors' courses are found in this easy to understand book.

This book is not a reference for Microsoft Excel. It is a learning guide for people of any age who are unfamiliar with the Microsoft Excel program, but is especially designed for seniors who want to be skilled in creating spreadsheets. It is like having a private instructor at your side as you walk through the basics of Excel with your book. It is full of common questions asked by beginners in actual classes, followed by easy to understand answers that have already helped thousands.

You only get so far by reading explanations and definitions. You need to actually use Microsoft Excel to learn to use it well. This book will help you do just that. It will help you get started using Microsoft Excel by walking you through the basic skills step-by-step while answering your "whys" and "whats" along the way.

Web Wise Seniors teaches basic computer classes every day. WWS instructors have seen first hand what works, what doesn't work, and what beginners want to know. We have draw on their knowledge, skills, and experience to write this book.

About the Authors

Web Wise Seniors is a company dedicated to teaching basic computer skills to individuals over the age of 50. Since 2000, Web Wise Seniors has filled over 25,000 classroom seats throughout Ohio and Pennsylvania, and has quickly become a premier computer education company for mature adults in the Midwest.

Classes have been designed for seniors by seniors and continually updated with the feedback of its students. By becoming an interactive part of the senior community and working closely with senior organizations throughout the Midwest, Web Wise Seniors has been able to develop a unique teaching style and curriculum that have been overwhelmingly successful.

Since 2000, over 97% of Web Wise Seniors students have stated they would recommend the program to their friends and family. 100% of affiliated teaching locations have been happy to work with the WWS program and, out of a 4 point scale, WWS received on average a 3.8 rating in student satisfaction.*

The same dedication and love of teaching that has made the WWS program so successful in the classroom is available for you in the pages of this book. Readers will find this book full of examples, illustrations, and easy to follow directions. This is a teaching guide, not just a manual or reference book.

*Student satisfaction as collected through WWS classes and events (2000 – 2008).

About this Book

Microsoft Excel for Beginners is designed to be read in order. Readers should begin with page one and continue through the book as if they were actually taking a computer course. The sections all relate and build upon each other.

Readers should keep a computer close at hand while reading *Microsoft Excel for Beginners*. We recommend you read through an entire section and then go back and try the steps outlined in the section.

Keep a pen or pencil handy too. Take notes and highlight any sections that you personally feel are important. This is your computer book and the more personal references you make within its pages, the better this course will work for you.

Above all, please enjoy *Microsoft Excel for Beginners*. Read at your own pace and keep at it. You'll be a spreadsheet wiz before you know it!

Meet Larry

Larry is the Web Wise Seniors mascot. He will be found throughout the pages of this book, helping you to "get the bugs out." Larry has been helping beginning computer users for over three years now. He runs the WWS help desk on www.WebWiseSeniors.com and often makes guest appearances in WWS publications.

In his spare time, Larry enjoys searching the Internet, e-mailing friends, and belly dancing.

Acknowledgements

We would like to thank the thousands of students who have challenged our computer instructors' minds in class. Your countless, and sometimes off-the-wall, questions and constructive feedback have made us better teachers. Without you, this book would not have been possible. Thank you!

We would also like to thank our family members for their insight, feedback and support.

Credits

Authors
Mary Pelton
Stephen Pelton

Book Design and Production
Michael Douglas
Stephen Pelton

Proof Reading
Jean Pelton

Clip Art
Microsoft Clip Art Gallery

Screen Shots
Microsoft Excel

Table of Contents

 Chapter 1: Let's Get Started!

Table of Contents

Chapter 2: Entering Data!

Chapter 3: Copying and Pasting!

Table of Contents

Chapter 4: Formulas and Calculations!

Table of Contents

Chapter 5: Saving, Opening, and Closing!

Chapter 6: Formatting Cell Data!

Table of Contents

Chapter 7: Resizing Rows & Columns

Table of Contents

Chapter 8: Worksheets

Chapter 9: Practice Entering and Formatting Data!

Table of Contents

Chapter 10: Filling In and Repeating Data!

Table of Contents

Chapter 11: Linking Worksheets!

Table of Contents

Chapter 12: Inserting & Deleting Rows and Columns!

Chapter 13: Hiding Data!

Chapter 14: Printing!

Table of Contents

Chapter 1

Let's Get Started!

What You Will Learn in this Chapter

- ✓ What is Microsoft Excel?
- ✓ Acquiring Microsoft Excel
- ✓ Opening Microsoft Excel
- ✓ The Various Sections of the Microsoft Excel Window
- ✓ Switching Worksheets

Chapter 1: Let's Get Started

Section 1: What is Microsoft Excel?

Before the advent of computers, accountants diligently penciled in data on columnar pads, which had as many as 13 columns and 40 rows per sheet. If one sheet couldn't hold all the data, the accountant used a second sheet, and then a third, etc. The data in each column and row was usually subtotaled on each sheet, with a grand total at the end of the entire document. When a number had to be changed, the accountant would painstakingly re-add, re-subtotal, and re-total the row and column that held the revised number. Accountants penciled in their data and used up a lot of erasers.

Spreadsheet software revolutionized the process. Spreadsheets are documents laid out in rows and columns. One worksheet on Microsoft Excel can store 16,384 columns and 1,048,576 rows of data. It can be used to add, subtract, divide, multiply, average, count, create charts, and perform many more functions, some of which are highly complex. Best of all, if you change a number, the totals update automatically.

Microsoft Excel is the spreadsheet program most commonly used in business today. Companies use Microsoft Excel to prepare profit and loss statements, budgets, balance sheets, statistical analysis, etc. However, spreadsheets are also an incredible tool for individuals who need an easy way to prepare personal budgets, track investments, record expenses, balance checkbooks, keep lists which can be automatically sorted (rearranged), etc. It is a user-friendly software package. Once you understand the structure of spreadsheets, you will discover that keeping records can be an enjoyable process. You may find yourself volunteering to keep your club's or organization's records simply because you can do it easily and well. Let the fun begin!

Chapter 1: Let's Get Started

Section 2: How to Acquire Microsoft Excel

Microsoft Excel is part of both the Microsoft Office Standard and Microsoft Office Professional software packages. Microsoft Office also includes Microsoft Word (a word processing program) and Microsoft PowerPoint (a slide presentation program). Microsoft Professional includes Excel, Word, PowerPoint, as well as Microsoft Outlook (an e-mail program), Microsoft Access (a data base program), and Microsoft Publisher (a program used to create signs, newsletters, etc). The Microsoft products are designed to work together to create and combine letters, charts, mailing lists, etc. Individuals who are proficient in all the Microsoft Office products and who can produce professional integrated documents are prized by industry. Most personal computers now come equipped with Microsoft Office.

If your computer did not come with Microsoft Office or Microsoft Office Professional and you do not intend to use any of the other Microsoft products, you can purchase Microsoft Excel separately at any computer store.

Section 3: Starting Microsoft Excel

How do you start the Excel spreadsheet program? The first step is to open the Start menu. The Start menu is accessed through the round button, displaying the Microsoft Windows logo, called the START button, located in the lower left corner of your desktop screen. The Start menu contains the option ALL PROGRAMS which includes a list of all the available programs on your computer. To display the list, position your mouse arrow directly on top of the

Chapter 1: Let's Get Started

ALL PROGRAMS option. The ALL PROGRAMS option will become highlighted in blue. Click your left mouse button and the computer will display a list of programs you can access. There are so many programs on the computer that a scroll bar will be displayed on the right side of the programs list. Use the scroll bar to locate the option MICROSOFT OFFICE. A small yellow folder will be located on the left side of the MICROSOFT OFFICE option. The yellow folder symbol indicates there are more options located within the folder. In the list, find the MICROSOFT OFFICE folder. Highlight the MICROSOFT OFFICE folder with the mouse and click the left mouse button. The list of Microsoft Office programs will be displayed. Locate the option MICROSOFT OFFICE EXCEL in the new list. It will have a green X symbol in a square next to its name. Place your mouse arrow on top of the MICROSOFT OFFICE EXCEL option. It will become highlighted in blue. Click your left mouse button. The menu will disappear and a blank Excel spreadsheet will be displayed.

NOTE: If you did not purchase one of the Microsoft Office packages (also called suites) there won't be a folder for Microsoft Office in the ALL PROGRAMS list. If the Microsoft Excel program was bought separately, the program's name will be displayed in the ALL PROGRAMS list. Place your mouse arrow on top of the MICROSOFT OFFICE EXCEL option and click the left mouse button to open Excel.

Starting Microsoft Excel: Step by Step Instructions
1. **Click the START button to open the Start menu.**
2. **Click the ALL PROGRAMS option.**
3. **Click the MICROSOFT OFFICE option.**
4. **Click the MICROSOFT OFFICE EXCEL option.**

Chapter 1: Let's Get Started

Starting Microsoft Excel: Visual Guide

**Step 1:
Click the
START button.**

**Step 2:
Click the ALL
PROGRAMS
option.**

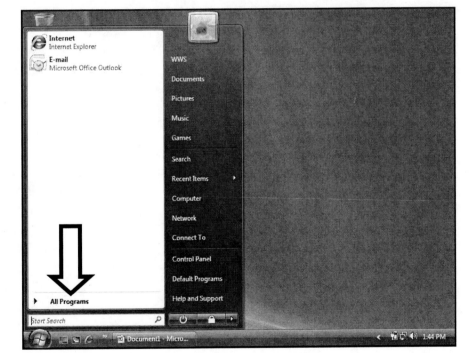

Step 3:
Click the
MICROSOFT
OFFICE
option.

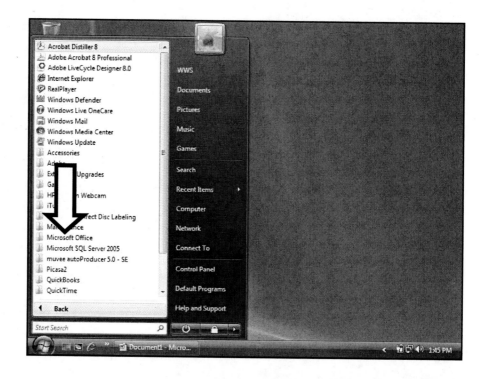

Step 4:
Click the
MICROSOFT
OFFICE
EXCEL option.

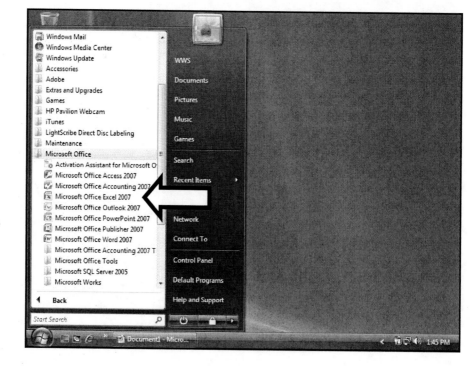

Chapter 1: Let's Get Started

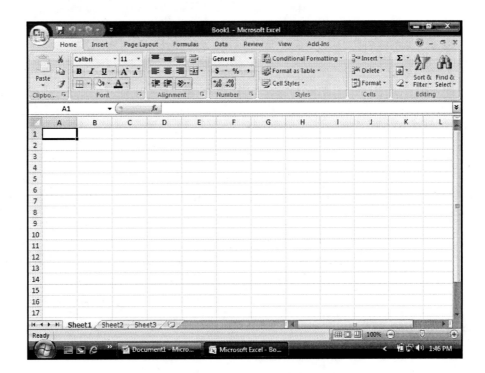

Microsoft Excel

Section 4: Microsoft Excel Screen Layout

Microsoft Excel is now open on your computer screen. Before you start typing data, take a moment to look at the basic layout. Look at the Title Bar of the program window. It is a bar at the top of your open screen/window. The title bar will read "Book1-Microsoft Excel." "Book1" is the generic name given to the blank spreadsheet. If you open another new blank spreadsheet, it will be assigned the name "Book2." The words Book, Workbook, or Spreadsheet are used interchangeably to describe a file created using Microsoft Excel. When you save the book for the first time, Excel will ask you to give the spreadsheet a new name. After completing the save process, the new name you selected will be displayed in the title bar of the Excel window.

Located in the upper left corner of the Microsoft Excel screen is a round circle adorned with the Microsoft Office symbol which consists of four multi-colored squares. This button is known as the Office button. It provides access to a *list* of very important functions which will be discussed throughout this book.

Just to the right of the Office button is the Quick Access Toolbar that displays buttons which work independently of the ribbons. The Quick Access Toolbar contains the Save button, the Undo typing button, and the Repeat typing symbol (commonly called the Redo button). If you make an error, you can simply click the Undo button and your latest instruction to the computer will be undone. This incredibly useful button will be discussed in more detail later in this book.

Office Button, Quick Access Toolbar, and Title Bar

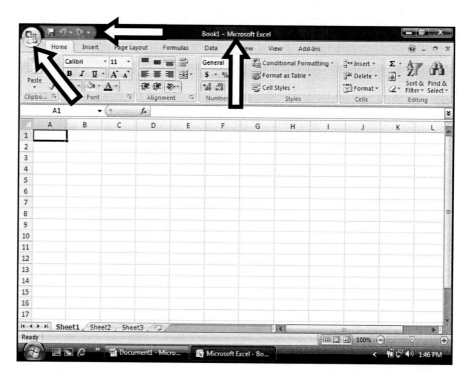

Located just below the title bar is the ribbon. The top of the ribbon contains a group of tabs which allows you to change the options being displayed on the ribbon. The ribbon has eight different tabs: Home, Insert, Page Layout, Formulas, Data, Review, View, and Add-Ins. If you look just below the tabs, you will see an area filled with tiny symbols and pictures. These tiny symbols and pictures make up the remainder of the ribbon. Each symbol on the ribbon represents a different function of Microsoft Excel. As you can see, Microsoft Excel has the ability to perform many different functions. As this book progresses, we will review many aspects of this ribbon.

Chapter 1: Let's Get Started

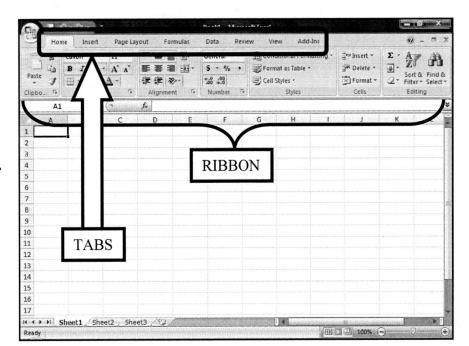

The RIBBON.

NOTE: The menus and toolbars used in earlier versions of Microsoft Office have been replaced by the Ribbon.

Overview of the Ribbon

The tabs located at the top of the ribbon control which symbols are displayed on the ribbon. If you place the mouse arrow on top of the Insert tab and click the left mouse button, a new set of symbols will be displayed on the ribbon. If you click on the Page Layout tab, another set of symbols will be displayed on the ribbon, and so on. In summary, the different tabs help categorize the numerous functions of Microsoft Excel.

Chapter 1: Let's Get Started

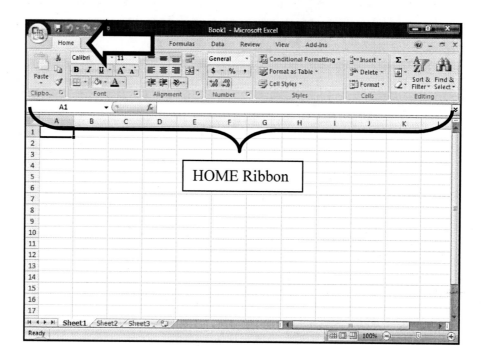

The HOME tab ribbon.

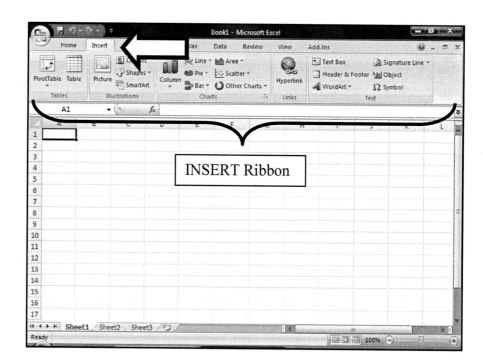

The INSERT tab ribbon.

Chapter 1: Let's Get Started

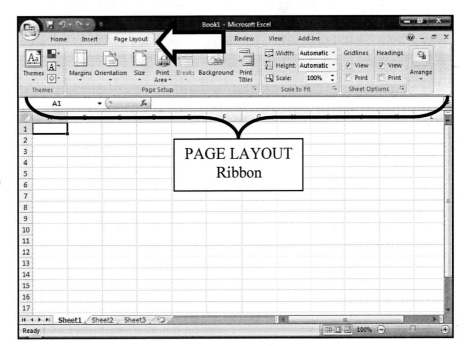

The PAGE LAYOUT tab ribbon.

You can select any of the options located on the ribbon by placing your mouse pointer over the desired option and clicking the left mouse button. When you position the mouse pointer over an option, it will become highlighted in orange. If you hold the mouse steady, without moving, a small balloon will appear to tell you the name of the option and a brief description of its use. To make the selection, just click the left mouse button and the action will be performed. At the bottom of the ribbon are category titles which give you a hint of what a particular set of options does.

Using the Ribbons: Step by Step Instructions
1. **Click a ribbon tab. (Example: The HOME tab.)**
2. **Move the mouse arrow over the ribbon.**
3. **Place the mouse arrow on top of the desired option.**
4. **Click the left mouse button.**

Chapter 1: Let's Get Started

Summary of the Ribbon Functions by Selected Tab

Overview of the Home Tab

1. **Clipboard** – Cut, Copy, Paste, Format Painter
2. **Font** – Font, Font size, Bold, Italicize, Underline, Color, etc.
3. **Alignment** – Alignment, Merge, Change Indent etc.
4. **Number** – Type of Number, Dollar, Percent, Increase/Decrease Decimal Point, etc.
5. **Styles** – Overall cell formatting using predetermined settings
6. **Cells** – Insert, Delete, Format
7. **Editing** – Sum, Sort, Find, Replace, Select

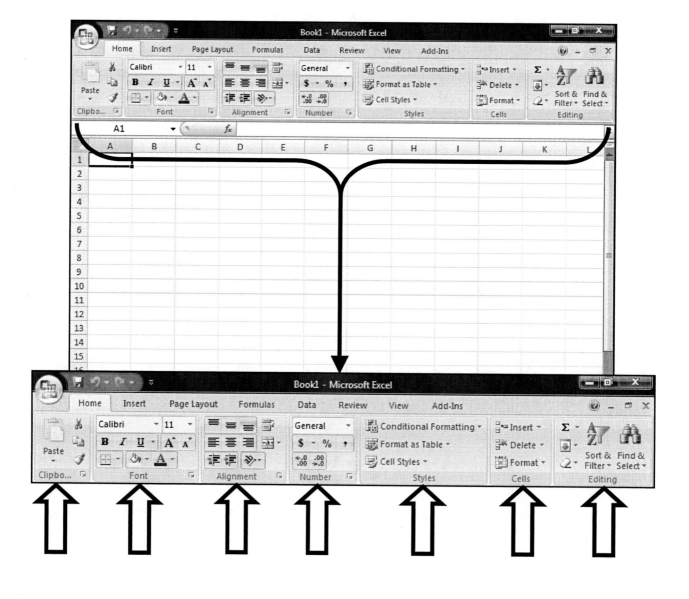

Chapter 1: Let's Get Started

Overview of the Insert Tab

1. **Tables – Insert a Table**
2. **Illustrations – Pictures, Clip Art, Shapes, etc.**
3. **Charts – Insert a Chart and other Chart options**
4. **Links – Hyperlink**
5. **Text – Word Art, Text Boxes, Signature Lines, Date, Time, Etc.**

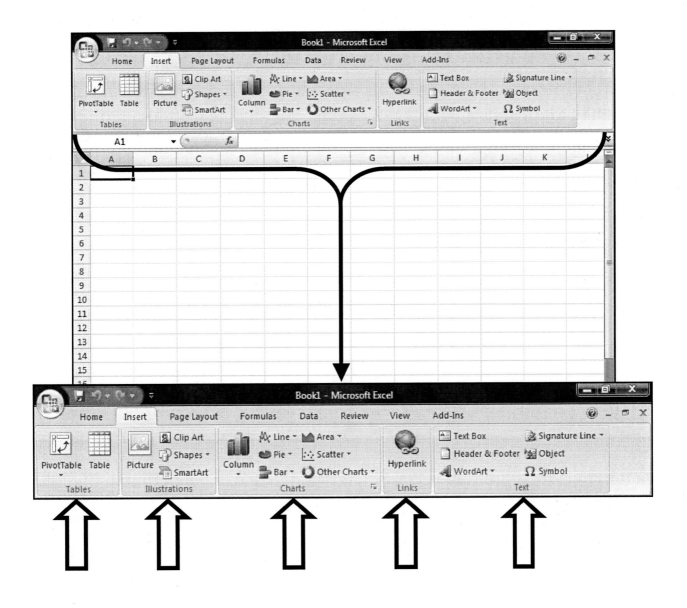

Chapter 1: Let's Get Started

Overview of the Page Layout Tab

1. **Themes** – Change the overall design of the document including colors, fonts, and effects
2. **Page Setup** – Margins, Page Orientation, Breaks, Print Area, etc.
3. **Scale to Fit** – Width, Height, Scale
4. **Sheet Options** – Guidelines, Headings
5. **Arrange** – Bring to front, align, etc.

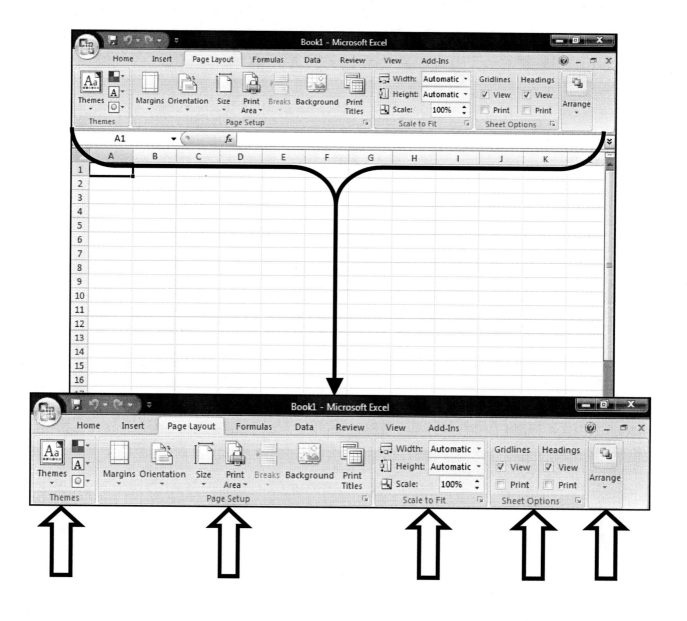

Chapter 1: Let's Get Started

Overview of the Formulas Tab

1. **Function Library** – Insert Function, AutoSum, Functions grouped by type
2. **Defined Names** – Define Name – a name is shorthand that makes it easier to understand the purpose of a cell reference, formula, etc.
3. **Formula Auditing** – Trace Precedents, Trace Dependents, etc.
4. **Calculations** – Calculation options

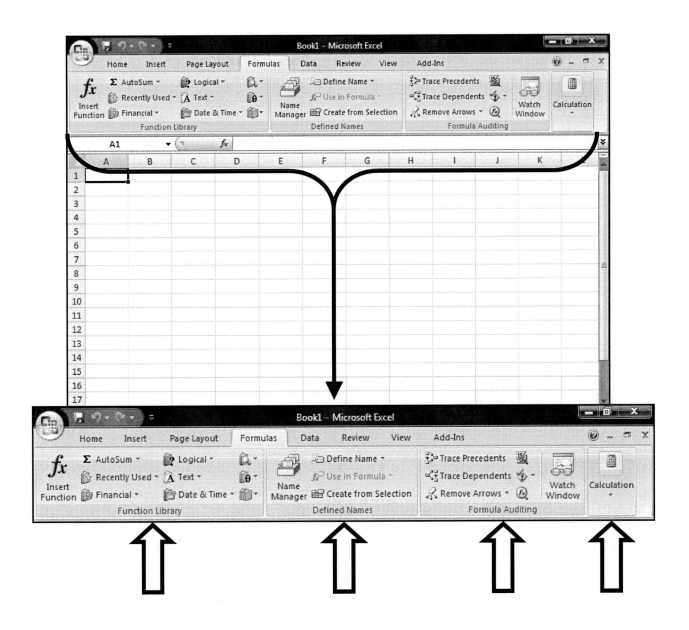

Chapter 1: Let's Get Started

Overview of the Data Tab

1. **Get External Data** – Import data options
2. **Connections** – Create and edit connections to external data sources that are stored in a workbook
3. **Sort & Filter** – Ascending/Descending Sort and Filter options
4. **Data Tools** – Text to Columns, Consolidate, etc.
5. **Outline** – Group, Ungroup, Subtotal

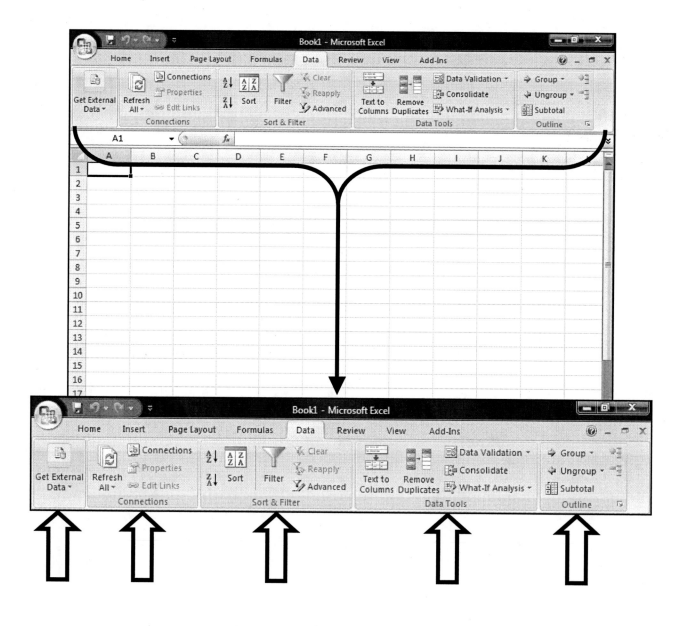

Chapter 1: Let's Get Started

Overview of the Review Tab

1. **Proofing** – Spell Check, Thesaurus, etc.
2. **Comments** – Add/delete/show comments on the spreadsheet
3. **Changes** – Track your revisions to the document and restrict other people from making specified changes to the document

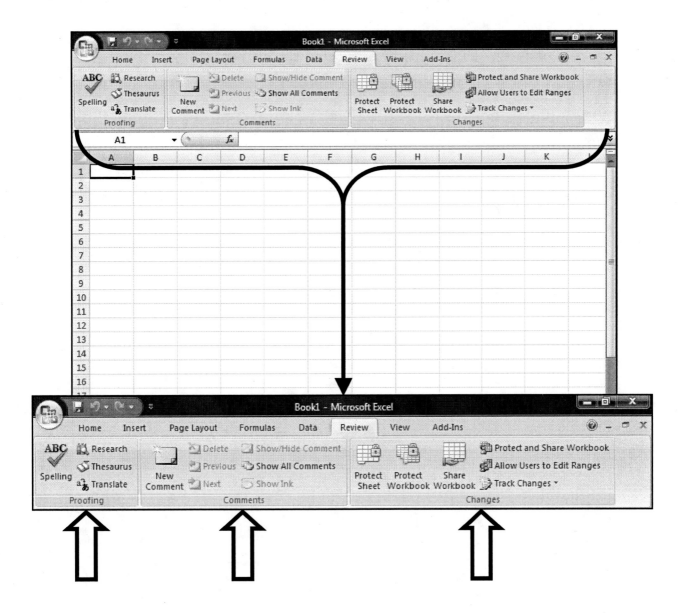

Chapter 1: Let's Get Started

Overview of the View Tab

1. **Workbook Views** – Normal, Page Layout, Page Break Preview, etc.
2. **Show/Hide** – Gridlines, Formula Bar, Headings
3. **Zoom** – Magnify or Shrink pages
4. **Windows** – Open New Window, Freeze Panes, Split Window, Tile All Windows on the Screen, etc.
5. **Macros** – Macro options

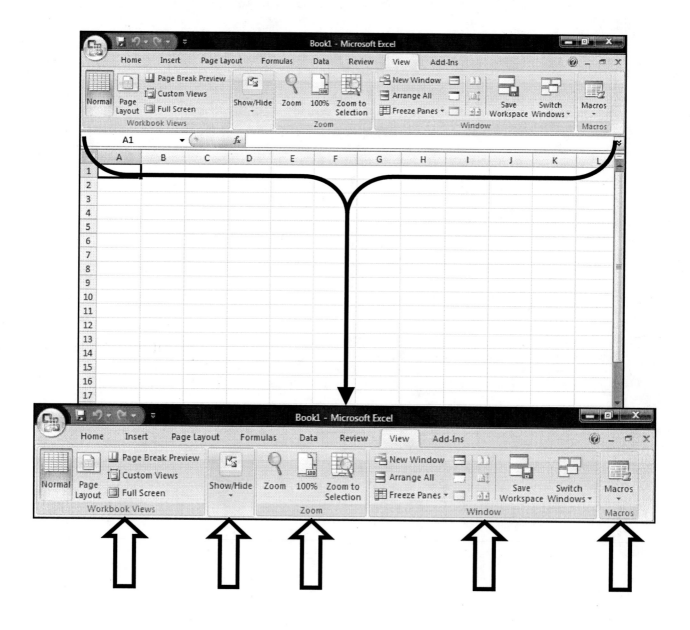

Chapter 1: Let's Get Started

Overview of the Add-Ins Tab

1. **Menu Commands** – Load or unload available add-ins into Excel. An add-in is a supplemental program that adds custom commands or features to a program.

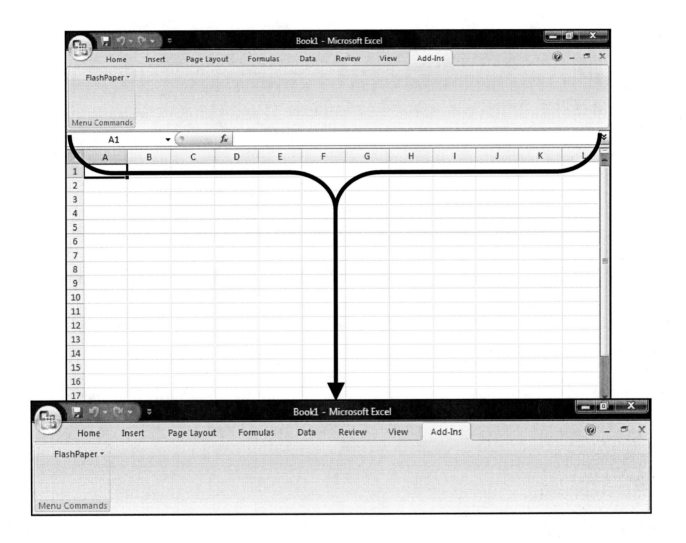

Chapter 1: Let's Get Started

Overview of the Office Button

Clicking the left mouse button one time on the OFFICE button will display a vertical list of options. The vertical list is divided into two sides. The left side consists of nine "file" options that enable you to open new spreadsheets, close spreadsheets, save your work, and more. The right side of the Office menu consists of a list of the most recently used Microsoft Excel documents.

Using the Office Button: Step by Step Instructions

1. Place the mouse arrow on top of the OFFICE button.
2. Click the left mouse button one time.
   - A vertical list of options will be displayed.
3. Place your mouse arrow over the desired option.
4. Click the left mouse button.

Using the Office Button: Visual Guide

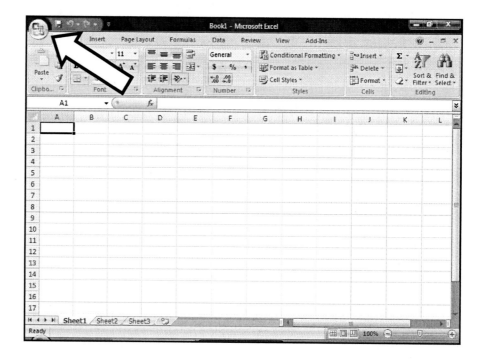

Click the OFFICE button.

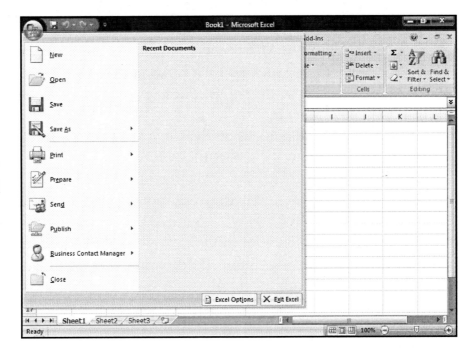

A vertical list of options will be displayed.

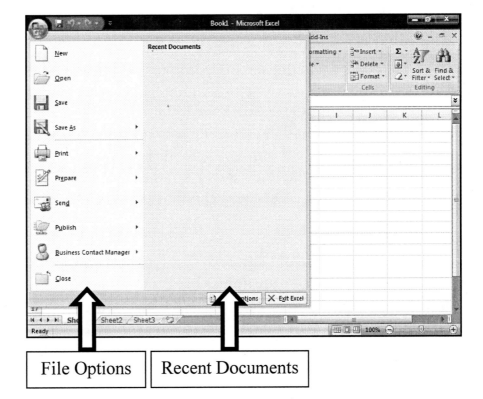

File options

File Options   Recent Documents

Chapter 1: Let's Get Started

Using the "File" Options under the Office Button

The left-hand side of the Office menu contains nine different "file" topics. Notice that some topics such as SAVE AS and PRINT have arrows next to them that are pointing to the right. These arrows tell you there is more information underneath that topic heading. To see the additional topics, take your mouse arrow and place it on the topic with the arrow. In this example, place your mouse arrow on top of PRINT. PRINT will become highlighted in orange and a submenu will appear displaying the various available print options. In this case there are three additional options: PRINT, QUICK PRINT, and PRINT PREVIEW. To move your mouse arrow into the submenu, you must slide your mouse arrow into the submenu without moving outside of your orange highlight. If you move the mouse arrow outside of the orange highlight, the submenu will disappear. If the submenu disappears, simply move your mouse arrow on PRINT and try again.

Once you have moved your mouse arrow into the submenu, you may then move your mouse arrow up and down within the submenu. Move your mouse arrow until it is directly on top of the desired option, and the option will become highlighted in orange. Click the left mouse button one time to activate the selected option. In this example, move your mouse arrow on top of the option PRINT. It will become highlighted when your arrow is on top of it. Once PRINT is highlighted, click the left mouse button one time to tell the computer that you would like to print your document. If you click successfully on the option PRINT, the print screen will open on your computer screen. Since we were only using the PRINT option as an example, click the close button to exit the print screen and continue on to the next section.

Using the "Formula" Bar

Located below the ribbon is another bar containing the Name Box and the Formula Bar. The Name Box displays the position of a selected cell. The Formula Bar shows the details of any data contained in a cell. As you enter data into a cell, the Formula Bar will display what you are typing. Immediately below the Formula bar is the Excel Work Area, displaying a blank spreadsheet where you will enter your data.

Chapter 1: Let's Get Started

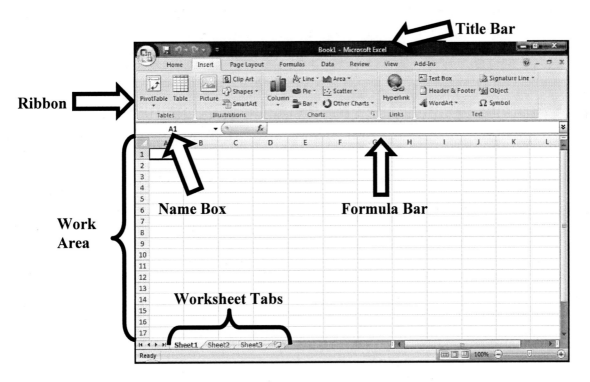

Below the work area is another bar which contains the worksheet tabs and a scroll bar. Each workbook (Excel document) is divided into worksheets (commonly called spreadsheets) which can be used to separate your data into sections. The worksheets start with the generic names of Sheet1, Sheet2, and Sheet3. Take a look at the worksheet tab named Sheet1. The Sheet1 tab has a white background indicating that Sheet1 is the active sheet. The active sheet is visible on screen at the present time, waiting for you to enter data. The tabs for Sheet2 and Sheet3 are light blue, indicating that they are inactive. Position the mouse pointer over the Sheet2 tab and click the left mouse button one time. The Sheet2 tab will turn white, and the Sheet1 tab will turn light blue. Sheet2 is now the visible/active worksheet. You can enter data on multiple worksheets and use the worksheet tabs to switch easily from one sheet to another. You will learn how to rename the worksheets, add additional worksheets, and link data contained on multiple worksheets later in this book.

Switching Worksheets: Step by Step Instructions
1. **Position the mouse pointer over the desired worksheet tab located near the bottom left side of the Excel window.**
2. **Click on the left mouse button and the corresponding worksheet will be displayed on the screen.**

Chapter 1: Let's Get Started

Switching Worksheets: Visual Guide

Step 1:
Position the mouse pointer over the desired worksheet tab.

Step 2:
Click the left mouse button to display the worksheet.

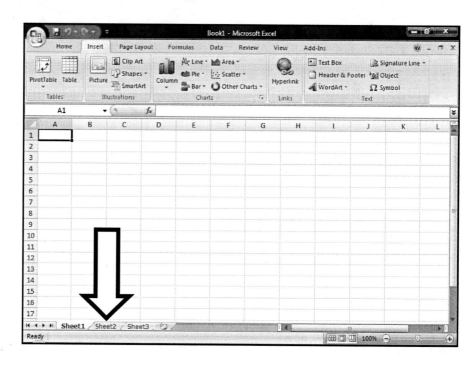

Repeat Steps 1 and 2 to display another worksheet.

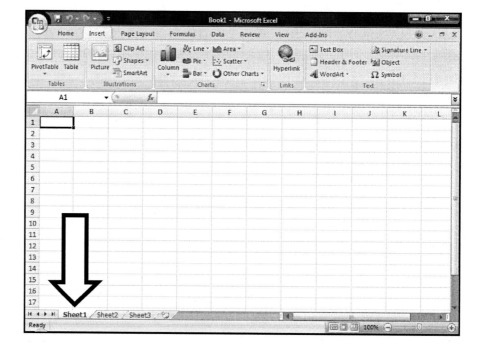

Chapter 1: Let's Get Started

To the right of the worksheet tabs is the horizontal scroll bar. The horizontal scroll bar is used to move your screen to the right and left (horizontally). When you are working on a large spreadsheet, you will not be able to see all the columns and rows on the screen at one time. The number of columns and rows you can see depends upon your screen size, settings, and the length of the data contained in the cells. You should be able to view approximately 12 columns and 24 rows on a blank worksheet. You can view the data which is not visible on the screen by using the scroll bar. By moving the horizontal scroll bar, you will be able to see the remaining 16,362 columns available on the Excel worksheet.

To the far right side of the Work Area is the vertical scroll bar. The vertical scroll bar enables you to move the viewing area of the worksheet up and down (vertically) to display additional rows of the worksheet. The vertical scroll bar provides the means to view the remaining 1,048,532 rows available on the current worksheet.

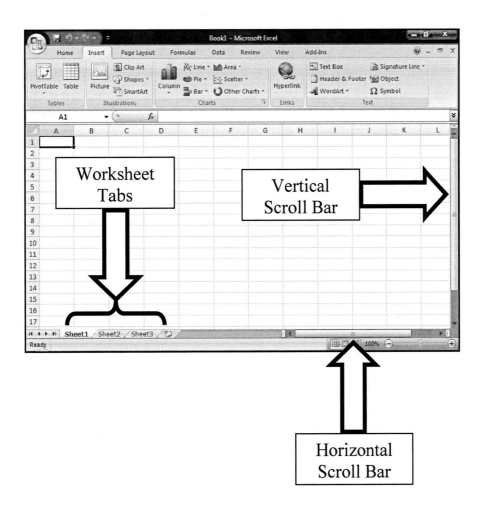

Spreadsheet Layout

- **Office Button** – contains the main features of the program including Save, Print, Open, and Close.
- **Ribbon** – contains pictures/icons used for easy access to the options/features of Excel including Formatting, Copy, Paste, Insert, Insert Function, etc.
- **Name Box** – displays the selected cell's position.
- **Formula Bar** – displays the details of the data you are entering into the selected cell.
- **Work Area** – contains the cells in which you will be entering data.
- **Worksheet Tabs** – separate your data into sections (each spreadsheet initially has three worksheets).
- **Horizontal Scroll Bar** at the bottom of the worksheet – moves your screen to the right and left so that you can see data that is outside of the screen viewing area.
- **Vertical Scroll Bar** on the right side of the worksheet – moves your screen up and down so that you can see data that is above or below the screen viewing area.

Chapter 2

Entering Data!

What You Will Learn in this Chapter
- ✓ Entering Data Into Excel
- ✓ Selecting Cells
- ✓ Correcting Data

Chapter 2: Entering Data!

Section 5: Entering Data

To understand Microsoft Excel, you must understand the worksheet layout. The basic worksheet layout of Microsoft Excel consists of columns (vertical) rows (horizontal) and cells (where the column and row join). You must select a cell to tell the computer where on the worksheet you desire to enter data.

- Columns are named using letters, from A through XFD
- Rows are named using numbers, from 1 through 1,048,576.
- Cells are named by the intersection of the column letter and the row number. For example, C5 = column C, row 5. F16 = column F, row 16.

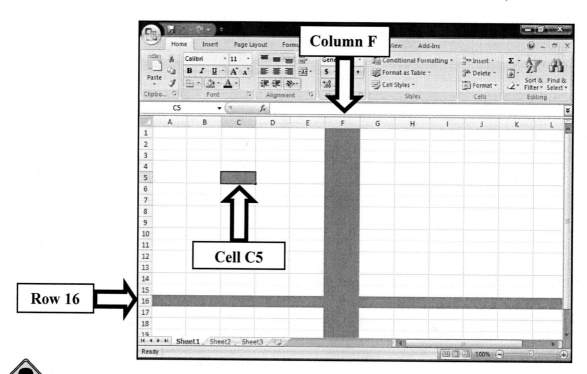

WARNING: Older versions of Microsoft Excel only have 256 columns and 65,536 rows. If you save a Microsoft Excel 2007 worksheet to an older version, all data that is outside the limits of the older versions will be lost.

Section 6: Selecting Cells Using the Arrow Keys

First, you need to learn how to move from one cell to another. When you start a new Excel spreadsheet, your cursor will automatically be on cell A1. Look at the upper left corner of the spreadsheet – there is a black border around the first cell in Column A, Row 1. Also, the cell address "A1" is shown in the Name Box located immediately above and to the left of the main work area. Use your arrow keys to move your cursor around the screen and note how the cell address changes each time you move. The arrow keys are the simplest way to move around the spreadsheet.

NOTE: You can also move to another cell by using your mouse. Simply move your cursor to the cell you want to select, and click your left mouse button once.

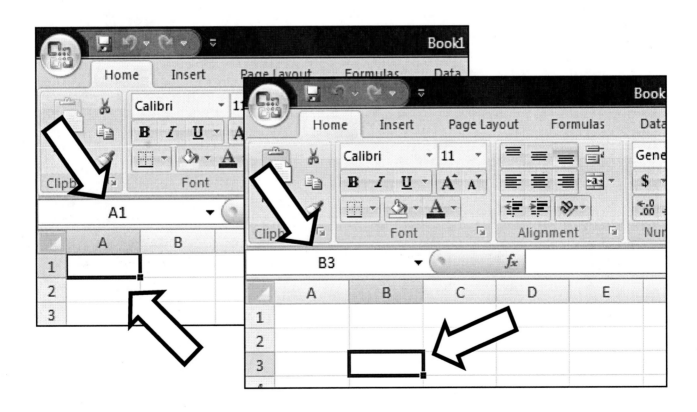

Chapter 2: Entering Data!

Section 7: What Can You Type Into A Cell?

You can type words (text), numbers, and/or symbols into a cell. A cell that contains only words or letters is considered a text cell. Text cells are commonly used to label rows and columns on a worksheet. In a few moments you are going to begin creating a budget for a typical household. Before you begin typing in the specific numbers, you will label the rows and columns. The labels will indicate what the data in each specific row or column represents. Labels are text cells placed at the top of a column or to the far left of a row. If you enter numbers without labels, when you look back later you may not know what those numbers represent.

A spreadsheet cell can also contain numbers. A cell which contains only numbers can be used in calculations. The majority of the data entered into a spreadsheet are numbers. In the example budget, you will enter both income and expenses for a household. After the specific numbers are input, you will calculate how much extra money is left. Any cell which consists of numbers only can be used in the calculation.

Symbols (+ - / * @ %) can also be typed into a spreadsheet cell. Symbols are used in Excel to perform mathematical calculations. Limit the use of symbols until you are ready to perform a calculation.

NOTE: You may combine text and numbers in one cell, for instance "M28468" or "Salary 1,000" but Excel will identify the cell containing text and numbers as a text cell. A cell which contains text cannot be used in calculations. So, if you intend to use specific cells in a calculation, it is important to keep the text in other, separate cells.

Chapter 2: Entering Data!

NOTE: If you want to type a number or symbol into a cell and not have it treated as a typical number or calculation, you should begin by typing in a single quotation mark '. The single quotation mark indicates that the number or symbol in the cell should be treated as text. The single quotation mark will not appear in the cell, but can be seen in the Formula Bar.

Excel aligns the data in a cell differently depending on which type of data the cell contains. Text will be aligned to the left side of the cell. Numbers will automatically be aligned to the right side of the cell. The alignment of the data within the cell helps you identify whether the data is considered text or a number.

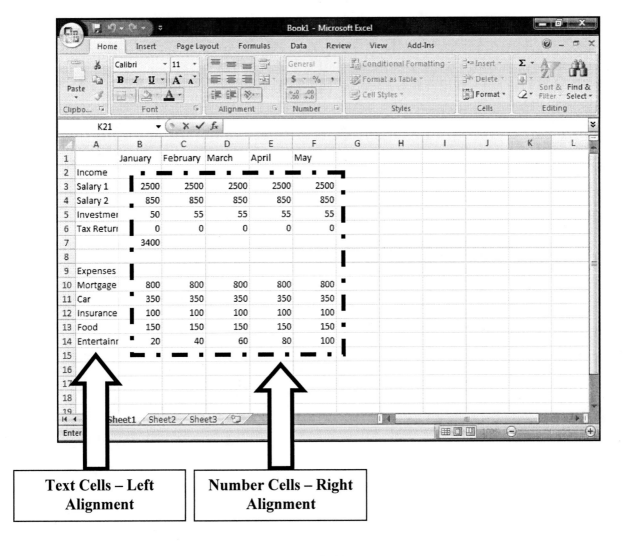

Text Cells – Left Alignment

Number Cells – Right Alignment

Chapter 2: Entering Data!

Now that you understand the basic layout of an Excel spreadsheet, you can begin entering data for the example household budget. The first step is always to select the cell in which you desire to type. Remember the selected cell will have a thick bold black border. Use the arrow keys on the keyboard to move the cell selection indicator (cursor) to cell B1. The bold black border around the cell will indicate the cell is selected.

To begin the example, add labels at the top of columns B through E. Each column will represent one month of the year. Once cell B1 is selected, type the word "January" into the cell. Using the right arrow key on the keyboard, move to cell C1. Label column C "February" by typing the month in cell C1. Continue to use your right arrow key to move to the adjacent cells. Type "March" into cell D1 and "April" into cell E1. Later, you will learn how to automatically fill-in the dates/months instead of having to type in each one.

Entering Data into a Cell: Step by Step Instructions
1. Select the cell where you desire to type.
   - The selected cell will have the bold black border.
2. Type the data in the cell.
3. Repeat steps 1 and 2 to add additional data to the spreadsheet.

Chapter 2: Entering Data!

Entering Data into a Cell: Visual Guide

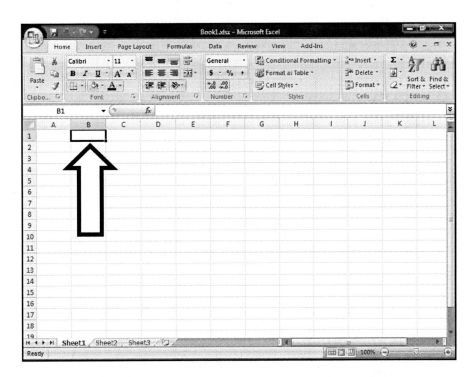

Step 1:
Select the cell where you desire to type. The selected cell will have the bold black border.

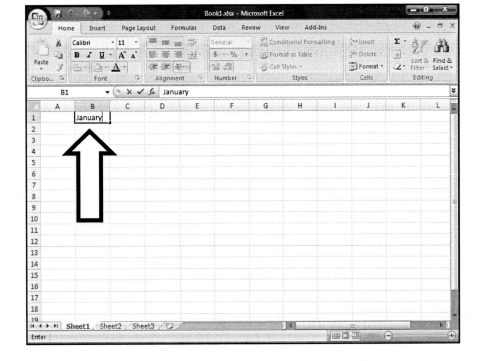

Step 2:
Type the data into the cell.

Repeat steps 1 & 2 to add additional data to the spreadsheet.

Step 1:
Select the cell where you desire to type.

Step 2:
Type the data into the cell.

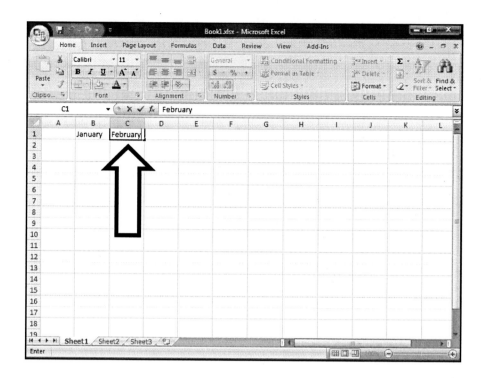

Repeat steps 1&2 to add additional data to the spreadsheet.

Step 1:
Select the cell where you desire to type.

Step 2:
Type the data into the cell.

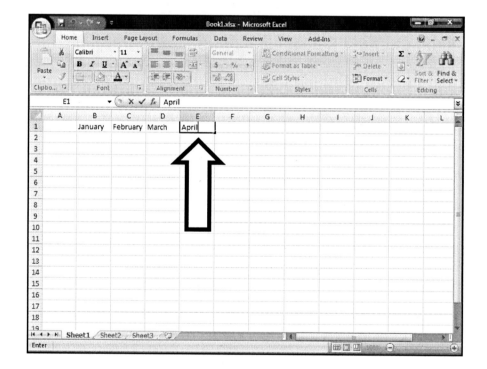

Now, add labels to the rows on the spreadsheet to indicate what income and expenses will be included in the example household budget. Using the left arrow key on the keyboard, move back into the first cell in Column 1. Look at

Chapter 2: Entering Data!

the Name Box. A1 should be displayed in the box. Use the down arrow key to move to cell A2. Type the word "Income."

NOTE: While you are typing the data into a cell, what you are typing is also being displayed in the Formula Bar located at the top of the screen. The Formula Bar allows you to see the entire contents of the selected cell.

Repeat the steps to enter the data, listed in the following table, into the spreadsheet. Remember to use the arrow keys to move the cell selector to the appropriate cell before you begin typing.

Cell	Data
A3	Salary 1
A4	Salary 2
A5	Investments
A6	Tax Return
Skip two lines (cells A7&A8)	
A9	Expenses
A10	Mortgage

Cell	Data
A11	Car
A12	Insurance
A13	Food
A14	Entertainment
Skip two lines (cells A15&A16)	
A17	Net Income

You may notice that the word "Entertainment" does not fit into cell A14. That is okay. If there is nothing in the adjoining cell, the word "Entertainment" will overflow into the adjacent cell. If there is something in the adjoining cell, the overflowing word will be cut off at the edge of the cell. You will learn how to increase the size of the columns and rows to fit the entire text later in the book. Congratulations, you have completed the basic budget outline.

Entering Data into a Cell: Step by Step Instructions
1. **Select the cell where you desire to type.**
   - **The selected cell will have the bold black border.**
2. **Type the cell data.**
3. **Repeat steps 1 and 2 to add additional data on the spreadsheet.**

Chapter 2: Entering Data!

Entering Data into a Cell: Visual Guide

Step 1:
Select the cell
where you
desire to type.

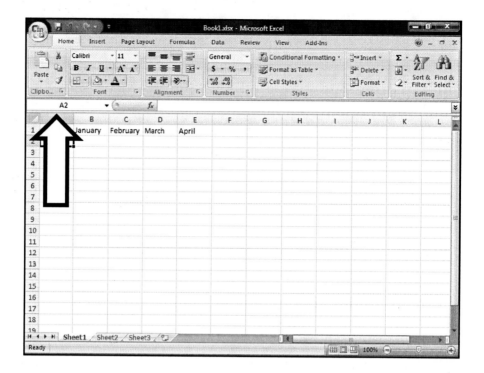

Step 2:
Type the data
into the cell.

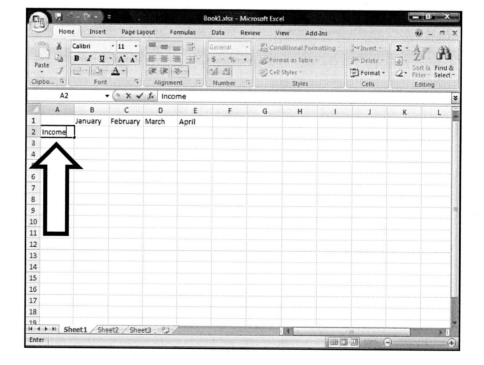

Chapter 2: Entering Data!

Repeat steps 1 & 2 to add additional data to the spreadsheet.

Step 1:
Select the cell where you desire to type.

Step 2:
Type the data into the cell.

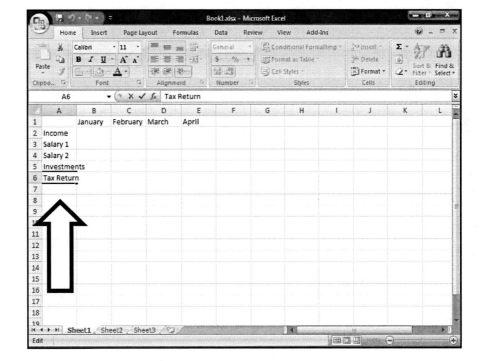

Repeat steps 1 & 2 to add additional data to the spreadsheet.

Step 1:
Select the cell where you desire to type.

Step 2:
Type the data into the cell.

Chapter 2: Entering Data!

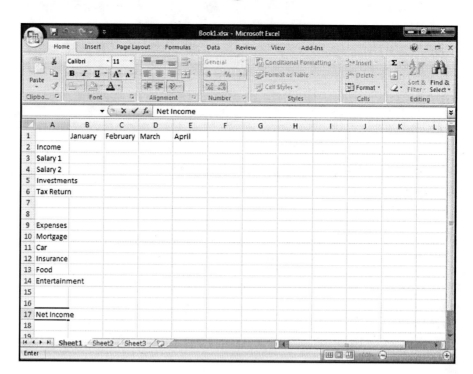

Repeat steps 1 & 2 to add additional data to the spreadsheet.

Finished Budget Outline.

Section 8: Correcting Mistakes

Occasionally you will misspell a word while you are typing and not notice until later. At that point, you have two options. The first option is to select the cell containing the misspelled word and simply retype the word. Anything currently contained within the cell will automatically be replaced when you begin typing. The newly typed word will replace the misspelled word.

If the data you have typed in the cell is long or cumbersome to retype, you may prefer a second option. Since the data contained within a selected cell is displayed in the Formula Bar, you can move the cursor into the Formula Bar to the position of the mistake. The Formula Bar is just like a sheet of paper, and the cursor can be repositioned to the appropriate location within the text. You can use the Backspace key or the Delete key on the keyboard to erase the mistake and type the correction. The best way to understand this principle is with a demonstration. If you want to change the word "Entertainment" in cell

Chapter 2: Entering Data!

A14 to "Entertaining" without typing the whole new word, you have to use the Formula Bar.

To do this, first select cell A14 using the arrow keys. Look in the Formula Bar at the top of the screen. The word "Entertainment" will be displayed in the Formula Bar. Move the mouse pointer over the Formula Bar and position the mouse pointer between the n and m in the word "Entertainment." The location of the mouse pointer will determine the position of the blinking cursor. Click the left mouse button. The Formula Bar will become the active work area, and the blinking cursor will appear.

If the cursor is not positioned next to the letter m, use the arrow keys on the keyboard to move the cursor to the correct position. Press the delete key until the letters "ment" are erased, and then type in the letters "ing." When you have made the correction, and "Entertainment" has been changed to "Entertaining," press the Enter key on the keyboard to tell the computer you are finished and to exit the Formula Bar. Your correction will now be displayed in the cell A14.

Option 1:
Correcting Mistakes within a Cell: Step by Step Instructions
1. Select the cell where the mistake occurred. The selected cell will have the bold black border.
2. Type the correct data into the cell.

Option 2:
Correcting Mistakes within a Cell: Step by Step Instructions
1. Select the cell where the mistake occurred. The selected cell will have the bold black border.
2. Position the mouse pointer over the Formula Bar at the location of the mistake.
3. Click the left mouse button to activate the Formula Bar and to drop the blinking cursor at the location of the mouse pointer.
4. Erase the mistake using the Delete or Backspace key on the keyboard. (Remember: The Backspace key erases to the left of the cursor and the Delete key erases to the right.)
5. Type the correction.
6. Press the Enter key on the keyboard.

Chapter 2: Entering Data!

Correcting Mistakes within a Cell: Visual Guide

Step 1:
Select the cell where the mistake occurred.

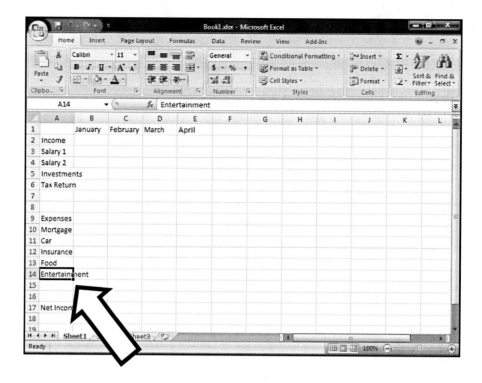

Step 2:
Position the mouse pointer over the Formula Bar at the location of the mistake.

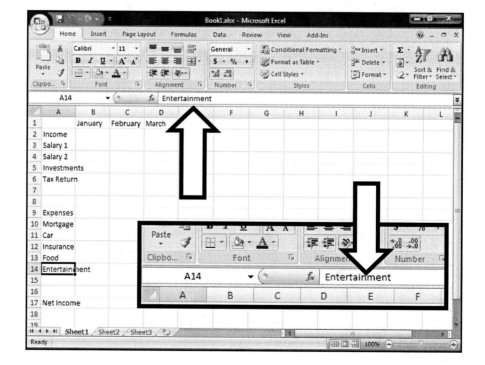

Chapter 2: Entering Data!

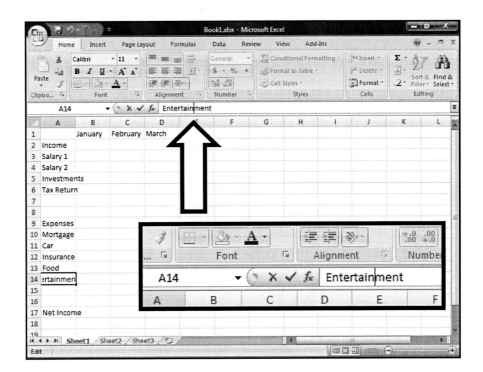

Step 3:
Click the left
mouse button.

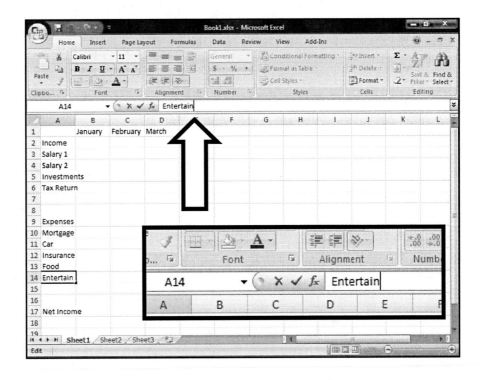

Step 4:
Erase the
mistake using
the Delete or
Backspace key
on the
keyboard.

Chapter 2: Entering Data!

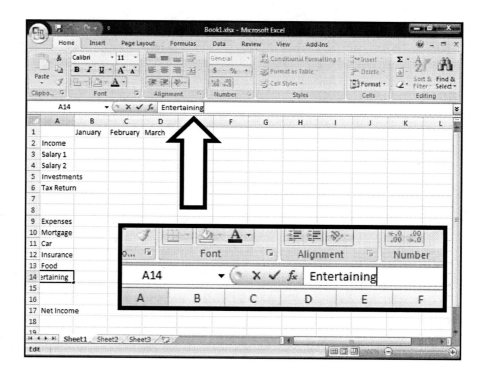

Step 5:
Type the
correction.

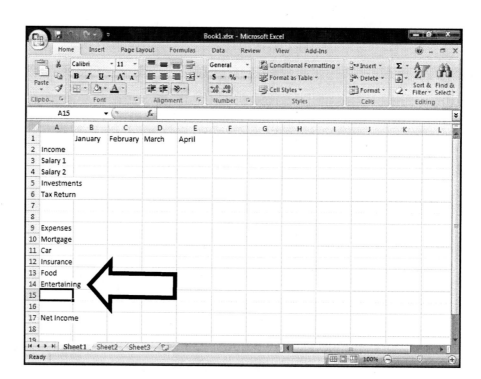

Step 6:
Press the Enter
Key on the
keyboard.

Using Option 1 for correcting mistakes, change "Entertaining" back to "Entertainment" by selecting cell C14 and retyping the word.

Chapter 2: Entering Data!

Section 9: Selecting Cells Using the Mouse

Now, begin to enter the specific budget numbers into the spreadsheet. This time, instead of using the arrow keys to select the cell in which to type, try using the point and click method via the mouse.

The point and click method is accomplished by moving the mouse pointer over the cell you desire to select. When the mouse is in the correct location on the spreadsheet, click the left mouse button to select the cell. The bold, black selection box will appear around the chosen cell. Once the cell has been selected, you can type in the cell data. For the example, move your mouse pointer over cell B3 and click your left mouse button. Notice, cell B3 will have the thick black box surrounding the cell. Type the monthly salary -- in this example 2,500. To move to another cell, simply move your mouse onto the cell and click your left mouse button to select it.

To continue with the example, select cell B4. Position your mouse pointer over cell B4 and click the left mouse button. Type the number 850 in cell B4. Continue using the point and click method to select cells and enter the values found in the following table. Remember, if you not sure which cell is currently selected, look at the Name Box located at the top of the screen.

Cell	Data
B5	50
B6	0
Skip three lines (cells B7&B9)	
B10	800

Cell	Data
B11	350
B12	100
B13	150
B14	20

Entering Data into a Cell: Step by Step Instructions

1. Select the cell where you desire to type. The selected cell will have the bold black border.
2. Type the data into the cell.
3. Repeat steps 1 and 2 to add additional data to the spreadsheet.

Chapter 2: Entering Data!

Entering Data into a Cell: Visual Guide

Step 1:
Select the cell where you desire to type.

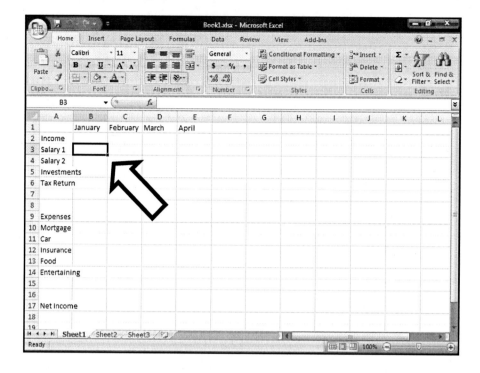

Step 2:
Type the data into the cell.

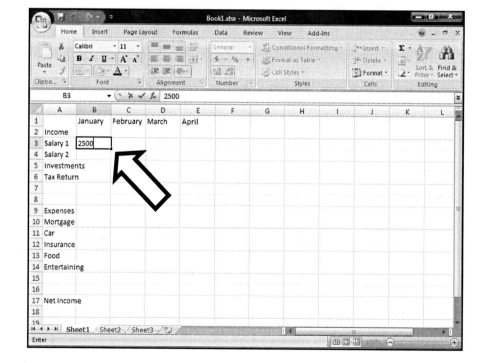

Chapter 2: Entering Data!

Repeat steps 1 & 2 to add additional data to the spreadsheet.

Step 1:
Select the cell where you desire to type.

Step 2:
Type the data into the cell.

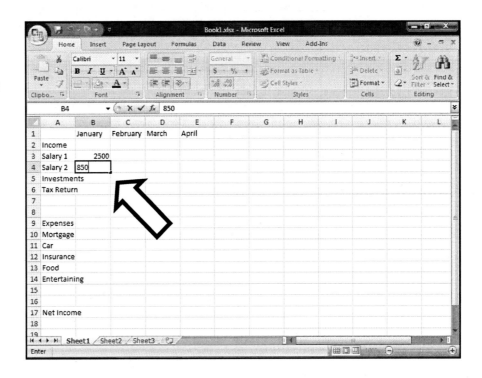

Repeat steps 1 & 2 to add additional data to the spreadsheet.

Step 1:
Select the cell where you desire to type.

Step 2:
Type the data into the cell.

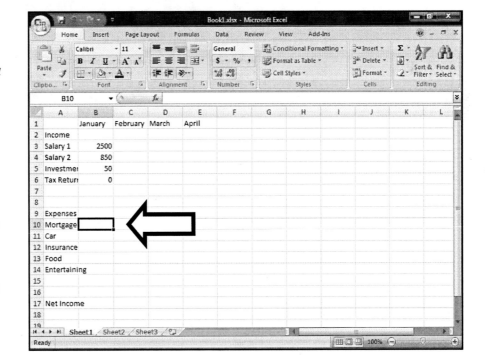

Chapter 2: Entering Data!

Repeat steps 1 & 2 to add additional data to the spreadsheet.

Step 1:
Select the cell where you desire to type.

Step 2:
Type the data into the cell.

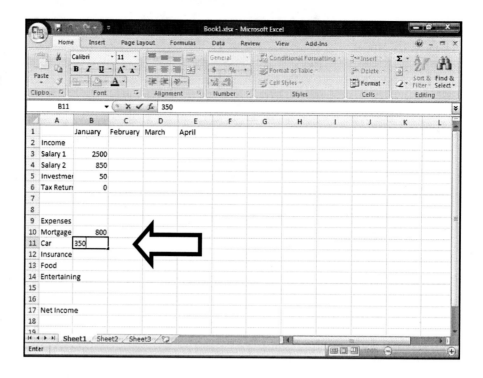

Finished January Budget

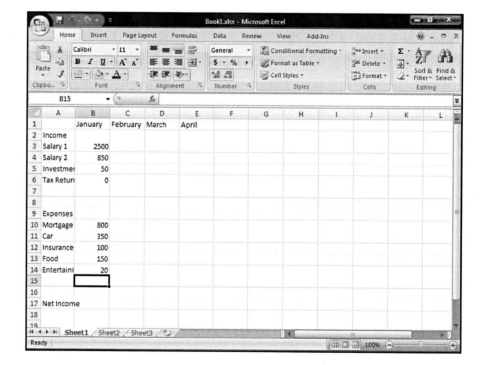

Section 10: Entering Data Using the Enter Key

Move into the next column. Position the mouse pointer over the cell you desire to select, in this example cell C3, and click the left mouse button to select the cell. The bold, black selection box will appear around cell C3. Once the cell has been selected, type in the monthly salary -- in this example 2,500. Now, instead of using your arrow key or cursor to select the next cell, simply press the Enter key on the keyboard. Excel is programmed to move down to the cell immediately below the selected cell each time you press the Enter key.

Continue with the example and type in the data located in the following table. Remember to press the Enter key on the keyboard to move the next cell. If you are not sure which cell is currently selected, look at the Name Box located at the top of the screen.

Cell	Data
C4	850
C5	55
C6	0
Skip Three lines (cells C7-C9)	
C10	800

Cell	Data
C11	350
C12	100
C13	150
C14	40

Entering Data into a Cell: Step by Step Instructions
1. Select the cell where you want to type. The selected cell will have the bold black border.
2. Type the data into the cell.
3. Press the Enter key located on the keyboard.
4. Repeat steps 1, 2, and 3 to add additional data to the spreadsheet.

Chapter 2: Entering Data!

Entering Data into a Cell: Visual Guide

Step 1:
Select the cell where you desire to type.

Step 2:
Type the data into the cell.

Step 3:
Press the Enter key.

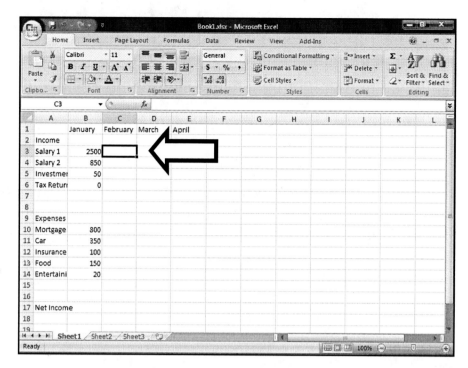

Repeat steps 1, 2, & 3 to add additional data to the spreadsheet.

Step 1:
Select the cell where you desire to type.

Step 2:
Type the data into the cell.

Step 3:
Press the Enter key.

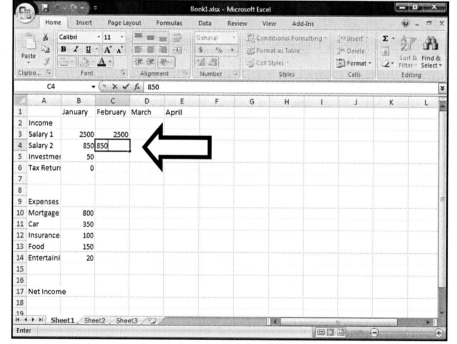

Chapter 2: Entering Data!

Repeat steps 1, 2, & 3 to add additional data to the spreadsheet.

Step 1:
Select the cell where you desire to type.

Step 2:
Type the data into the cell.

Step 3:
Press the Enter key.

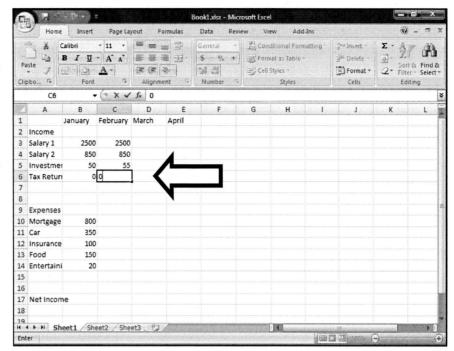

Repeat steps 1, 2, & 3 to add additional data to the spreadsheet.

Step 1:
Select the cell where you desire to type.

Step 2:
Type the data into the cell.

Step 3:
Press the Enter key.

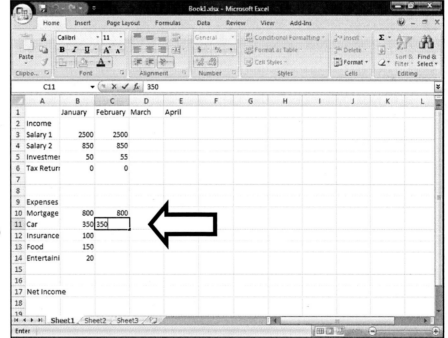

Chapter 2: Entering Data!

Repeat steps 1, 2, & 3 to add additional data to the spreadsheet.

Step 1:
Select the cell where you desire to type.

Step 2:
Type the data into the cell.

Step 3:
Press the Enter key.

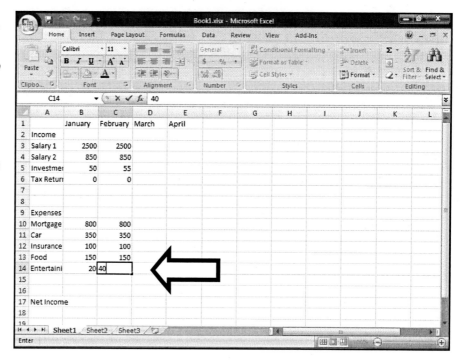

Chapter 3

Copying and Pasting!

What You Will Learn in this Chapter
- ✓ Copying and Pasting
- ✓ Copying and Pasting Cell Data
- ✓ Highlighting Cell Data
- ✓ Copying and Pasting Multiple Cells

Chapter 3: Copying and Pasting!

Section 11: Copying and Pasting Cell Data

Assume your budget is the same for the remaining months. Instead of retyping the data in the remaining cells, you can use the Copy and Paste option in Excel. The Copy and Paste option allows you to select data, copy it into the computer's memory, and then paste the data into another cell, or multiple cells, on the spreadsheet.

In the example, you are going to use the mouse to select and copy the data located in cell B3. Move the mouse pointer over cell B3 and press the left mouse button. The bold, black selection box will appear around the chosen cell. Once the cell has been selected, move your mouse pointer over the copy button located on the ribbon. The copy option looks like two pieces of paper, one on top of the other.

Position the mouse pointer over the COPY option and click the left mouse button one time. The selected cell data will be copied into the computer's memory. Take a moment to look at the selected cell. The cell border is moving, indicating that you have successfully copied the data contained within the cell. The computer is now awaiting instructions to specify where the copied data should be placed.

Move your mouse pointer over cell D3 and click your left mouse button. The bold, black selection box will appear around cell D3 indicating the cell has been selected. Once the cell has been selected, move your mouse pointer over the Paste option located on the left side of the ribbon. The paste option looks like a clipboard with a sheet of paper on it. Position the mouse pointer over the PASTE option and click the left mouse button once. Notice the data from cell B3 has been copied into cell D3.

Chapter 3: Copying and Pasting!

Copying & Pasting: Step by Step Instructions
1. Highlight the cell containing the data you want to copy.
2. Click on the COPY option.
3. Select the cell where you want the copied text to be placed.
4. Click on the PASTE option.

Copying & Pasting: A Visual Guide

Step 1:
Highlight the cell containing the data you want to copy.

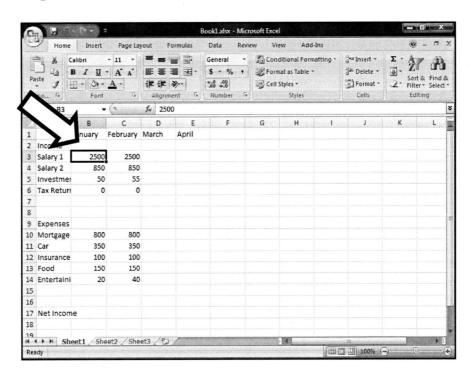

Chapter 3: Copying and Pasting!

Step 2:
Click the COPY
option.

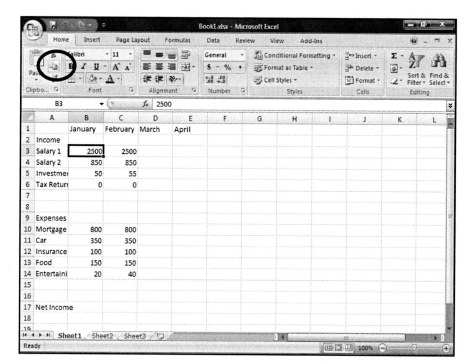

Step 3:
Select the cell
where you want
the copied text
to be placed.

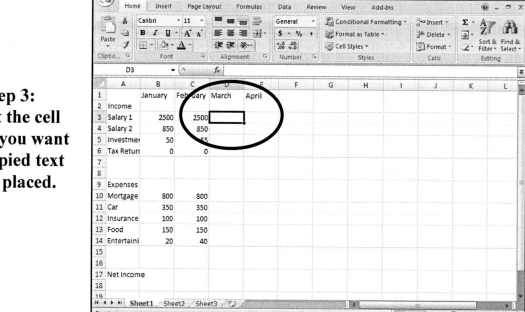

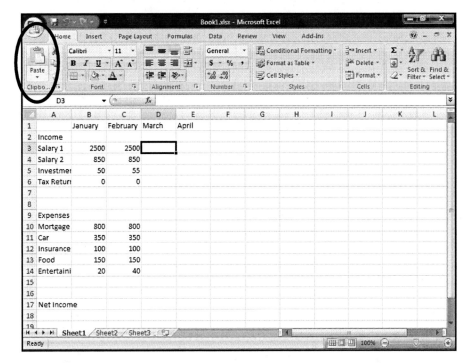

Step 4:
Click the
PASTE option.

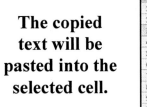

The copied
text will be
pasted into the
selected cell.

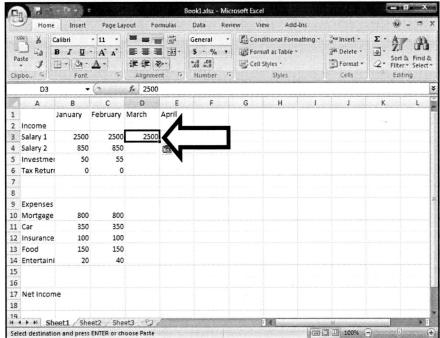

Chapter 3: Copying and Pasting!

For practice, move the mouse pointer over cell E3 and click the left mouse button. Cell E3 will become highlighted. Then select the PASTE option on the ribbon using the mouse. Notice, the same data you copied from cell B3 has been pasted into cell E3. As long as the cell you copied the data from still has the rotating border, the data is still stored in the computer's memory.

Copying & Pasting: Step by Step Instructions

1. **Highlight the cell containing the data you want to copy.**
2. **Click on the COPY option.**
3. **Select the cell where you want the copied text to be placed.**
4. **Click on the PASTE option.**

Copying & Pasting: A Visual Guide

Steps 1 and 2 were completed in the last example.

Step 3: Select the cell where you want the copied text to be placed.

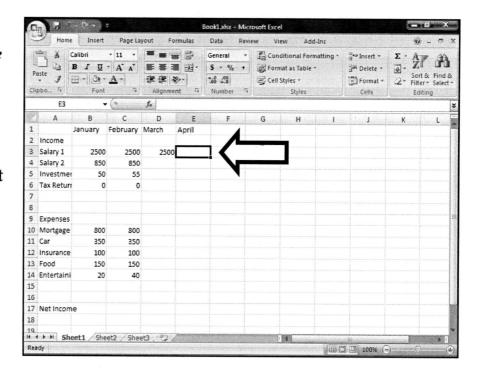

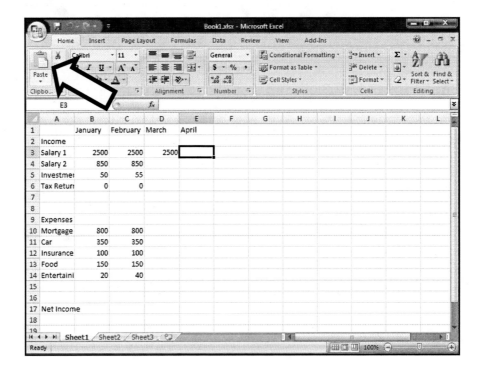

**Step 4:
Click on the
PASTE option.**

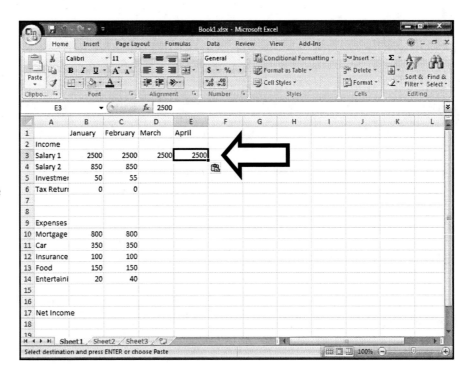

**The copied
text will be
pasted into the
selected cell.**

Now that you have successfully copied and pasted the value of "Salary 1" from cell B3 into cells D3 and E3, you can either repeat the process to fill in the data for the remaining cells or you can copy and paste data from multiple cells at one time. Copying and pasting data from multiple cells uses the same basic steps as are used to copy and paste data from one cell to another. The only exception is that you need to select multiple cells before you copy the data into the computer's memory. The process of selecting multiple cells is called highlighting. Once you have selected/highlighted the desired cells, the values can be copied into the computer's memory at one time and then pasted into the spreadsheet. You will quickly see that the process of copying and pasting data from multiple cells helps save time and effort.

Section 12: Highlighting Data

Highlighting is the process used to tell the computer what data on your spreadsheet you intend to work with. When text is highlighted, it may be cut, copied, bolded, italicized, and more. To highlight data, position your mouse arrow at the first cell you desire to select. Click and HOLD DOWN the left mouse button. While holding down the mouse button, move your mouse arrow to the last cell containing data you want to highlight. As the mouse moves over the cells, they will become highlighted (will change background color). After reaching the last cell of the desired data, release the mouse button. The selected cells will remain highlighted until you click your mouse on another cell in the spreadsheet. The computer is now ready for you to work with this selected data.

When you highlight data, the computer is only concerned with the data between where you began holding down the left mouse button and the exact point at which you released the left mouse button. Think of these positions as two dots. Anything between these dots will be highlighted. How you move from one location to another (left to right, or right to left) doesn't matter. The computer only focuses on the area between those two dots.

When you highlight more than one cell, you are selecting a "range" of cells. Now, try to highlight cells B4 thru B14 using the mouse. To begin the highlighting process, position the mouse pointer over cell B4. Click and hold down your left mouse button. While holding down the mouse button, move the mouse pointer over the desired cells ending on cell B14. The first cell will remain white, but all of the other cells will change color (become highlighted). Release the mouse button when the mouse arrow is positioned over cell B14. Cells B4 through B14 are highlighted.

Highlighting these cells will enable you to copy the cell data into the computer's temporary memory. Once the data is copied, you can paste it into cells D4 through D14. Copying and pasting the data into these cells will quickly enable you to fill in the values for the month of March on the example budget.

WARNING: Don't release the left mouse button until all of the desired cells have been highlighted. Releasing the button will stop the highlighting process before you have included all the desired cell data, and you will have to start the highlighting process over again.

NOTE: The only thing more important than knowing how to highlight cell data is knowing how to un-highlight the cells. If you accidentally highlight an area, click your mouse once anywhere in the spreadsheet. Clicking in an unhighlighted area will remove all the highlighting on the spreadsheet.

Highlighting Your Data: Step by Step Instructions

1. Position the mouse at the first cell you desire to select.
2. Click and hold down the left mouse button.
3. Move the mouse to the last cell you desire to select.
4. Release the mouse button.
   - The thick black outline surrounding the cells indicates the cells have been highlighted.

Chapter 3: Copying and Pasting!

Highlighting Your Data: Visual Guide

Step 1:
Position the mouse at the first cell you desire to select.

Step 2:
Click and hold down the left mouse button.

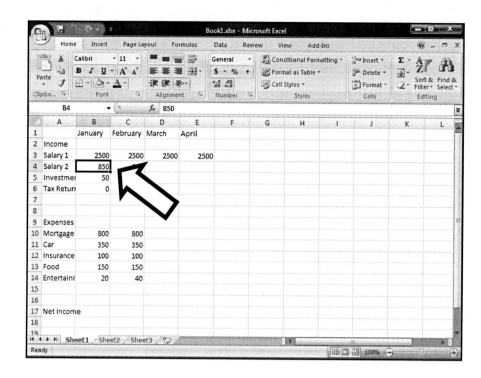

Step 3:
Move the mouse to the last cell you desire to select.

Step 4:
Release the left mouse button

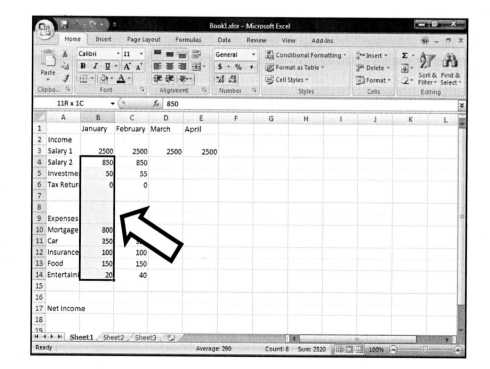

Chapter 3: Copying and Pasting!

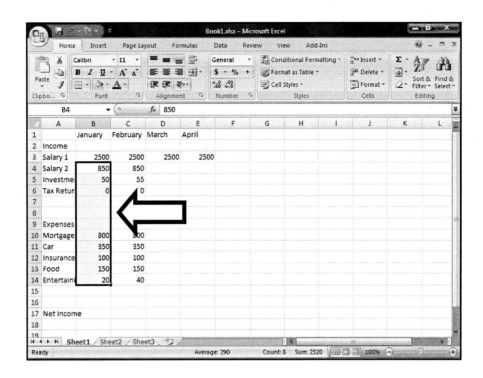

The thick black outline surrounding the cells indicates the cells have been highlighted.

Section 13: Copying and Pasting Data from Multiple Cells

In the last section you successfully highlighted cells B4 through B14. Use the mouse to copy the highlighted data located in cells B4 through B14. When the cells have been selected, position the mouse pointer over the COPY option and click the left mouse button one time. The menu will close and the selected cell data will be copied into the computer's memory. Take a moment to look at the selected cells. The cell border is moving, indicating that you have successfully copied the data contained within the cells. The computer is now awaiting instructions to specify where the copied data should be placed.

Chapter 3: Copying and Pasting!

Move your mouse pointer over cell D4 and click your left mouse button. The bold, black selection box will appear around the cell D4 indicating the cell has been selected. Once the cell has been selected, position the mouse pointer over the PASTE option and click the left mouse button one time. Notice the data from cells B4 through B14 has been copied into cells D4 through D14.

Copying & Pasting: Step by Step Instructions
1. **Highlight the cells containing the data you want to copy.**
2. **Click the COPY option.**
3. **Select the cell where you want the copied data to be placed.**
4. **Click the PASTE option.**

Copying & Pasting: A Visual Guide

Step 1:
Highlight the cells containing the data you want to copy.

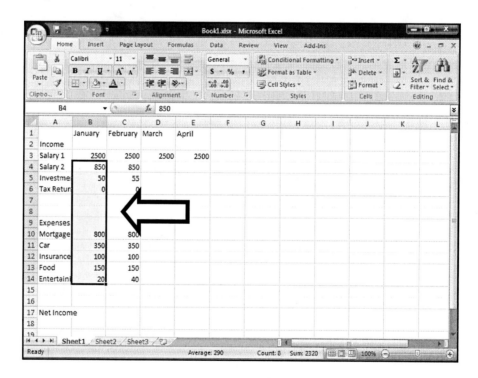

**Step 2:
Click the
COPY option.**

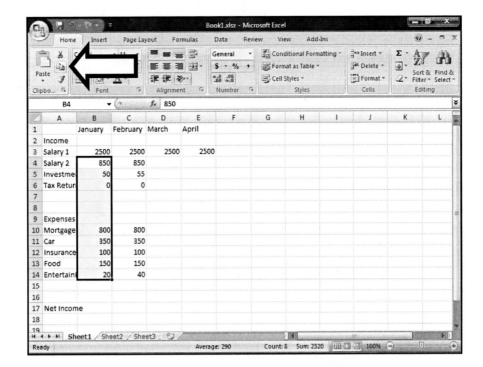

**The copied cells
will have a
moving dashed
line
surrounding
the cells.**

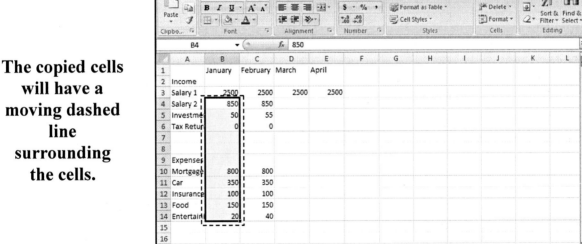

Chapter 3: Copying and Pasting!

Step 3:
Select the cell where you want the copied data to be placed.

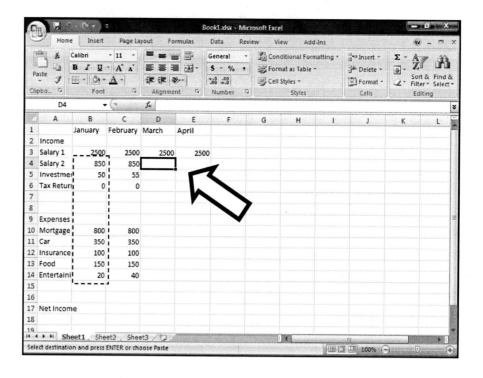

Step 4:
Click the PASTE option.

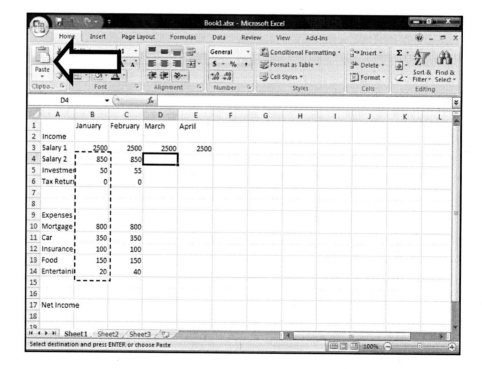

Chapter 3: Copying and Pasting!

The copied cell data will be pasted into the new cells.

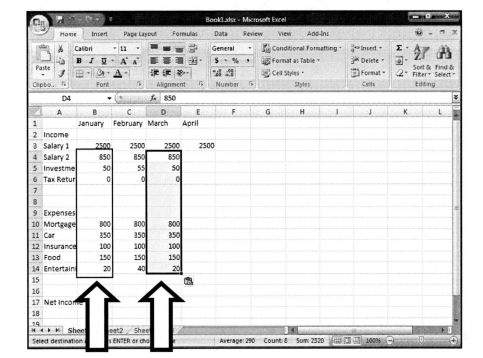

You still need to enter the data into the cells for the month of April in the example budget. Since the data contained in cells B4 thru B14 is still in the computer's memory, move the mouse pointer over to cell E4 and click the left mouse button. The bold, black selection box will appear around cell E4 indicating the cell has been selected. Once the cell has been selected, position the mouse pointer over the Paste option and click the left mouse button one time. Notice the data from cells B4 through B14 has been copied into cells E4 through E14.

Chapter 3: Copying and Pasting!

Step 3:
Select the cell
where you want
the copied data
to be placed.

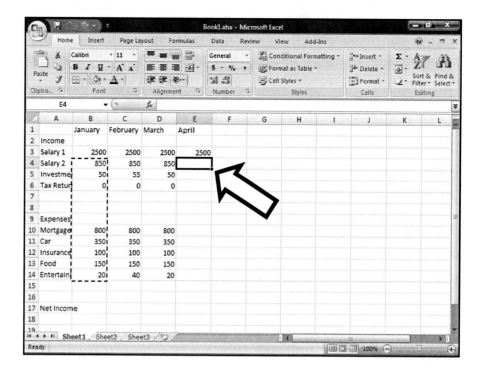

Step 4:
Click the
PASTE option.

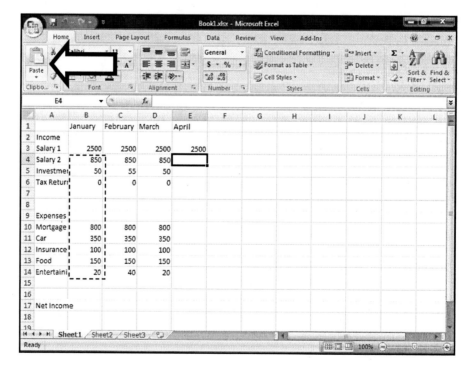

Chapter 3: Copying and Pasting!

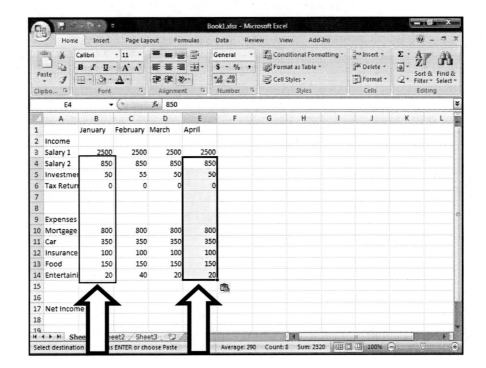

The copied cell data will be pasted into the new cells.

The data in the example spreadsheet is perfect, with one exception. Row 14 (Entertainment) should not repeat the same data each month. It increases monthly, as often happens with monthly expenses. You previously entered 20 in cell B14 and 40 in cell C14. Cell D14 should contain the number 60 and cell E14 should contain the number 80. Utilizing what you learned in Chapter 2, use your mouse to select the cell in which you desire to enter or edit data. Once the cell is selected, type in the correct value. Type 60 in cell D14; then type 80 in cell E14.

Entering Data into a Cell: Step by Step Instructions
1. Select the cell where you desire to type. The selected cell will then have the bold black border.
2. Type the data into the cell.
3. Repeat steps 1 and 2 to add additional data to the spreadsheet.

Chapter 3: Copying and Pasting!

Entering Data into a Cell: Visual Guide

Step 1:
Select the cell where you desire to type.

Step 2:
Type the data into the cell.

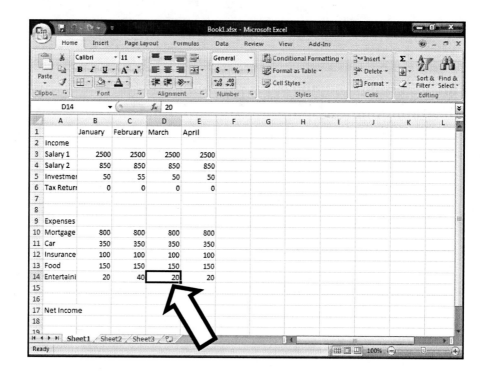

Repeat steps 1 & 2 to add additional data to the spreadsheet.

Step 1:
Select the cell where you desire to type.

Step 2:
Type the data into the cell.

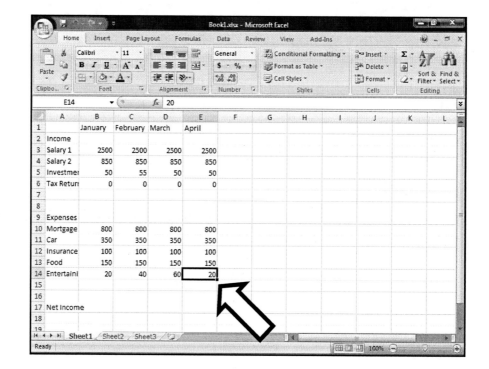

Example Budget

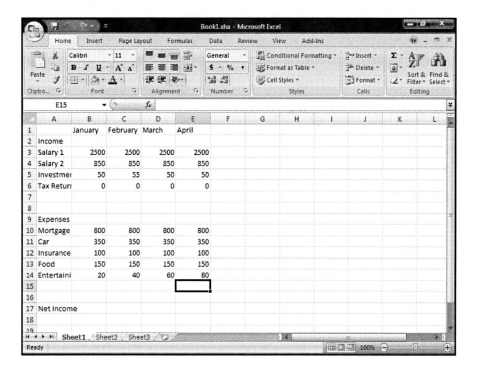

Chapter 3: Copying and Pasting!

Chapter 4

Formulas and Calculations!

What You Will Learn in this Chapter
- ✓ Performing Basic Calculations
- ✓ Creating a Formula by Manually Typing Values
- ✓ Creating a Formula by Manually Inputting Cell References
- ✓ Creating a Formula by Selecting Cells
- ✓ Copying and Pasting Formulas
- ✓ The Standard Symbols Used in Mathematical Calculations

Chapter 4: Formulas and Calculations!

Section 14: Basic Calculations

The true power of the Microsoft Excel becomes apparent when you perform calculations on data entered into a spreadsheet. Excel can perform basic calculations like addition and subtraction or very complicated calculations such as payment schedules and financial ratios. The level of complexity depends on what information you need to obtain from the data.

Before you can begin to create a formula, you must first decide which cell will display the answer. Don't be intimidated with the term formula – it is simply a set of instructions, usually directing the computer to calculate data. It is not uncommon for Excel enthusiasts to use the terms formula and calculation interchangeably. Using the mouse, position the mouse pointer over the desired cell and click the left mouse button. A thick black boarder will appear around the cell indicating the cell has been selected. After the cell has been selected, you can begin to enter the formula.

Begin the new formula by typing either an equal = sign or a plus + sign. Either of these symbols at the beginning of the line indicates that you are about to create a formula. The equal = sign and plus + sign are located on top line of your keyboard (just to the left of your backspace key). You may also use the plus + key located on your number pad at the far right of your keyboard. Once you have typed in the equal = sign or a plus + sign, you can enter or select the values you want to use in the calculation.

NOTE: Although it does not matter whether you use an equal = or plus + sign to start your formula, Excel will automatically change the first symbol to an equal = sign when you leave the cell.

Chapter 4: Formulas and Calculations!

NOTE: The plus + sign is called a mathematical operator. It instructs the computer to add the numbers. Other mathematical operators are the minus – sign (subtract), the asterisk * (multiply) and slash / (divide).

Section 15: Creating a Formula by Manually Typing in Values

The easiest way to learn how to create a formula in Excel is to walk through an example. Using the sample budget, you will calculate the total income for January. Move your mouse pointer to cell B7 and click the left mouse button to select the cell. You will calculate the answer by typing in the income values (numbers) manually. To tell the computer you are going to create a formula, type in an equal = sign. After the equal sign, type in the values for the calculation manually. Between each number, type a plus sign to indicate you want to add the numbers together. The example calculation for the month of January is =2500+850+50+0. After you have typed in all the values, press the Enter key on the keyboard to tell the computer to perform the calculation. The total 3400 will appear in cell B7. To view the equation for the cell, click the mouse on the cell B7. Look at the Formula Bar near the top of the Excel window and to the right of the Name Box. The Formula Bar will display the entire mathematical equation you typed in the cell.

Manually Typing a Formula: Step by Step Instructions
1. Click on the cell in which you want to place a formula.
2. Type an "equal sign" (=) to indicate that you are creating a formula.
3. Type in the formula manually (example: =300+50+200+800).

Chapter 4: Formulas and Calculations!

4. Press the Enter key on the keyboard. The computer will calculate the answer.

Manually Typing a Formula: Visual Guide

Step 1:
Click on the cell in which you want to place a formula.

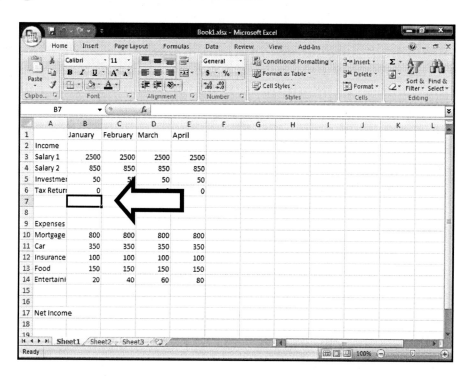

Step 2:
Type in an "equal sign" (=).

Step 3:
Type the formula manually.

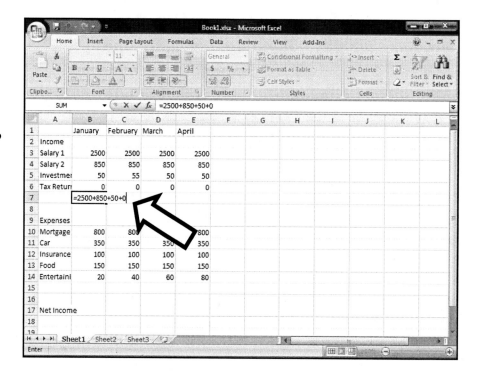

Chapter 4: Formulas and Calculations!

Step 4:
Press the Enter
key on the
keyboard.

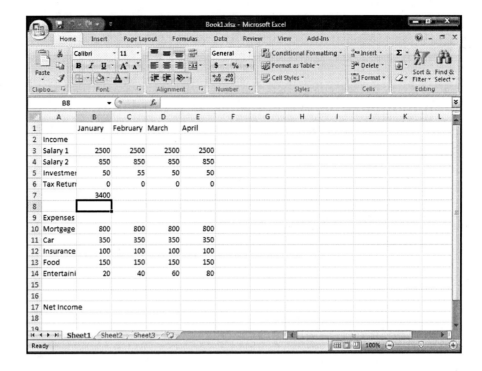

Viewing a Formula: Step by Step Instructions
1. Click on the cell that contains the formula.
2. Look at Formula Bar to view the equation.

Chapter 4: Formulas and Calculations!

Viewing a Formula: Visual Guide

Step 1:
Click on the cell that contains the formula.

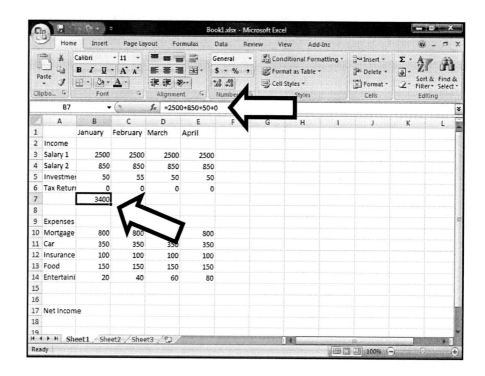

Step 2:
Look at Formula Bar to view the equation.

Congratulations you have created your first formula and completed your first calculation in Excel. The total income for January is 3400. Manually typing in the values used in a mathematical equation is very easy, but can lead to future problems on your spreadsheet. The problem arises when one of the values used in the formula changes. Consider the example budget, what if Salary 1 changed to 3500 instead of 2500. The total income calculated for January would be incorrect unless you remembered to manually correct the formula.

Test this out. Go back and select cell B3 with your mouse. Change the number 2500 to 3500. Note that the total income displayed in cell B7 did not change. The total for January still shows 3400 even though the correct answer is now 4400. To obtain the correct total, you must retype the formula to include the correct value for Salary 1. The mathematical formula in cell B7 must be changed to =3500+850+50+0 to calculate the correct total income for January. To avoid the problems associated with manually entering values (numbers) into calculations, Excel allows you to use cell references, rather than values when creating formulas. If you changed the value in cell B3 to 3500, please change cell B3 back to 2500 before continuing.

Chapter 4: Formulas and Calculations!

NOTE: When you type values (numbers) into a formula, the answer will not change automatically when you change one of the numbers used in the calculation.

Section 16: Creating a Formula by Manually Inputting Cell References

When creating a formula, the best practice is to reference the cells containing the values, rather than to type in the actual numbers. Remember each cell on a spreadsheet has a name. The cell name is the combination of the letter of the column and the number of the row where the cell is located. The cell's name can be used to reference any cell on the spreadsheet. If you use cell references in a formula, you can change the values in the cells, and the system will automatically update the answer. It recalculates the result every time you change one of the cells in the formula. This concept might seem confusing, so it's best to look at an example.

To calculate the total income for the month of February, you will add the income values 2500, 850, 55, and 0. These values are located on the spreadsheet in cells C3, C4, C5, and C6 respectively. If you were going to calculate the total by typing in the values, the formula would be =2500+850+55+0. The answer for the calculation is 3405. If, instead, you use the cell reference method, you would type in the cell names instead of the specific values. The formula using cell references would be =C3+C4+C5+C6. The answer for the calculation is still 3405. The answers are identical. However, if you have to go back and change the value for Salary 1 located in cell C3 from 2500 to 3500, your calculation will automatically update to 4405 if you used cell references when you created the formula.

Chapter 4: Formulas and Calculations!

Using the sample budget, calculate the total income for February. Move your mouse pointer to cell C7 and click the left mouse button to select the cell. You are going to calculate the answer by manually typing the income cell references. To tell the computer you are creating a formula, type in an equal = sign. After the equal sign, type the names of the cells for the calculation. Between each cell name, type a plus sign to indicate you want to add the numbers together. The example formula for February is =C3+C4+C5+C6. After you have typed in all the cell references, press the Enter key on the keyboard to tell the computer to perform the calculation. The total 3405 will appear in cell C7. Now go back to cell C3 and change the number to 3500. Note that the total automatically changes to 4405 as soon as you change the number in cell C3. This is your first encounter with the extraordinary power of Excel.

Manually Typing Cell References in a Formula: Step by Step Instructions

1. Click on the cell in which you want to place a formula (calculation).
2. Type an "equal sign" = to indicate that you are creating a formula.
3. Type the formula manually using the cell references in place of the specific values (=C3+C4+C5+C6).
4. Press the Enter key on the keyboard. The computer will calculate the answer.

Chapter 4: Formulas and Calculations!

Manually Typing Cell References in a Formula: Visual Guide

Step 1:
Click on the cell in which you want to place a formula.

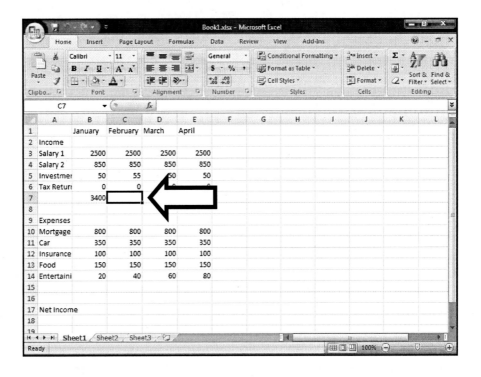

Step 2:
Type an "equal sign" (=).

Step 3:
Type the formula using cell references in place of the specific values.

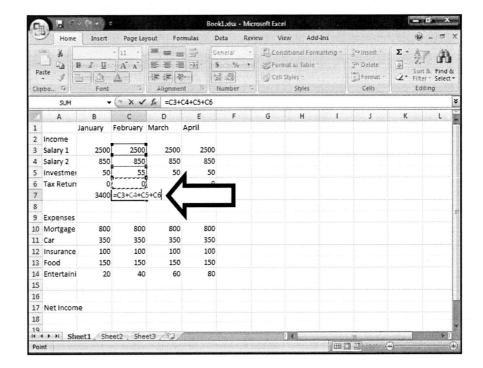

Chapter 4: Formulas and Calculations!

Step 4:
Press the Enter
key on the
keyboard.

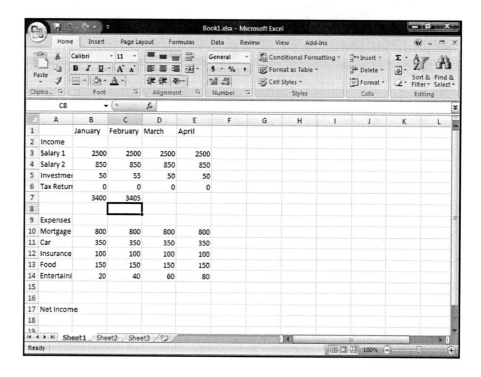

Test the calculation. Using your mouse, go back and select cell C3. Change the number 2500 to 3500. Note the total income displayed in cell C7 (February Salary 1) changes to 4405. The cell references worked perfectly.

Step 1:
Click on cell
C3.

Step 2:
Type the value
3500.

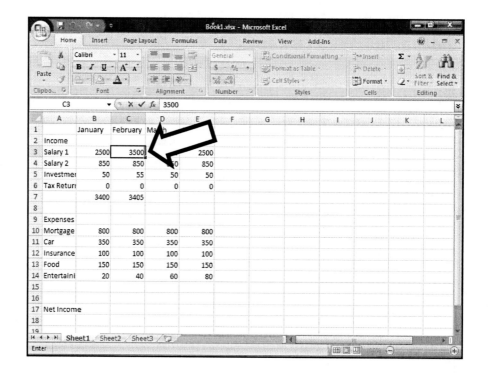

Chapter 4: Formulas and Calculations!

Step 3:
Press the Enter key on the keyboard.

Notice the answer updated automatically in cell C7.

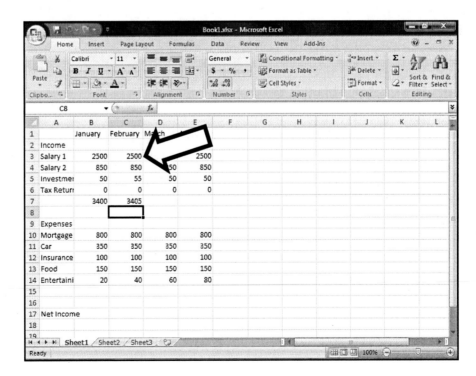

If you changed the value in cell C3, please change cell C3 back to 2500 before continuing.

Step 1:
Click on the cell C3.

Step 2:
Type 2500 in the cell.

Chapter 4: Formulas and Calculations!

Section 17: Creating a Formula by Selecting Cells

A slight variation to the previous method of creating a formula is to use the mouse to select each cell you want included in your calculation. You can try this method to calculate the total income for the month of March.

Move your mouse pointer to cell D7, and click the left mouse button to select the cell. You are going to select the cells used in the formula. To tell the computer you are going to create a formula, type an equal = sign. Instead of typing in the values or cell references, move the mouse to cell D3, the first cell you want to add, and press your left mouse button. The cell reference will now appear in the formula. After each cell selection, type a plus + sign to indicate you want to add the numbers together. Position the mouse over cell D4, the next cell you want to add to the calculation, and click the left mouse button. The cell reference has been added to the formula. Type a plus + sign. Continue to add cells D5 and D6 to the formula. Remember to type the plus sign between the cell references. After you have chosen the last cell, press the Enter key on the keyboard. (Make sure you end the formula with a cell reference and NOT a plus sign. If you end with a plus sign, the computer will tell you that you made an error and will not perform the calculation.) Once you have completed the formula and hit the Enter key, your total, 3500, will appear in cell D7. Selecting the cells using the mouse is typically easier and faster than typing the cell references manually, but you can use whichever process is easier for you. The results are the same.

Chapter 4: Formulas and Calculations!

Creating a Formula by Selecting Cells: Step by Step Instructions

1. Click on the cell in which you want to place a formula.
2. Type in an "equal sign" (=) to indicate that you are entering a formula.
3. Select a cell with your mouse.
4. Type in a mathematical operator (+,-,*, /).
5. Repeat steps 3 and 4 to add the remainder of the cells for the calculation.
6. Press the Enter key on the keyboard. The computer will calculate the answer.

Creating a Formula by Selecting Cells: Visual Guide

Step 1:
Click on the cell in which you want to place the formula.

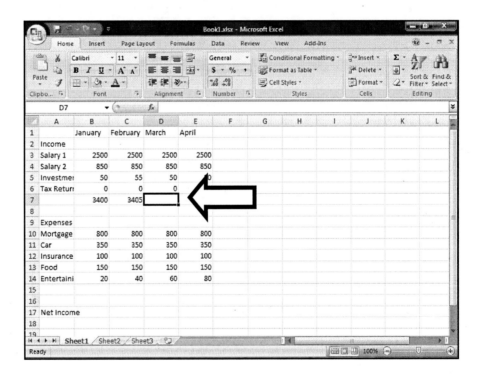

Chapter 4: Formulas and Calculations!

Step 2:
Type in an "equal sign" (=).

Step 3:
Select a cell with your mouse.

Step 4:
Type in a mathematical operator (+,-,*, /).

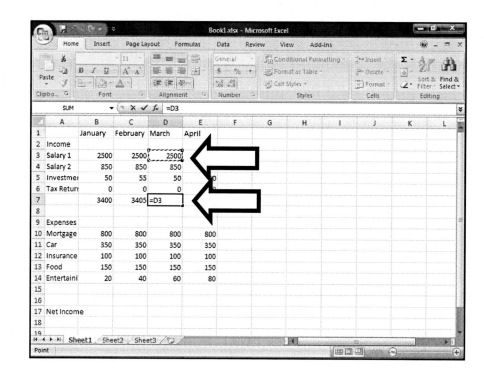

Step 5:
Repeat steps 3 & 4 to add the remainder of the cells for the calculation.

You will be able to see the formula in the formula bar.

Step 6:
Press the Enter Key.

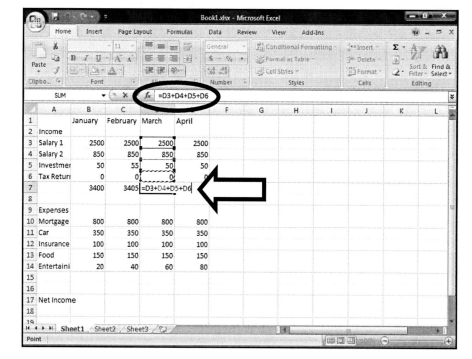

Finished Calculation.

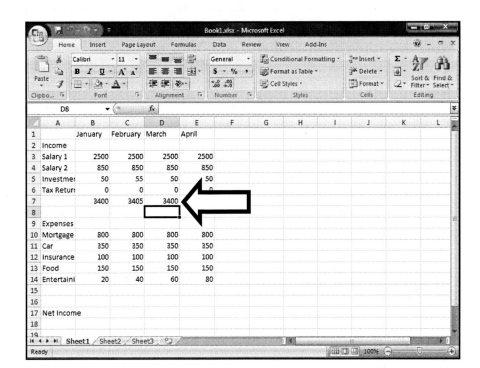

Now repeat the step to calculate the total revenue for April.

Finished spreadsheet displaying the Total Revenue from January through April.

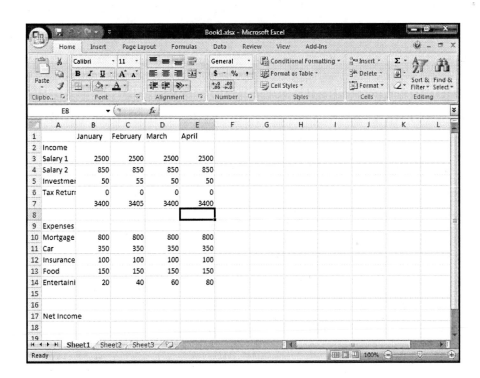

Chapter 4: Formulas and Calculations!

Section 18: Practice Creating Formulas by Selecting Cells

It is important to become comfortable creating formulas using the data on the spreadsheet. Before moving on to the next topic, use what you have learned to create new formulas to finish the example spreadsheet. First, you will total the expenses for each month and then calculate the net income for each month. Since selecting cells using the mouse is the most common way to create a formula, you should practice using this technique.

To begin, position the mouse over cell B15 and click the left mouse button. Cell B15 is now selected to display the answer to the calculation totaling January's expenses. To tell the computer you are going to create a formula, type an equal = sign. Move the mouse to cell B10, the first cell you want to add, and press your left mouse button. The cell reference will appear in the formula. Between each additional cell, type a plus + sign to indicate you want to add the cells together. Position the mouse over cell B11, the next cell you want add to the equation and click the left mouse button. The cell reference will be added to the formula. Continue to add cells B12, B13, and B14 to the formula. Remember to type the plus + sign between each cell reference. After you have chosen the last cell, press the enter key on the keyboard. Your total, 3500, will appear in cell B15.

Creating a Formula by Selecting Cells: Step by Step Instructions
1. Click on the cell in which you want to place a formula.
2. Type an "equal sign" (=) to indicate you are creating a formula.
3. Select a cell with your mouse.
4. Type a mathematical operator (+,-,*, /).
5. Repeat steps 3 and 4 to add the remainder of the cells to the formula.
6. Press the Enter key on the keyboard and the computer will calculate the answer.

Chapter 4: Formulas and Calculations!

Creating a Formula by Selecting Cells: Visual Guide

Step 1:
Click on the cell in which you want to place a formula.

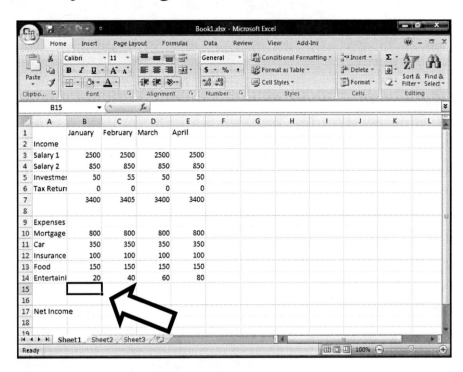

Step 2:
Type in an "equal sign" (=).

Step 3:
Select a cell with your mouse.

Step 4:
Type a mathematical operator (+,-,*, /).

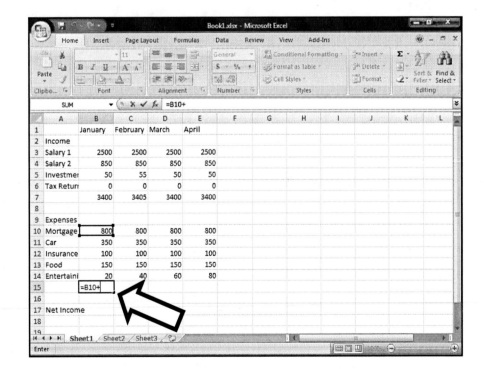

Chapter 4: Formulas and Calculations!

Step 5:
Repeat steps 3 & 4 to add the remainder of the cells for the calculation.

Step 6:
Press the Enter Key.

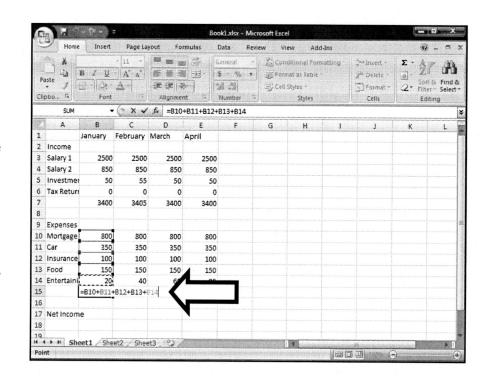

Finished Calculation.

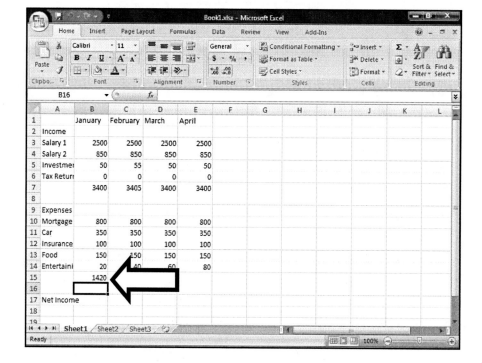

Chapter 4: Formulas and Calculations!

Repeat the steps to calculate the total expenses for February, March, and April. February's total expenses should be placed in cell C15, March's total should appear in D15, and April's total should be placed in cell E15.

Finished spreadsheet displaying the Total Expenses from January through April.

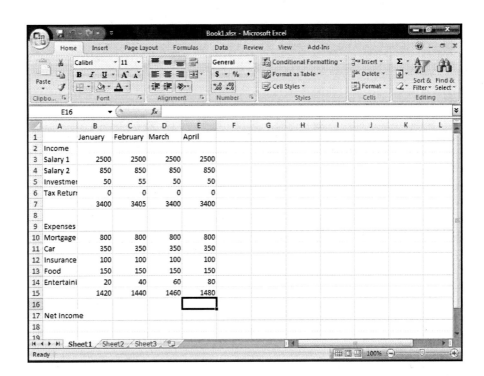

You have successfully completed totaling the expenses for each month on the example spreadsheet. With the revenue and expenses totaled, the last formula you need to add to the example spreadsheet will calculate the Net Income for each month. To correctly calculate the Net Income, you have to subtract your total monthly expenses from your total monthly revenue. For example, for the month of January you will subtract the expense total in cell B15 from the revenue total displayed in cell B7.

Position the mouse over cell B17 and click the left mouse button. Tell the computer you are going to create a formula by typing an equal = sign. Using the mouse, select cell B7, which contains the total revenue for January. The cell reference will appear in the formula. Since you are going to subtract the total expenses, type a minus (-) sign to indicate you want to subtract the numbers. Position the mouse over cell B15 and click the left mouse button. Press the Enter key. A Net Income of 1980 will appear in cell B17.

Chapter 4: Formulas and Calculations!

Step 1:
Click on the cell in which you want to place a formula.

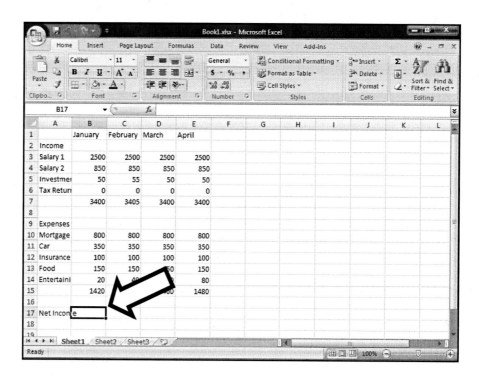

Step 2:
Type an "equal sign" (=).

Step 3:
Select a cell with your mouse.

Step 4:
Type a minus sign (-).

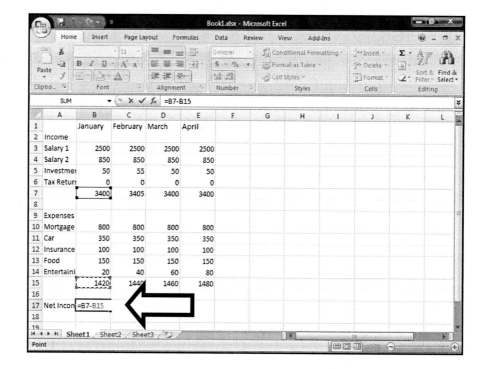

Chapter 4: Formulas and Calculations!

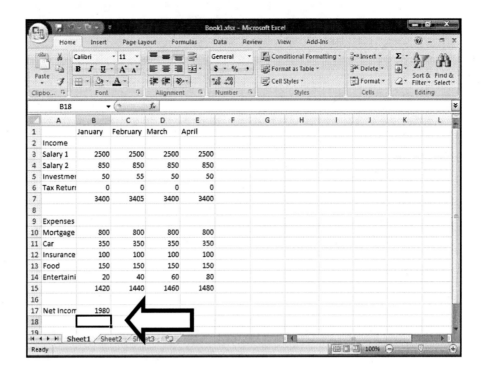

Step 5:
Press the Enter
Key.

Section 19: Copying and Pasting Formulas

The budget is going to utilize the same formula to generate the net income for each month as was used to calculate January's net income. Instead of retyping the formula in cells C17, D17, and E17, you can use the Copy and Paste option. The copy and paste option will allow you to select a cell containing a formula, copy the formula into the computer's memory, and then paste the copied formula into another cell on the spreadsheet. Since you used cell references in the formula, the computer will automatically adjust the cell references when the formula is pasted into the new cells.

In the example, you are going to use the mouse to select and copy the formula in cell B17. Move the mouse pointer over cell B17 and press the left mouse button. Once the cell has been selected, position the mouse pointer over the COPY option and click the left mouse button one time. The selected cell's formula will be copied into the computer's memory. Take a moment to look at

Chapter 4: Formulas and Calculations!

the selected cell. The cell border is moving, indicating that you have successfully copied the data contained in the cell.

Move your mouse pointer over cell C17 and click your left mouse button. The bold, black selection box will appear around cell C17 indicating the cell has been selected. Once the cell has been selected, position the mouse pointer over the PASTE option, and click the left mouse button one time. Notice a value appears in cell C17. The formula used in cell B17 has been copied to cell C17 and the net income for February has been calculated. Remember the net income for February will not be the same as the net income for January because the income and expenses for February are different from January's numbers.

Copying and Pasting: Step by Step Instructions
1. Select the cell containing the formula you want to copy.
2. Click the COPY option.
3. Select the cell where you want the copied formula to be placed.
4. Click the PASTE option.

Copying & Pasting: A Visual Guide

Step 1:
Select the cell containing the formula you want to copy.

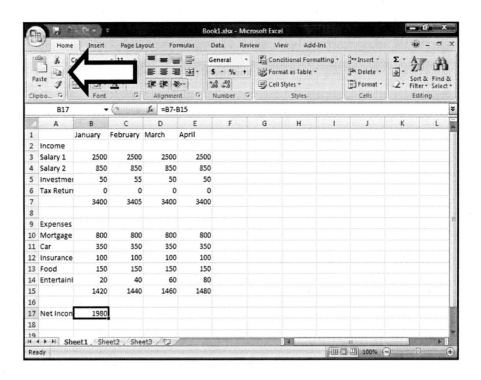

Step 2:
Click the COPY
option.

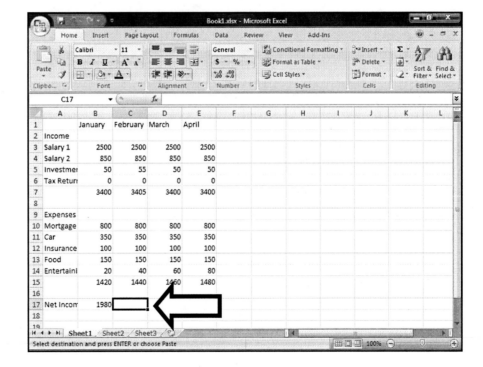

Step 3:
Select the cell
where you want
the copied text
to be placed.

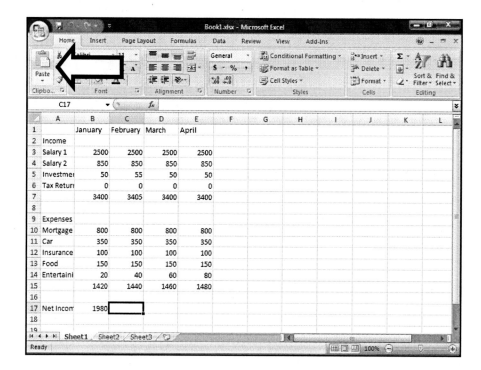

Step 4:
Click the
PASTE option.

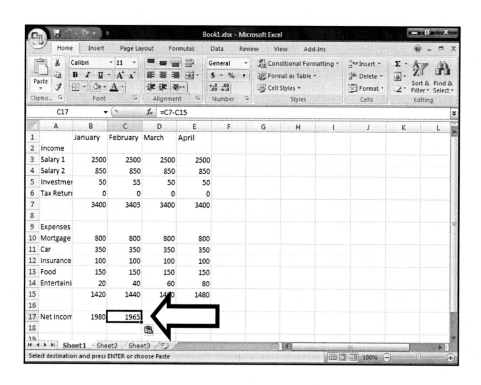

The copied
formula will
be pasted into
the selected
cell.

To verify that the formula was pasted into the cell, look at the Formula Bar located at the top of the screen. You will see the equation used to calculate the net income for February. Notice the cell references automatically updated to use the cells C7 and C15 in the calculation for February. Copying and Pasting calculations is another example of the power of Excel.

The calculation will be displayed in the Formula Bar.

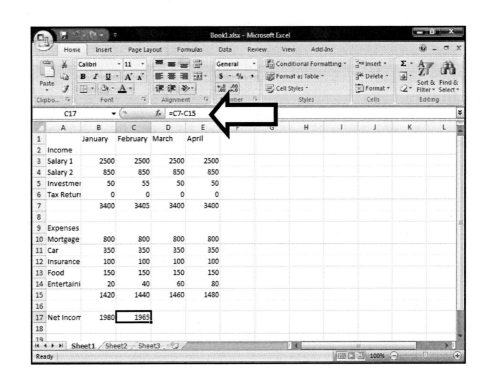

You still need to calculate the net income for the months of March and April. Since the calculation used in cell B17 is still in the computer's memory, move the mouse pointer to cell D17 and click the left mouse button. The bold, black selection box will appear around the cell D17 indicating the cell has been selected. Once the cell has been selected, position the mouse pointer over the PASTE option and click the left mouse button one time. Notice the calculation from cell B17 has been copied into cell D17.

Chapter 4: Formulas and Calculations!

The calculation is already in the computer's memory, so continue from Step 3.

Step 3:
Select the cell where you want the copied text to be placed.

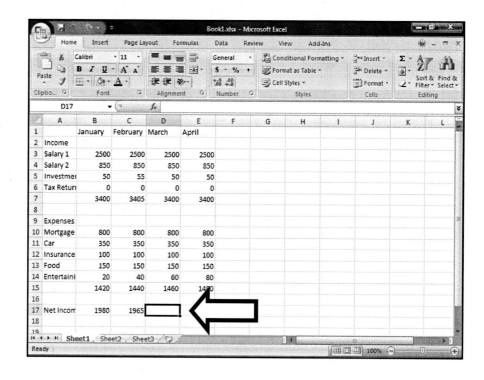

Step 4:
Click the PASTE option.

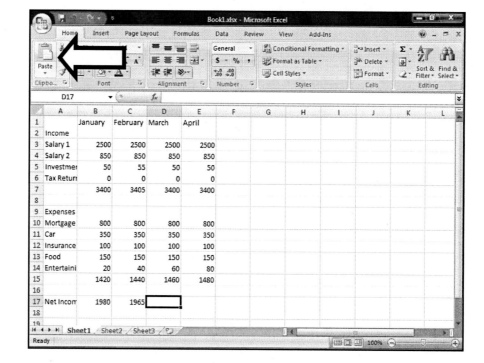

Chapter 4: Formulas and Calculations!

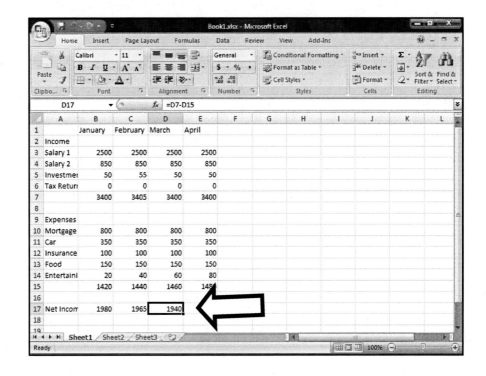

The copied calculation has been pasted into the selected cell.

Repeat the steps to paste the net income calculation in cell E17, and you will have completed the calculations on the example budget.

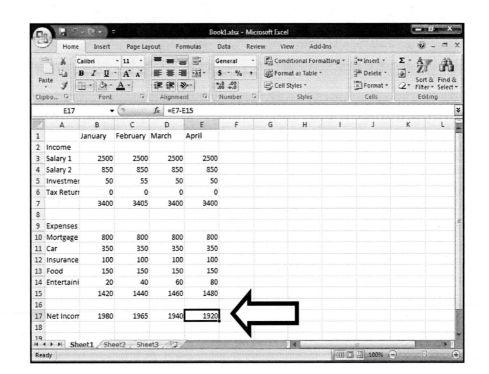

Step 3:
Select the cell where you want the copied text to be placed.

Step 4:
Click the PASTE option.

Chapter 4: Formulas and Calculations!

NOTE: Mathematical operations to be used in a calculation:
- **Addition: Use the plus + symbol**
- **Subtraction: Use the minus – symbol**
- **Multiplication: Use the asterisk * symbol**
- **Division: Use the slash / symbol**

NOTE: Each time you change one of the values in a calculation which utilizes cell references, the answer will update automatically.

Chapter 5

Saving, Opening, and Closing!

What You Will Learn in this Chapter
- ✓ Saving your Excel spreadsheet.
- ✓ Closing your spreadsheet.
- ✓ Opening a Saved spreadsheet.

Chapter 5: Saving, Opening, and Closing!

Section 20: Saving Your Work

The concept of "saving" can be best described through example. If you are working on a spreadsheet and the electricity goes out, your computer will shut down. When you turn your computer back on, the spreadsheet you were working on will be gone. You will have to start over. However, if you saved your work prior to the power outage, when you turn your computer back on, your spreadsheet will be safely stored, unchanged, in whatever location you had placed it during the "saving process." For this reason it is very important to save your work frequently.

After all the hard work you put into your spreadsheet, you run the risk of losing it. The budget is currently in the computer's temporary memory. If the computer loses power, the temporary memory will be erased, resulting in the loss of the budget. To avoid this potential problem, you must save the budget to the computer's main memory. Saving will enable you to return to the spreadsheet at a later time without the loss of any saved information.

Although you may think it unlikely that you will lose power, it seems as though everyone either has either personally experienced losing documents or knows someone who has. Business Information Services support staff normally have no compassion for employees who call in asking whether an "unsaved" document can be recovered. Their answer is usually a quick "no" followed by a sarcastic "you might want to consider saving from time to time." After all the work you put into preparing your spreadsheet, why risk losing it, especially since the saving process is relatively simple. The hardest part is remembering where you saved your files and what you named them so that you can quickly locate any file you need in the future.

Microsoft Excel is setup to store all your spreadsheets in a folder called Documents. This folder is located on the computer's main memory referred to as the Local Disk, C drive, or hard drive. You are going to save the example budget in the Documents folder.

Chapter 5: Saving, Opening, and Closing!

To start the save process, move the mouse arrow up to the Office button located in the upper left corner of the Excel window. Click the left mouse button once to open the OFFICE menu. Notice there are two save options in the Office menu. These options are SAVE and SAVE AS. The SAVE AS option is used to choose a location for the file and to give the file a name. The SAVE option is used after every update or change to the original saved file. Save As = Name and Location: Save = Update.

NOTE: The first time you try to save the Excel spreadsheet, the computer will ask you to give it a name. At this point, both SAVE AS and SAVE will open the Save As window.

Move the mouse arrow down to the SAVE AS option and click the left mouse button. This will close the Office menu and open the save screen. There are three additional steps to complete the save process. First, you must choose where to save the file. Second, you have to give the file a name and, third, you must click the save button.

The first objective is to tell the computer where you want to save the file. At the top of the save screen is a white box currently displaying the path to your Documents folder. The Documents folder is the default, automatically selected, folder used for the Office programs. It is good practice to save all of your work in the Documents folder to make it easy for you to find your information in the future. This also eliminates the chance of you getting your documents mixed up with the program files used to run the computer.

If the white box currently displays DOCUMENTS, you are in the right location. If it does not display DOCUMENTS, you need to choose the DOCUMENTS option from the list provided. Position the mouse pointer over the DOCUMENTS option, located on the left side of the save screen, and click the left mouse button. DOCUMENTS will be displayed in the "Save In" input box.

The second step is to choose a name for the Excel spreadsheet. Located near the bottom of the save screen is the heading FILE NAME. To the right of the heading FILE NAME is a white input box containing the generic name BOOK1. The name in the input box is the computer's suggestion for a name and, as you will quickly learn, the computer's suggestions for file names are usually poor. To change the suggested name, move your mouse arrow to the end of the name and click the left mouse button. Clicking the mouse activates the box and drops the cursor (blinking line) at the location the mouse was clicked. Use the Backspace key on the keyboard to erase the name. When the name has been erased, type in the desired name using the keyboard. For this sample spreadsheet, use the name Budgets.

NOTE: When choosing a file name, you can use up to 256 characters. The name may include any numbers (0-9) and letters (A-Z) but not colons, semicolons, slashes, or mathematical operators (for example, plus and minus signs). We recommend you use a maximum of three or four short words. If the name is too long, it will be truncated (only part of the name will show followed by three dots) when displayed in lists. By keeping it short, you have a better chance of seeing the entire name displayed when you search through the computer for your file in the future.

Finally, click the SAVE button located on the bottom right side of the save screen. When you click the SAVE button, the computer will close the save screen, and the file will be successfully saved in the computer's main memory.

QUESTION: How do you know the spreadsheet was saved successfully?

ANSWER: If you look in the title bar of the workbook window, you will see the name you chose for the workbook followed by words Microsoft Excel. This verifies the workbook was saved correctly. In this example, the title bar will have changed from "Book1" to "Budgets."

Saving Your Work: Step by Step instructions
1. **Click the OFFICE button.**
2. **Click the SAVE AS option.**
3. **Click the DOCUMENTS option.**
4. **Click in the FILE NAME box and type the name of your workbook.**
5. **Click the SAVE button.**

Chapter 5: Saving, Opening, and Closing!

Saving Your Work: Visual Guide

Step 1:
Click the
OFFICE
button.

Step 2:
Click the
SAVE AS
option.

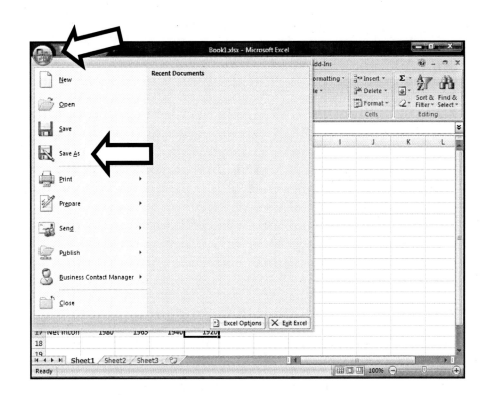

Step 3:
Click the
DOCUMENTS
option.

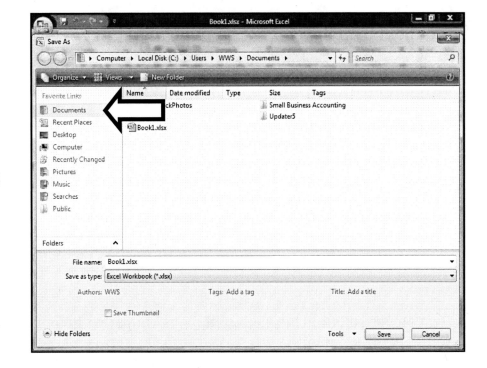

Step 4:
Click in the
FILE NAME
box and type
the name of
your
workbook.

Step 5:
Click the
SAVE button

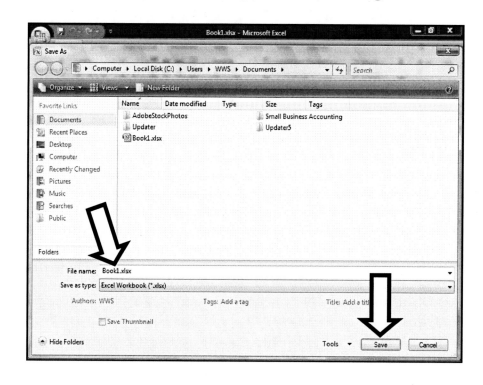

Successfully
saved
workbook.

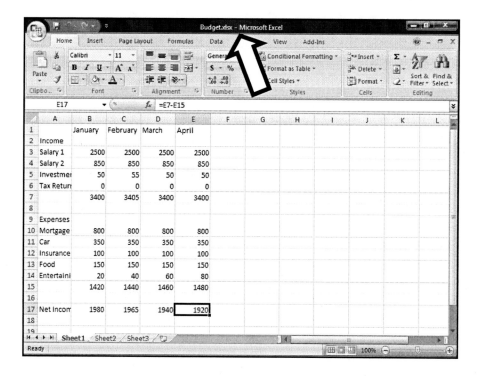

Now, you can return to working with your budget without worrying about the loss of any information.

Chapter 5: Saving, Opening, and Closing!

NOTE: In the future when you want to update the Budgets spreadsheet you saved to the computer's main memory, you can use the Save option in the Office menu. Left click on OFFICE button. Move your cursor down to the SAVE option and click the left mouse button. Your spreadsheet, including all the changes you made since you first saved your spreadsheet, will be saved.

Section 21: Closing Your Spreadsheet

Two Ways to Close a Spreadsheet

Assume for a moment that you have to stop what you are doing and go on an errand. You do not want to leave your spreadsheet displayed on the screen, so you will close your file. When you have finished working with your spreadsheet and successfully saved it to the computer's main memory (the Documents Folder) you are ready to close the workbook. There are two ways to close an Excel file. The first is to use the Office menu. The CLOSE option, found under the Office menu, will close the workbook but leave the Microsoft Excel program open. The second is to click the X found in the upper right corner of the program window. This will close both the spreadsheet and the Microsoft Excel program.

Chapter 5: Saving, Opening, and Closing!

QUESTION: Why are there two X's in the upper right corner of my program window?

ANSWER: The X in the title bar will close the Microsoft Excel program as well as any spreadsheet you are currently working on. The bottom X will only close the spreadsheet, leaving the Microsoft Excel program open.

NOTE: As a safety feature, when you attempt to close a workbook, the computer will ask you whether or not you want to save the workbook. This safety prompt only appears if you have made any changes to your spreadsheet since your last save. If you want to save the changes you made, click YES. If you do not want to save the changes, click NO.

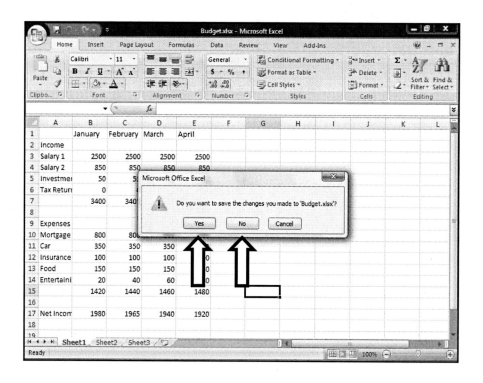

Chapter 5: Saving, Opening, and Closing!

Closing a Spreadsheet: Step by Step Instructions

1. Click the OFFICE button.
2. Click the CLOSE option.
   - If a message box appears asking if you would like to save your work, you must answer the question by clicking either the YES or NO button with the mouse. If you click No, any work you completed after the last time you saved your file will be gone.

Closing a Spreadsheet: Visual Guide

Step 1: Click the OFFICE button.

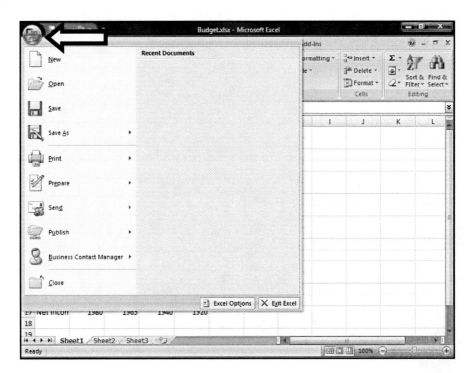

Chapter 5: Saving, Opening, and Closing!

**Step 2:
Click the
CLOSE option**

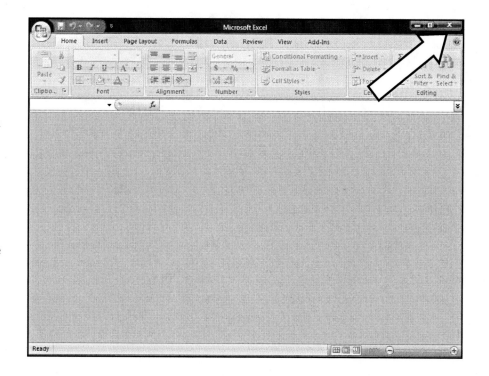

**The file closes
leaving the
Excel program
open.**

**Click the "X"
in the upper
right corner to
close the entire
program.**

Chapter 5: Saving, Opening, and Closing!

Section 22: Opening a Saved Spreadsheet

Now, reopen the spreadsheet you just closed. If you exited Microsoft Excel after closing the file, the first step to retrieve the file is to open Microsoft Excel using the Start menu.

Once you open Microsoft Excel, move the mouse arrow directly to the OFFICE button and click the left mouse button once to open the menu. Move your mouse arrow down the list to the option OPEN. When "Open" is highlighted, click your left mouse button. The menu will close and the OPEN screen will be displayed. Except for the Title bar, the open screen will look exactly like the save screen. There are two ways to access your file. The one you use depends on whether or not the name of your file is listed in the OPEN screen.

The OPEN screen always starts at the place you last saved a file in Microsoft Excel. If you see the file name you want listed in the OPEN screen, select it by clicking it with the left mouse button. The name will turn blue, indicating you have successfully selected it. After you select the file, click on the OPEN button found in the lower right corner of the OPEN screen. The spreadsheet will open and be displayed for you in the Excel window.

If the file is not in the list shown on the OPEN screen, you will have to find it. This process will be simplified if you save all your work in the same location. In this example, you saved the Budgets spreadsheet in the Documents folder. At the left of the OPEN screen is a list of common places on the computer where information is saved. Look for the option DOCUMENTS in the list, and click it with your mouse arrow. The DOCUMENTS option will open to display the contents of the folder.

Chapter 5: Saving, Opening, and Closing!

Listed in the middle section of the OPEN screen will be the contents of the DOCUMENTS folder. Since you saved the Budgets spreadsheet in the DOCUMENTS folder, it will be listed on the OPEN screen. Click on the name "Budgets" once. It will turn blue. Click the OPEN button located in the lower right corner of the screen. The spreadsheet will open.

Opening a Spreadsheet: Step by Step Instructions
1. **Open MICROSOFT EXCEL.**
2. **Click the OFFICE button.**
3. **Click the OPEN option.**
4. **Click the DOCUMENTS folder option.**
5. **Click the name of the file that you want to open (it will turn blue).**
6. **Click the OPEN button.**

Opening a Saved Spreadsheet: Visual Guide

Step 1:
Open
MICROSOFT
EXCEL.

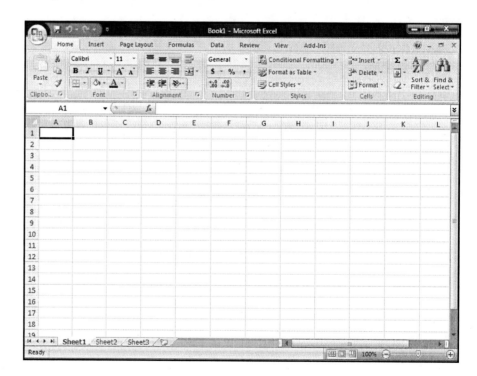

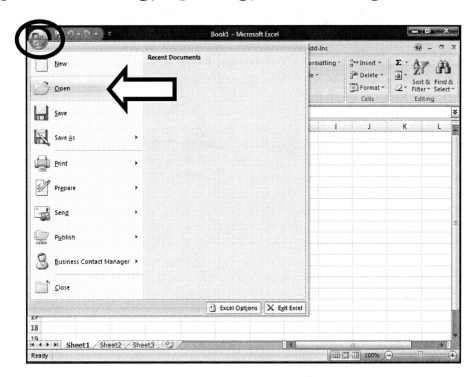

**Step 2:
Click the
OFFICE
button.**

**Step 3:
Click the OPEN
option.**

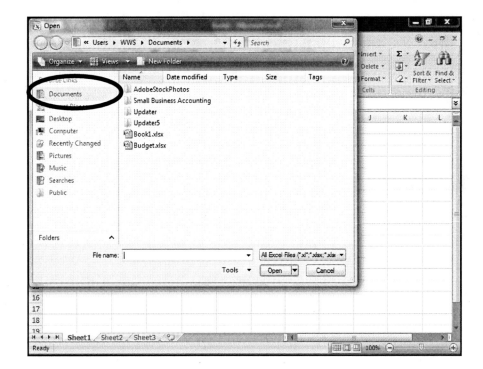

**Step 4:
Click the
DOCUMENTS
folder option.**

Step 5:
Click the
Budgets
workbook.

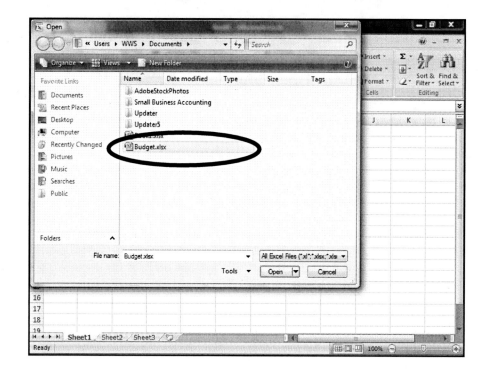

Step 6:
Click the OPEN
button.

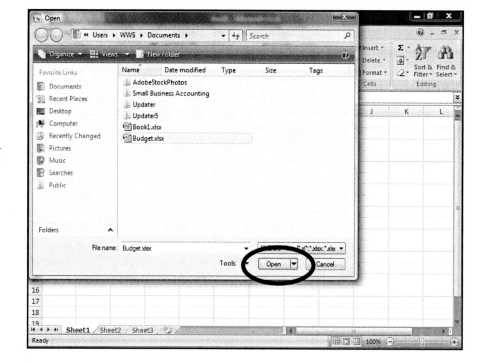

The Budgets workbook will open.

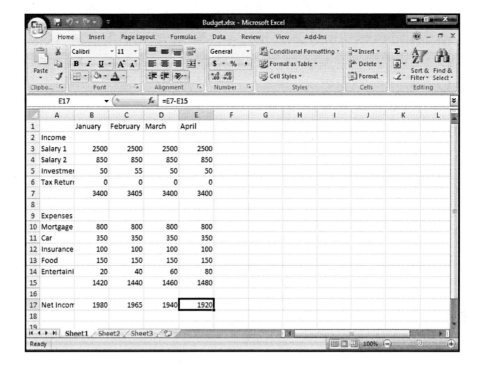

Chapter 5: Saving, Opening, and Closing!

Chapter 6

Formatting Cell Data!

What You Will Learn in this Chapter
- ✓ Formatting
- ✓ Formatting Cells
- ✓ Formatting Numbers
- ✓ Formatting Numbers as Dates
- ✓ Additional Options Available when Formatting Numbers
- ✓ Changing Text Alignment
- ✓ Changing a Cell's Background
- ✓ Formatting Lines
- ✓ Formatting Text, Text Style, Size, and Color

Chapter 6: Formatting Cell Data!

Section 23: Formatting Cells

You have completed the basic spreadsheet, but now you want to give the budget a more professional and aesthetically pleasing look. Turning an ordinary spreadsheet into a professional spreadsheet is accomplished by formatting the text, numbers, dates, and cells on the spreadsheet. Perhaps you'd like the letters and numbers to be larger, the titles to be bold, the cells to be different colors, or have your numbers appear displaying dollars and cents. You can do all of these things, and much more, by formatting your text.

NOTE: Formatting your spreadsheet will change the way the spreadsheet appears on the screen, as well as, how it will appear when printed.

The first step to formatting any part of the spreadsheet is to select the cell or cells you would like to change. Once the cells are selected, you can use the Format options located on the ribbon to select the type of formatting you wish to apply to the selected cells. It's best to make the formatting changes after you have finished creating the basic spreadsheet. You will save time and effort by making all your formatting changes at one time.

Section 24: Review of Highlighting

Highlighting is the process used to tell the computer what data on your spreadsheet you intend to use. When text is highlighted, it may be cut, copied, bolded, italicized, formatted, and more. To highlight data, position your mouse arrow on the first cell you want to select. Click and HOLD DOWN the left mouse button. While holding down the mouse button, move your mouse arrow to the last cell you want to select. As the mouse moves over the cells, they will become highlighted (the background color will change). When you reach the last cell, release the mouse button. The selected cells will remain highlighted until you click your mouse on another cell in the spreadsheet. You are now ready to work with the selected data.

REMEMBER: When you highlight data, the computer is only concerned with the data between where you began holding down the left mouse button and the exact point at which you released the left mouse button. Anything in between these two points will be highlighted.

In this example, highlight all of your numbers. Place your mouse pointer on cell B3, and click and hold down your left mouse button. Move your mouse to cell E17. The first cell, B3, will remain white, but all of the other cells will change color.

WARNING: Don't release the left mouse button until all the desired cells have been highlighted. Releasing the button prematurely will stop the highlighting process before you have included all the desired cells, and you will have to start the highlighting process over again.

NOTE: If you accidentally highlight an area, click your mouse anywhere in the spreadsheet once. A click in any area of the worksheet (other than the highlighted section) will remove all the highlighting on the spreadsheet.

Chapter 6: Formatting Cell Data!

Highlighting Your Data: Step by Step Instructions

1. Position the mouse at the first cell you desire to select.
2. Click and hold down the left mouse button.
3. Move the mouse to the last cell you desire to select.
4. Release the mouse button.
   - The thick black outline surrounding the cells indicates the cells have been highlighted.

Highlighting Your Data: Visual Guide

Step 1:
Position the mouse at the first cell you desire to select.

Step 2:
Click and hold down the left mouse button.

Chapter 6: Formatting Cell Data!

Step 3:
Move the mouse to the last cell you desire to select.

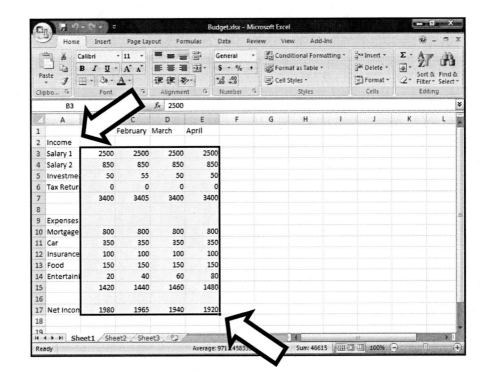

Step 4:
Release the mouse button.

Section 25: Formatting Numbers

You have completed the first step in the formatting process – highlighting the cells you want to change. The next step is to open the Format window (dialog box) from the ribbon at the top of the screen. Click your left mouse button on the Show Format Dialog Box button located in the bottom right corner of the Font section of the ribbon.

NOTE: Many of the formatting options can be selected directly from the options displayed on the ribbon. However, if you desire to see all the available options on the screen at one time, you need to open the Format Dialog Box.

Chapter 6: Formatting Cell Data!

After you select the Show Format Dialog Box button, the "Format Cells" window will appear on screen. At the top of the Format Cells window are multiple tabs. Each tab allows you to view a different formatting option which you can use to change your highlighted cells. For this example, you will use the NUMBER tab to change the appearance of the numbers.

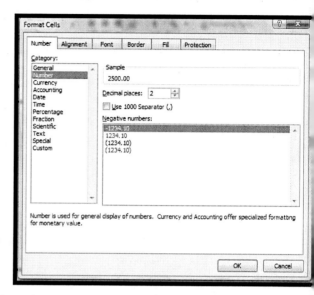

On the left side of the Format Cells window is a list of options for numbers. Click the Currency option. The right side of the Format Cells window will change depending on which selection you make in the main category list. The right side of the window will display a sample of the selected formatting. Below the sample will be additional options for further customizing the formatting.

By looking at the "Sample" number displayed at the upper right side of the screen, you can decide if you would like to select any additional changes from the options displayed below the sample. The "Sample" illustrates how the numbers you have highlighted will appear in your spreadsheet. The decimal option permits you to change how many decimals will be displayed. You can use the arrows located to the right of the decimal list to increase (up arrow) or decrease (down arrow) the number of decimal places. Typically for financial calculations, like the budget, the decimal point option is set at two decimal places.

Below the decimal option is an option that can be used to insert a dollar sign, pound sign, euro sign, etc. or no sign at all in the highlighted cells. To select a currency symbol, click on the drop-down arrow (little blue arrow) located to the right of the Symbol drop down box. A list of available currency symbols will appear. Click your mouse on any of the available symbol options to select it. The symbol you selected will appear in the "Symbol" box.

The final selection you can make to the currency format is designating how the computer will display negative numbers. The "Negative Number" list will allow you to choose whether negative values will be displayed in black or red and whether or not parenthesis will be displayed. Select the last option in the list using the mouse. The selection specifies that all negative numbers

Chapter 6: Formatting Cell Data!

displayed within the highlighted cells will be red and in parenthesis. This selection will make the negatives readily noticeable. Once you have finished making the specific change to the highlighted cells, click on the OK button located at the bottom of the "Format Cells" window. All of the numbers you highlighted on your spreadsheet will change to show the new formatting. Each number should have a dollar sign in front of the number, two decimal places, and negative numbers will appear in red and in parentheses.

Formatting Numbers: Step by Step Instructions

1. **Highlight the desired cells using the mouse.**
2. **Click the SHOW FORMAT DIALOG BOX button.**
3. **Click the NUMBER tab.**
4. **Select the desired category of formatting.**
   - **For example: currency**
5. **Select the specific details of the cell formatting.**
   - **For example: # of decimal places, symbols, etc.**
6. **Click the OK button.**

Formatting Numbers: Visual Guide

Step 1: Highlight the desired cells using the mouse.

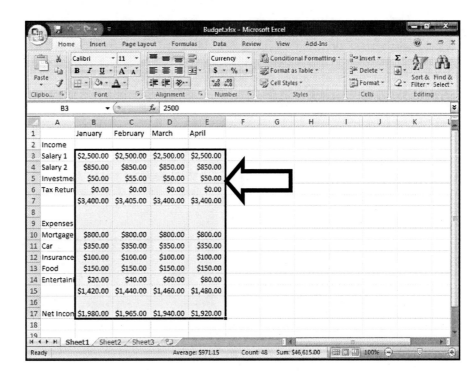

**Step 2:
Click the
SHOW
FORMAT
DIALOG BOX
button.**

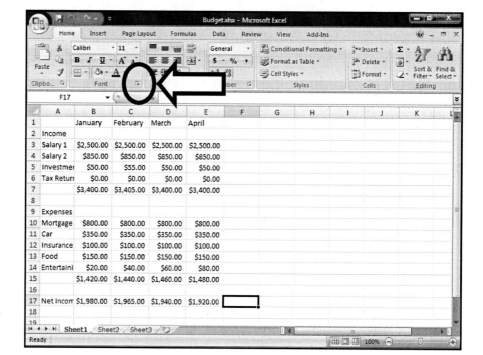

**Step 3:
Click the
NUMBER
tab.**

**Step 4:
Select the
desired
category of
formatting.**

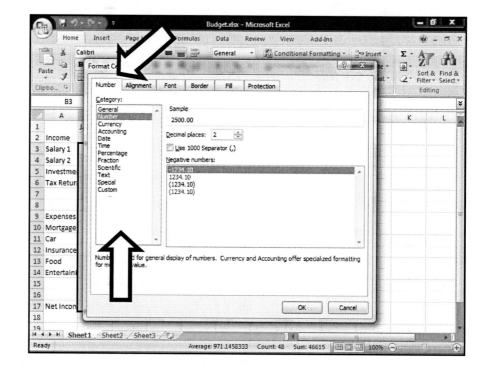

Chapter 6: Formatting Cell Data!

Step 5:
Select the specific details of the cell formatting.

Step 6:
Click the OK button.

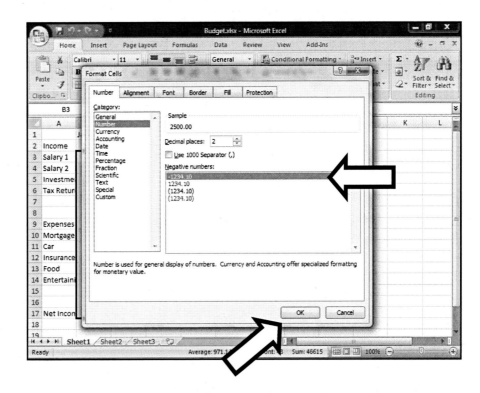

Applied Formatting.

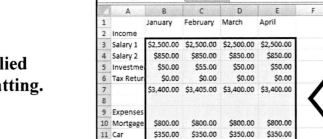

Chapter 6: Formatting Cell Data!

Section 26: Formatting Numbers as Dates

Frequently, you will want to type dates on a spreadsheet. The same process used to format your numbers into currency is used to format dates. In the example budget, you didn't use any dates written in number format so the steps will be reviewed for future reference.

In this example, you don't want to apply any of the date formats to the current numbers on the spreadsheet. However, it would be a good idea to go through the steps to better understand the process. Move the mouse over a blank cell, like F17, and click the left mouse button to select the cell. Open the Format Cells window by clicking on the SHOW FORMAT DIALOG BOX button. The Format Cells window will appear on the screen. Click on the NUMBER tab, if it is not currently selected, and look down the category list to locate the DATE option. Click once on the date option, and the date format options will appear on the right side of the window. You can use the scroll bar to move up and down the formatting list to become familiar with the available options.

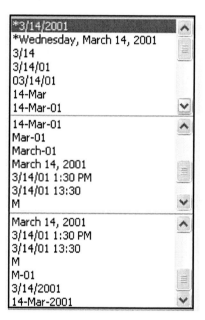

Formatting Numbers as Dates: Step by Step Instructions
1. **Highlight the desired cells using the mouse.**
2. **Click the SHOW FORMAT DIALOG BOX button.**
3. **Click the NUMBER tab.**
4. **Select the DATE OPTION from the category list.**
5. **Select the specific date formatting from the list provided.**
6. **Click the OK button.**

Chapter 6: Formatting Cell Data!

Formatting Numbers as Dates: Visual Guide

Step 1:
Select/Highlight the desired cells.

Step 2:
Click the SHOW FORMAT DIALOG BOX button.

Step 3:
Click the NUMBER tab.

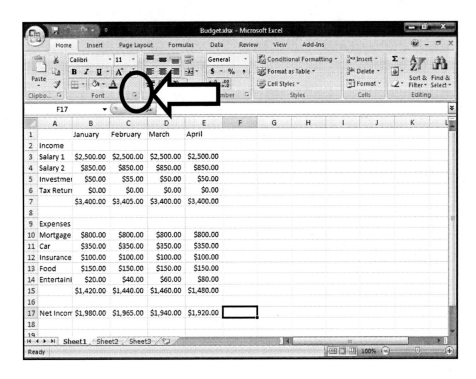

Step 4:
Select the DATE option from the Category List.

Step 5:
Select the specific date formatting from the list provided.

Step 6:
Click the OK button.

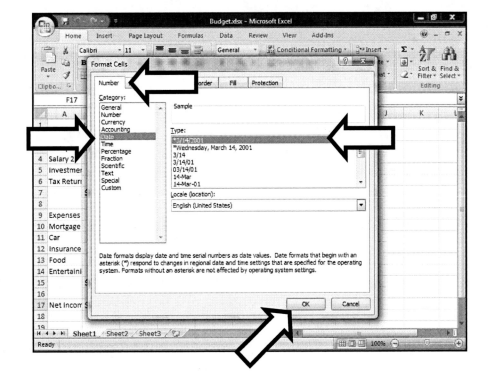

Chapter 6: Formatting Cell Data!

NOTE: If you choose the format option that abbreviates the month followed by the last two digits of the year, even if you type 3/31/07, the month will be displayed as Mar-07.

Section 27: Other Formatting Options for Numbers

Numbers as Text

A popular option for number formatting is Text. If you input a number, but don't intend to ever use it in a calculation, you can format the number as text. Formatting numbers as text is popular for account numbers, check numbers, employee identification numbers, etc. These numbers are not used in formulas.

Numbers as Percentages

You may find yourself needing to use a percentage in a spreadsheet. When you type a percentage, the number will look just like any of the other numbers on the page. If you select Percentage from the formatting options, the computer will automatically take the value (number) in the selected cell and multiple it by 100. After the new value is calculated, a percent sign will be placed to the right of the number in the cell.

Numbers as Special Text

You may also find yourself entering numbers that typically have a specific format such as phone numbers and social security numbers. You can find both of these formatting options located under the Special category of the Number tab on the Format Cell window. If you choose the phone number option and input the number 2165555555, it will appear as (216) 555-5555. If you chose the social security number option and input the number 555555555, it will be displayed as 555-55-5555.

Chapter 6: Formatting Cell Data!

Formatting Numbers: Step by Step Instructions

1. Highlight the desired cells using the mouse.
2. Click the SHOW FORMAT DIALOG BOX button.
3. Click the NUMBER tab.
4. Select the desired category of formatting.
5. Select the specific formatting options from the list provided.
6. Click the OK button.

Format	Description
General	This is the default number format. Numbers are formatted and displayed just the way you type them.
Number	This format allows you to specify the number of decimal places, whether to use a thousands separator, and how to display negative numbers.
Currency	This format is used for monetary values and allows you to specify the number of decimal places, whether to use a thousands separator, how to display negative numbers, and whether to display a currency symbol.
Accounting	This format is also used for monetary values, but will automatically align the currency symbols and decimal points of numbers in a column.
Date	This format displays date using standard notation.
Time	This format displays time using standard notation.
Percentage	This format multiplies the cell value by 100 and displays the result with a percent symbol. The format also allows you to specify the number of decimal places.
Fraction	This format displays a number as a fraction, according to your selection.
Scientific	This format displays a number in exponential notation.
Text	This format treats the content of a cell as text and displays the content exactly as you type it.
Special	This format displays a number as a postal code (ZIP Code), phone number, or Social Security number, based on your selection.
Custom	This format allows you to modify and create a new number formatting.

Chapter 6: Formatting Cell Data!

Section 28: Formatting: Text Alignment

Not only can you change the way numbers look, you can also change the way cells look. Excel always aligns numbers to the left of the cell and words to the right of a cell. You may want to change this alignment to make your spreadsheet look more balanced. To change the way information is aligned, you must highlight the desired cells.

To highlight/select the cells, position the mouse pointer over cell B1. Click and hold down your left mouse button. While holding down the mouse button, move the mouse pointer over the cells ending with cell E1. The first cell will remain white, but all of the other cells will change color. Release the mouse button. The cells should be surrounded by a thick black box indicating the cells have been highlighted/selected.

NOTE: You can highlight an entire row or column by clicking on the row number heading or the column letter heading.

NOTE: You can highlight an entire spreadsheet by clicking on the gray square located at the corner where the column headings and row headings begin.

	A	B	C
1		January	February
2	Income		
3	Salary 1	$2,500.00	$2,500.00
4	Salary 2	$850.00	$850.00

Chapter 6: Formatting Cell Data!

In this exercise, you will center align the months of the year in row 1. Highlight cells B1 through E1. The next step is to open the Format window (dialog box) from the ribbon at the top of the screen. Click your left mouse button on the SHOW FORMAT DIALOG BOX button located in the bottom right corner of the ALIGNMENT section of the ribbon.

After you select the Show Format Dialog Box button, the "Format Cells" window will appear on screen. At the top of the Format Cells window are multiple tabs. Select the ALIGNMENT tab. To change the horizontal alignment of text, click on the blue drop down arrow located at the end of the "Horizontal" drop down box. A list of alignment options will appear. Choose the CENTER option and click the OK button.

NOTE: Many of the formatting options can be selected directly from the options displayed on the ribbon. However, if you desire to see all the available options on the screen at one time, you need to open the Format Dialog Box.

Text Alignment: Step by Step Instructions
1. **Highlight the desired cells using the mouse.**
2. **Click the SHOW FORMAT DIALOG BOX button.**
3. **Click the ALIGNMENT tab.**
4. **Click on the Drop Down arrow to open the list of Horizontal alignment options.**
5. **Click on the desired alignment option.**
6. **Click the OK button.**

Chapter 6: Formatting Cell Data!

Text Alignment: Visual Guide

Step 1:
Select/Highlight
the desired cells.

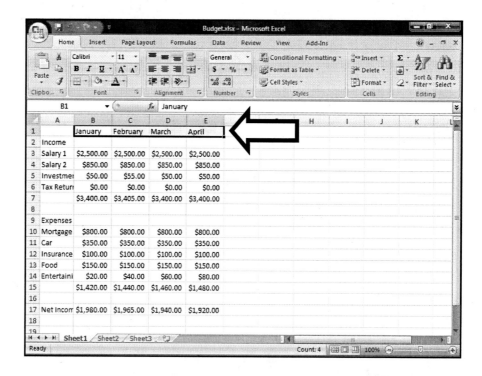

Step 2:
Click the
SHOW
FORMAT
DIALOG BOX
button.

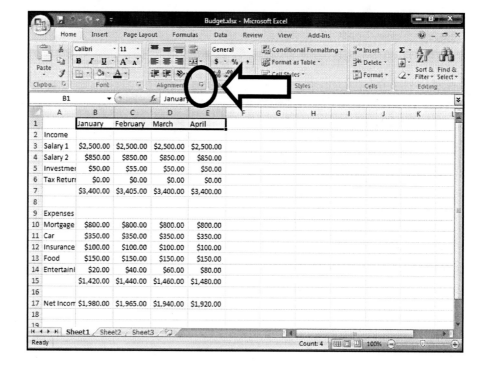

Chapter 6: Formatting Cell Data!

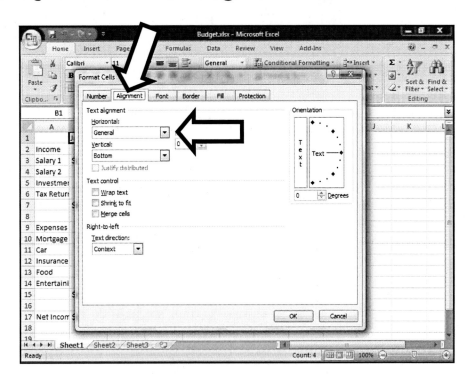

Step 3:
Click the
ALIGNMENT
Tab.

Step 4:
Click on the
Drop Down
arrow to view
the Horizontal
alignment
options.

Step 5:
Click on the
desired
alignment
option.

Step 6:
Click the OK
button.

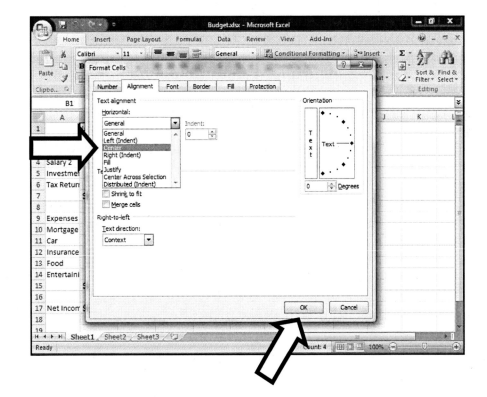

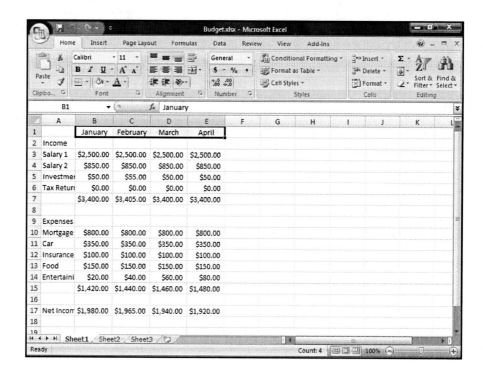

Position the mouse outside the highlighted area and click the left mouse button to view the formatting changes.

WARNING: If you change the alignment of your numbers, the dollar symbols and decimal points may not line up.

Section 29: Formatting: Cell Background

Occasionally people choose to change the background color of specific cells or information on a spreadsheet to make the spreadsheet more visually appealing or to enable them to pick out specific data at a glance. In the example budget, you are going to change the background color of the cells containing the month headings. Begin by highlighting cells B1 through E1 using the mouse. The months January through April should be highlighted.

Open the Format window (dialog box) by clicking on the SHOW FORMAT DIALOG BOX button located in the bottom right corner of the Font section of the ribbon.

When the Format Cells window appears, select the FILL tab located at the top of the window. The Format Cell window will change to display the Cell Shading options. To change the color of the cell, place your mouse pointer on one of the squares in the color palette, and click your left mouse button. The color you selected will appear in the "Sample" box. To the right of the color swatches, you can use the Pattern Style drop down box to see more shading options for the cell. The sample area at the bottom of the window will display the selected color or pattern. Once you have chosen the desired background, click the OK button to apply the change and return to the spreadsheet. Remember to click outside the highlighted area to release the highlighted cells and view the changes.

NOTE: If the color being displayed on the worksheet does not match the color you selected, the cells might still be highlighted. If you click in an empty cell, the highlighted selection will be un-highlighted, and the color you chose will be displayed correctly in the background of the selected cells.

Formatting the Cell Background: Step by Step Instructions
1. Highlight the desired cells using the mouse.
2. Click the SHOW FORMAT DIALOG BOX button.
3. Click the FILL tab.
4. Click on the desired color swatch from the list provided.
5. Click the OK button.

Chapter 6: Formatting Cell Data!

Formatting the Cell Background: Visual Guide

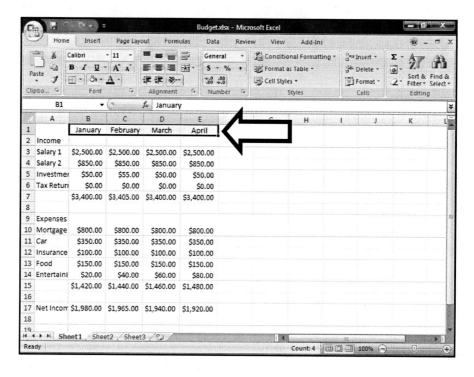

Step 1:
Select/Highlight
the desired cells.

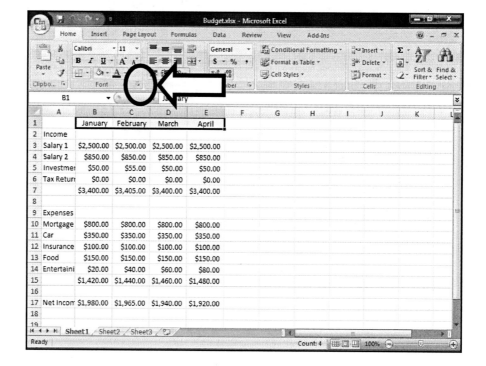

Step 2:
Click THE
SHOW
FORMAT
DIALOG BOX
button.

Chapter 6: Formatting Cell Data!

Step 3:
Click the
FILL Tab.

Step 4:
Click on the
desired color
swatch from
the list
provided.

Step 5:
Click on the
OK button.

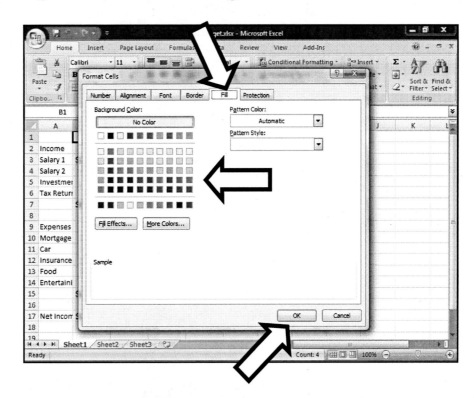

Position the
mouse outside
the highlighted
area and click
the left mouse
button to view
the formatting
changes.

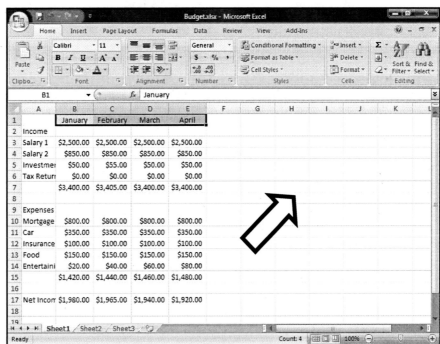

135

Chapter 6: Formatting Cell Data!

NOTE: If you intend to print your spreadsheet, you may not want to add color to the background unless you have color ink in your printer. If you do not have color ink, the printer will use various shades of gray in the background to simulate the colors you chose. This may make it difficult to read printed material.

Section 30: Formatting: Lines

One of the most common formatting changes used on a spreadsheet is adding lines. Typically the lines are used to separate the numbers used in a calculation from the answer, just like in math. You have the option of adding a single line, a bold line, double lines, and even complete borders to cells depending on your formatting preference. Using the example budget, you will add three lines to the spreadsheet. The first line will be used to separate the income lines from the total income. The second line will separate the individual expenses from the total expense line. The last line will be a double line to separate the Net Income from the rest of the spreadsheet.

To place the first dividing line, highlight all the contents of row 6. The new line will be placed at the bottom of row 6. Remember, to highlight an entire row, position the mouse pointer over the row heading number and click the left mouse button. The entire row should become highlighted. Now open the Format window (dialog box) by clicking on the SHOW FORMAT DIALOG BOX button located in the bottom right corner of the Font section of the ribbon. When the Format Cells window appears, click on the BORDER tab. The window will change displaying a list of available line and border options.

Chapter 6: Formatting Cell Data!

The Border tab options allow you to place a complete or partial border around the highlighted cells. Located near the top of the box are a number of preset borders you can choose from. Below the presets under the Borders heading are individual buttons which can be used to add specific lines to the selected cells. Located between the individual buttons is a sample area to view the selections before applying them to the highlighted cells. You are going to select the third button on the left side to place a line at the bottom of the highlighted cells. Click on the desired border option, and then click the OK button to apply the changes to the highlighted cells. You will see a black line appear at the bottom of row 6 separating the values above and below the line.

Adding Lines: Step by Step Instructions
1. **Highlight the desired cells using the mouse.**
2. **Click the SHOW FORMAT DIALOG BOX button.**
3. **Click the BORDER tab.**
4. **Click on the desired border option from the list provided.**
5. **Click the OK button.**

Adding Lines: Visual Guide

Step 1:
Select/Highlight the desired cells.

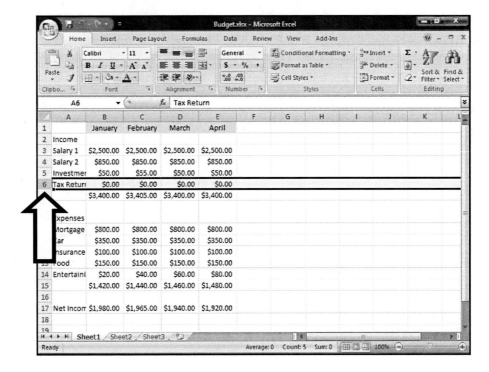

Chapter 6: Formatting Cell Data!

Step 2:
Click the
SHOW
FORMAT
DIALOG BOX
button.

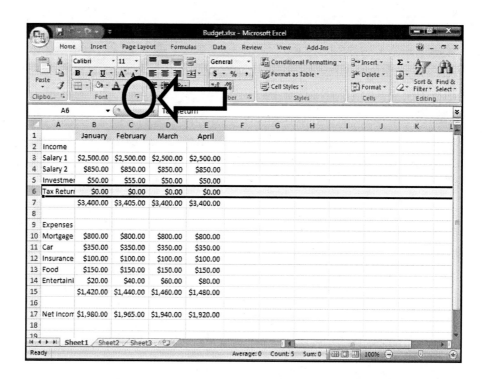

Step 3:
Click the
BORDER Tab.

Step 4:
Click on the
desired border
option from
the list
provided.

Step 5:
Click the OK
button.

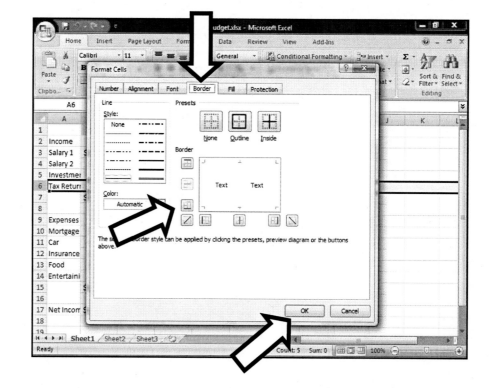

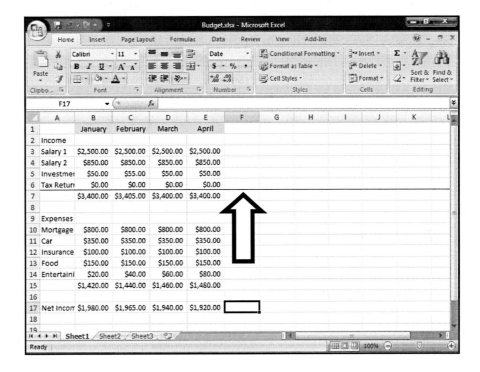

A dividing line has been successfully added to the spreadsheet.

Repeat the steps to add a line at the bottom of row 14. Once the new line is created, you can repeat the steps to add a line at the bottom of row 16. Make the line located at the bottom of row 16 a double line by using that border options located under Style on the right side of the Format Cell window.

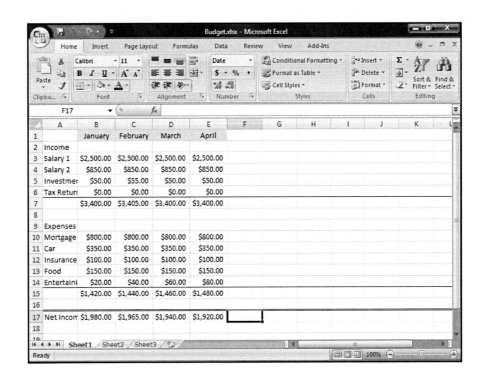

Dividing lines have been successfully added to the spreadsheet.

Chapter 6: Formatting Cell Data!

NOTE: If you don't want the lines to extend past the columns containing values, highlight only the cells you want the border applied to instead of selecting the entire row via the row heading. Later in the book you are going to expand the budget, so the dividing lines will be useful.

Section 31: Formatting: Text Style, Size, and Color

In addition to providing options to format numbers and cells, Excel also provides formatting options for text. You can format the text by changing the font, style, size, and color. First, highlight the cells that contain the data you want to format. In this example, highlight all the income and expense headings. Place your mouse pointer on cell A2, and click and hold down your left mouse button. Move your mouse to cell to A17 and release the button. The first cell, A2, will remain white, but all of the other cells will change color. Once the text is highlighted, open the Format window (dialog box) by clicking on the SHOW FORMAT DIALOG BOX button located in the bottom right corner of the Font section of the ribbon. When the Format Cells window appears, click on the FONT tab located at the top of the box.

Changing the Text Font
FONT refers to the appearance of your text. The Font tab provides options to change the Font, Font Style, Size, Color, and Underline style. Notice a "Preview" box is located near the bottom right corner of the window to preview any changes you make to your text.

Chapter 6: Formatting Cell Data!

Using the options provided on the Font tab, choose the font you would like by clicking on the name of that font with your left mouse button. If you do not know the name of the font you want, click a font that sounds appealing. The "Preview" box will display a sample of the selected font. You can use the scroll bars to view other font options. Use the scroll bar to select the option Times New Roman. Until you click the OK button, your text will not change.

**NOTE:** The standard fonts are Ariel, Courier, and Times New Roman.

Changing the Text Font Style

Once you have changed the Font, the next step is to decide whether you want to change the Font Style. You may prefer to make all the income and expense headings bold. Use the Font Style list located on the Font tab of the Format Cells window to make this change. Click on the BOLD option. Look in the Preview area to check whether you like the new style. If not, choose another or click on REGULAR to revert to the standard text style.

Changing the Text Size

You can also change the size of the text. The third option on the Font Tab of the Format Cells window provides multiple text size options. Choose a text size from the list by clicking your mouse on the number. The smaller the number, the smaller the text; the larger the number, the larger the text. As you make selections, the text in the preview box will change so you can see how your selection will affect the text. The standard sizes for fonts are 10 or 12. For those familiar with typewriters, 10 corresponds to elite type and 12 to pica type. For the row headings choose size 12.

Chapter 6: Formatting Cell Data!

Changing the Text Color

You can also change the color of your text. The Color options are located in a drop down box in the middle of the window. Currently, the box should display the word "Automatic" for black. Located to the right of the box is the blue drop down arrow. Click on the blue drop down arrow to display the palette of colors. Choose the color you want by clicking on the color swatch. The color will then be displayed in the "Color" box. The text in the Preview will also change to illustrate your selection.

After you have made all of the desired changes, click on the OK button located at the bottom of the window. The selections will be applied to the highlighted text on the spreadsheet.

Formatting Text: Step by Step Instructions

1. **Highlight the desired cells using the mouse.**
2. **Click the SHOW FORMAT DIALOG BOX button.**
3. **Click on the FONT Tab.**
4. **Select the desired options from the lists provided.**
   - **Font, Font Style, Size, Color, etc.**
5. **Click the OK button.**

Chapter 6: Formatting Cell Data!

Formatting Text: Visual Guide

Step 1:
Select/
Highlight the
desired cells.

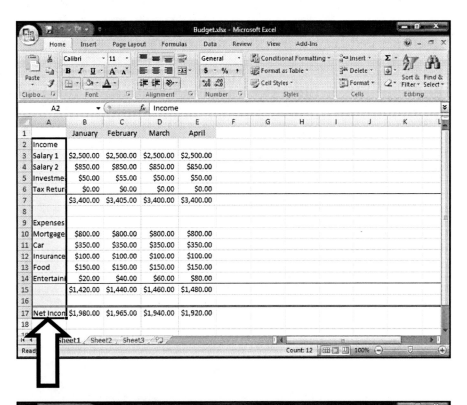

Step 2:
Click the
SHOW
FORMAT
DIALOG BOX
button.

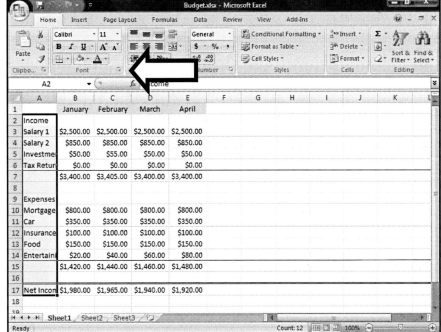

Step 3:
Click the FONT
Tab.

Step 4:
Click on the
desired options
from the lists
provided.

Step 5:
Click the OK
button.

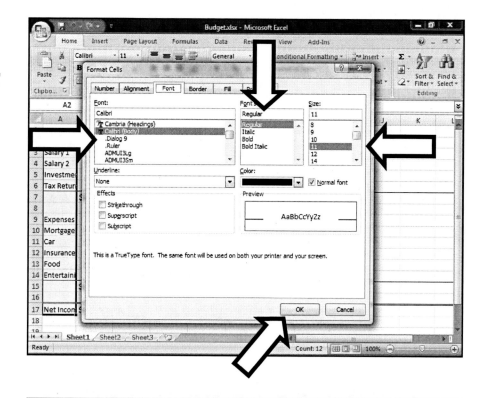

The Income and
Expense
headings have
been changed.

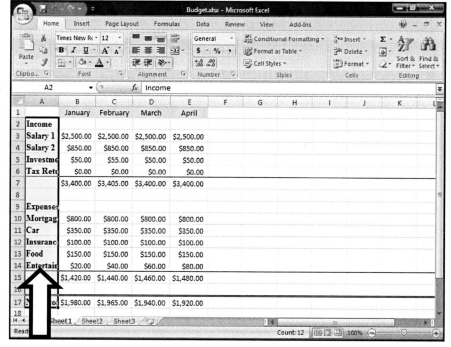

Chapter 7

Resizing Rows and Columns!

What You Will Learn in this Chapter
✓ The Purpose of Resizing a Row or Column
✓ Resizing a Row or Column

Chapter 7: Resizing Rows & Columns!

Section 32: Resizing Rows and Columns

Look at the example budget you have been creating. Notice the income and expense lists in Column A do not completely fit in the cells. You need to adjust the size of Column A. The process of adjusting the size of a column or row is called resizing.

The first step is to highlight/select the column or row you want to resize. Remember, to select an entire column or row, place your mouse in the row or column heading, and click the left mouse button once. When the row or column is highlighted, click on the FORMAT button located in the Cells section of the ribbon to view the cell formatting options. Position the mouse pointer over the desired option, and click the left mouse button to make the selection.

The Format list provides multiple resizing options. The first option, ROW HEIGHT or COLUMN WIDTH, lets you type in the exact size for the highlighted row or column. Selecting Column Width or Row Height will open a new window providing an input box to type in the desired size and an OK button to apply the change to the highlighted items. If the column or row is still too small, you can simply repeat the steps, input a larger number in the Size input box, and click OK.

The second option, AUTOFIT, automatically resizes the highlighted row or column to fit the text contained in the cells. AutoFit looks at the data you selected and resizes the selected row or column to fit the longest or widest word. The row or column will expand or shrink to fit the data entirely within the cell. Typically, AutoFit is the preferred option used to resize a row or column.

Using the example budget, highlight the contents of Column A by clicking the mouse on the Column A heading. The entire column will be highlighted. Open the FORMAT option list, and click the AUTOFIT COLUMN WIDTH option. Column A will be resized to fit the income and expense headings.

Chapter 7: Resizing Rows & Columns!

Resizing Rows and Columns: Step by Step Instructions

1. Highlight the row or column you want to resize.
2. Click the FORMAT button on the ribbon.
3. Click ROW HEIGHT or COLUMN WIDTH to manually type in the size and Click the OK button. Or Click AUTOFIT to let the computer automatically control the resizing.

Resizing Rows and Columns: Visual Guide

Step 1:
Select/Highlight
the desired
Rows or
Columns.

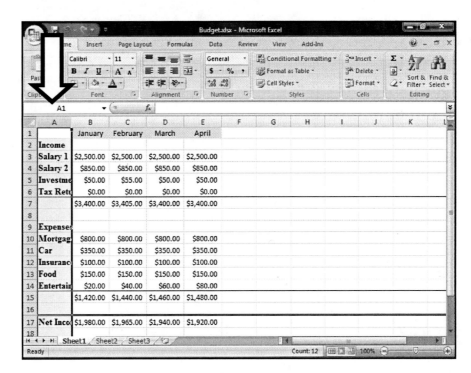

Chapter 7: Resizing Rows & Columns!

Step 2:
Click the
FORMAT
button on the
ribbon.

Step 3:
Click
AUTOFIT
COLUMN
WIDTH.

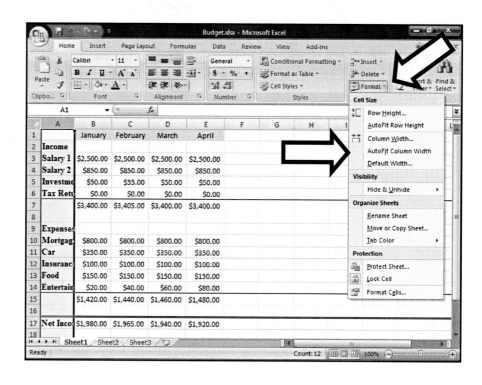

The column has
been resized to
fit the text.

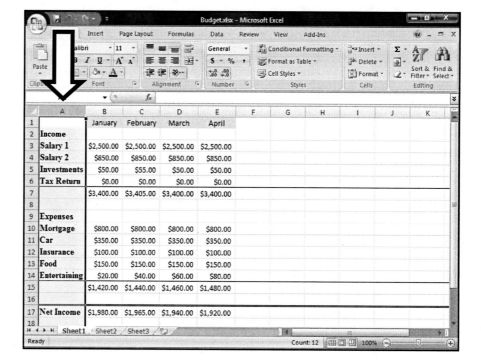

Chapter 7: Resizing Rows & Columns!

 NOTE: There is one more way to change the size of a row or column. Look at the Column or Row headings. Notice there are lines between each heading. These lines can be used to increase or decrease the size of the row or column using the mouse. If you need to widen a column, place your mouse pointer on the line between the two columns. The mouse pointer will change from a white plus sign into a black line with two arrows pointing to the sides. Click and hold down your left mouse button. Drag your mouse to the right to widen the column or to the left to shrink the column. The same process can be used to increase or decrease the height of rows on the spreadsheet.

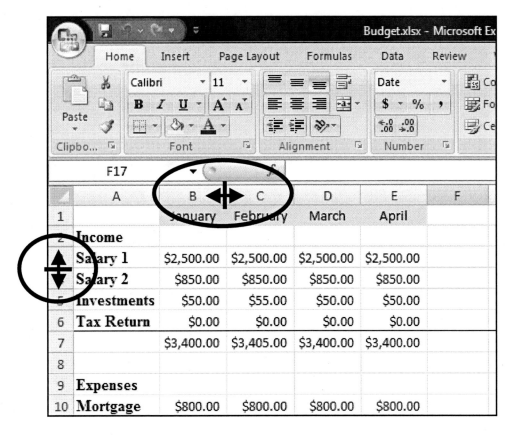

REMEMBER: Save your work.

Chapter 7: Resizing Rows & Columns!

Chapter 8

Worksheets!

What You Will Learn in this Chapter
- ✓ What are Worksheets?
- ✓ Renaming Worksheets
- ✓ Adding Worksheets
- ✓ Moving Worksheets
- ✓ Deleting Worksheets

Chapter 8: Worksheets!

Section 33: Multiple Worksheets

An Excel spreadsheet can have multiple worksheets. Think of a worksheet as one individual page, of a number of pages, which make up the spreadsheet. Utilizing multiple worksheets allows you to separate data onto different pages, while keeping the data together in one overall spreadsheet. Using multiple worksheets can help keep data organized and limit the amount of scrolling necessary to view large amounts of data on a single worksheet.

Look at the bottom left side of the Excel window. Notice the three tabs labeled Sheet1, Sheet2, and Sheet3. These tabs provide easy access to all the worksheets within the example budget spreadsheet. To move between worksheets, simply position your cursor over the tab representing the worksheet you want to access and click your left mouse button. Open the worksheet named Sheet2. Then open Sheet3. The worksheet with the White Tab is the active sheet; the worksheet is being displayed on the screen and is waiting for you to enter data. The other worksheets, with gray tabs, are temporarily inactive. When you want to input data on another worksheet, you must activate that worksheet by clicking on its name tab. Return to the worksheet containing the budget by clicking on the tab Sheet1.

9	Expenses					
10	Mortgage	$800.00	$800.00	$800.00	$800.00	
11	Car	$350.00	$350.00	$350.00	$350.00	
12	Insurance	$100.00	$100.00	$100.00	$100.00	
13	Food	$150.00	$150.00	$150.00	$150.00	
14	Entertaining	$20.00	$40.00	$60.00	$80.00	
15		$1,420.00	$1,440.00	$1,460.00	$1,480.00	
16						
17	Net Income	$1,980.00	$1,965.00	$1,940.00	$1,920.00	
18						

Sheet1 Sheet2 Sheet3

Ready

Chapter 8: Worksheets!

Section 34: Renaming Worksheets

Typically, when you use multiple worksheets, it is preferable to rename each worksheet so you can easily identify what information each one contains. To change the name of a worksheet, move the mouse pointer over the tab, and double click your left mouse button. The worksheet name will change color from black to white, and the background color will change to black indicating you can rename the worksheet. Type in the new name and, when finished, press the Enter key.

Using the example spreadsheet, rename worksheet Sheet1 to "Budget." To begin the process, position the mouse pointer over the tab labeled Sheet1 and double click the left mouse button. When the background color has changed to black, type in the new name. When you have finished typing, hit the Enter key on the keyboard.

Renaming a Worksheet: Step by Step Instructions
1. **Double click on the desired worksheet tab.**
2. **Type the new name for the worksheet.**
3. **Press the Enter key on the keyboard.**

Chapter 8: Worksheets!

Renaming a Worksheet: Visual Guide

Step 1:
Double click
on the desired
worksheet tab.

Step 2:
Type the new
name for the
worksheet.

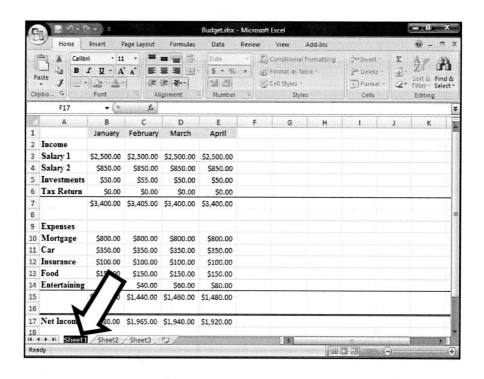

Step 3:
Press the Enter
key on the
keyboard.

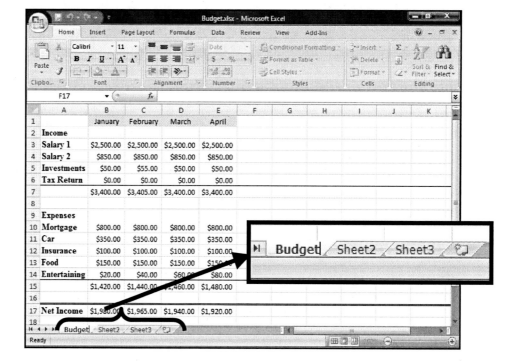

Chapter 8: Worksheets!

When you have finished renaming the first worksheet, repeat the steps to rename worksheet Sheet2 "Retirement" and worksheet Sheet3 "List." Remember the first step is to double click on the worksheet tab. When the tab changes color, type in the new name and press the Enter key on the keyboard to apply the change. You have now successfully renamed all three worksheets contained in your Excel spreadsheet file.

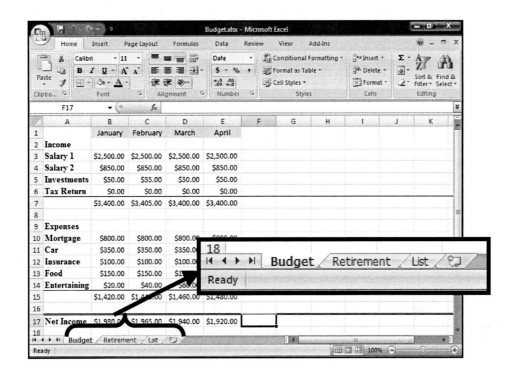

NOTE: You cannot assign the same name to multiple worksheet tabs. There must be at least one letter or number that is different in each worksheet name. For instance, you may decide to project your retirement income for various scenarios – one assuming early retirement, another assuming normal retirement, and a third assuming delayed retirement. You can either rename the worksheet by typing a longer description or by simply adding a letter, e.g. RetirementE, RetirementN, RetirementD.

Chapter 8: Worksheets!

NOTE: Renaming your worksheets does not affect the name you assigned to your Excel spreadsheet file. A spreadsheet file is also called a workbook. The names are separate and distinct.

Section 35: Adding Worksheets

Adding a worksheet to a spreadsheet is a very simple process. Depending on your computer's storage capacity and the volume of data you have in your current worksheets, you can add more than 100 worksheets to an Excel workbook.

Since you just finished renaming the third worksheet "List," the List worksheet is your active worksheet. Remember, the active worksheet is the worksheet currently being displayed on the screen waiting for you to enter data. As a result, the List worksheet tab should be white; the Budget and Retirement worksheets should be gray. Excel adds worksheets to the right of the last worksheet.

Move your mouse pointer over the fourth tab which has the picture of a piece of paper with a red starburst in the corner. This tab is called the INSERT WORKSHEET tab. Click your left mouse button one time, and a new worksheet will be added to the spreadsheet. Notice, the name on the worksheet tab is Sheet1. Excel automatically tracks the number of worksheets in a spreadsheet/ workbook, gives all new worksheets the generic name Sheet, and numbers them accordingly. To add an additional worksheet, repeat the process.

Chapter 8: Worksheets!

Adding a Worksheet: Step by Step Instructions

1. Click on the worksheet tab that should appear to the left of the worksheets in your workbook.
2. Click the INSERT WORKSHEET tab.
3. Optional: Rename the new worksheet.

Adding a Worksheet: Visual Guide

Step 1:
Click the worksheet tab to the left of the last worksheet in your workbook.

Step 2:
Click the INSERT WORKSHEET tab.

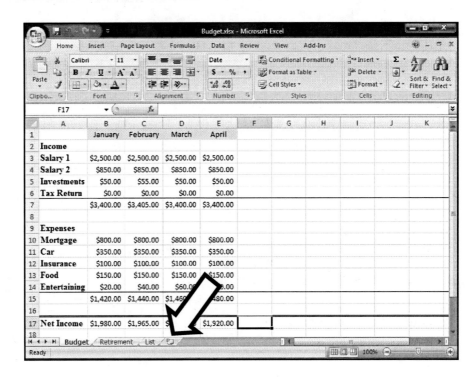

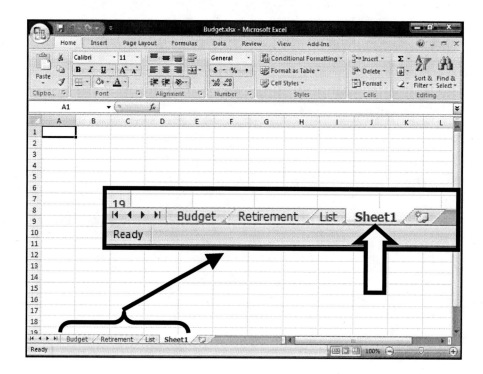

**Step 3:
Optional:
Rename the
new
worksheet.**

NOTE: Whenever you add a worksheet, it is inserted to the right of the current worksheets. The new worksheet automatically becomes the active worksheet. If you want to work in another worksheet, you must first activate it by clicking on the appropriate tab.

Section 36: Moving Worksheets

You have finished adding a new worksheet to the Budgets spreadsheet. After you add a new spreadsheet, you may decide that you would like to change the order of the worksheets. Typically people arrange their worksheets in

Chapter 8: Worksheets!

alphabetical order or in order by frequency of use. The most used worksheet is normally positioned to the extreme left side of the worksheet tabs.

Moving a worksheet is completed in the same manner you use to move a card while playing solitaire – the click and drag method. Position the mouse over the tab you desire to move, and click and hold down the left mouse button. By holding down the mouse button, you are grabbing a hold of the worksheet tab. Move the mouse into the position you want the worksheet placed, and release the mouse button. The worksheet will be moved to its new location.

As an example, move the worksheet named Sheet1 to the left of the worksheet named Retirement. Remember the first step is to position the mouse arrow over the Sheet1 tab. Click and hold down the left mouse button. Then move the mouse to the left of the Retirement tab and release the mouse button. The Sheet1 worksheet will now be located to the left of the Retirement worksheet. The same process can be used to change the order of the other worksheets.

Moving Worksheets: Step by Step Instructions
1. Click on the worksheet tab you desire to move.
2. Hold down the left mouse button.
3. Move the mouse to the new desired location within the worksheet tab list.
4. Release the mouse button.

Chapter 8: Worksheets!

Moving Worksheets: Visual Guide

Step 1:
Click on the worksheet tab you desire to move.

Step 2:
Hold down the left mouse button.

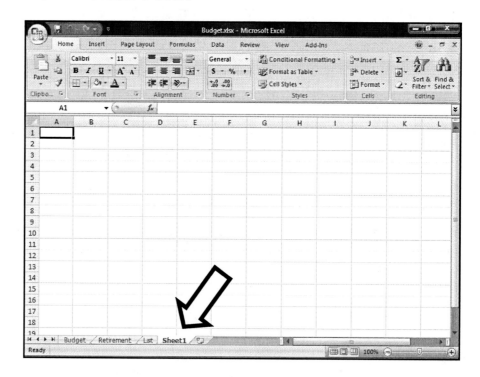

Step 3:
Move the mouse into the new desired location within the worksheet tab list.

Step 4:
Release the mouse button.

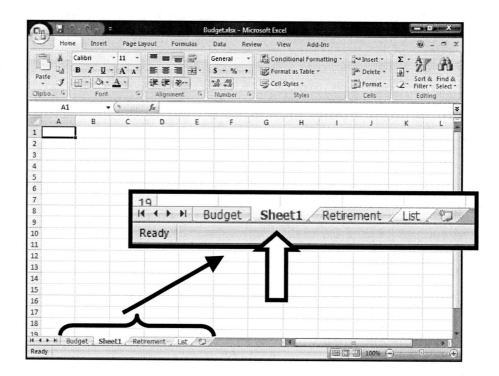

Chapter 8: Worksheets!

Section 37: Deleting Worksheets

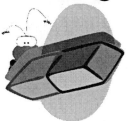

Deleting a worksheet is a simple task. However, you want to be absolutely certain the worksheet you are going to delete is the currently active worksheet and doesn't contain any data you need to keep. Once you delete a worksheet and save your spreadsheet/workbook, the worksheet and all of its data is gone. In this example, you will delete the worksheet named List.

To activate the worksheet, click on the List tab. The List tab will turn white, and the List worksheet will be displayed on the screen. Now, look at the screen and check the data to make sure it is safe to delete the worksheet. Click the DELETE button, located in the Cells section of the ribbon, to view the delete options.   Position the mouse pointer over the desired option, and click the left mouse button to make the selection.   The List worksheet will be removed from the spreadsheet.

Deleting a Worksheet: Step by Step Instructions
1. **Click on the worksheet tab you want to delete.**
2. **Click the DELETE button on the ribbon.**
3. **Click the DELETE SHEET option.**

Chapter 8: Worksheets!

Deleting a Worksheet: Visual Guide

Step 1:
Click on the
worksheet tab
you want to
delete.

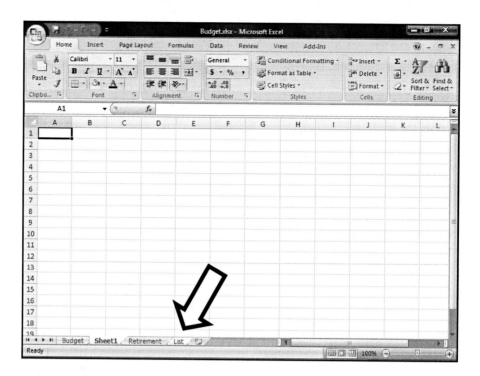

Step 2:
Click the
DELETE
button on the
ribbon.

Step 3:
Click the
DELETE
SHEET option.

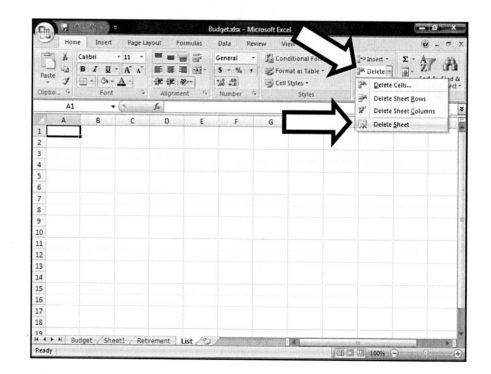

The List Worksheet has been deleted.

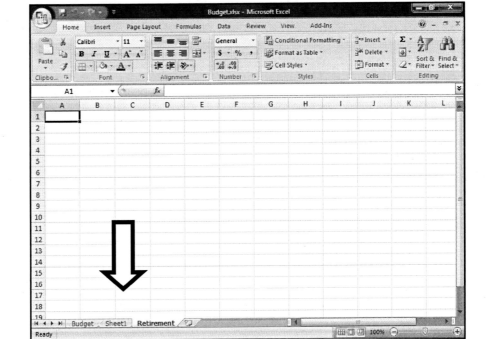

Please repeat the steps to delete worksheet Sheet1. Only two worksheets, Budget and Retirement, will be left when you are finished.

Worksheet Sheet1 has been deleted.

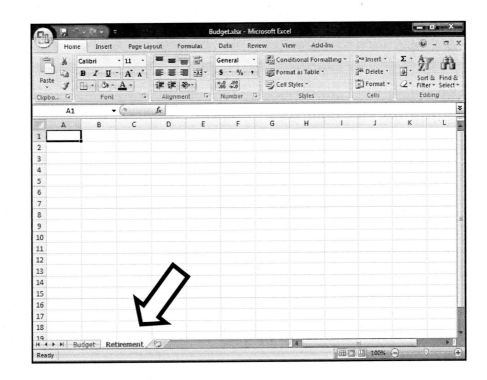

Chapter 8: Worksheets!

Chapter 9

Practice Entering and Formatting Data!

What You Will Learn in this Chapter

- ✓ Entering Data
- ✓ Creating Formulas to Calculate Mathematical Data
- ✓ Copying Formulas
- ✓ Using Toolbar Buttons
- ✓ AutoSum and How to Use It
- ✓ Formatting Data Using Toolbar Buttons

Chapter 9: Practice Entering & Formatting Data!

Section 38: Practice Entering Data and Creating Formulas to Perform Mathematical Calculations

To improve your Excel skills, practice entering and formatting data using the second worksheet, Retirement, in the example Budgets workbook. To activate the Retirement worksheet, click on the Retirement worksheet tab. The new worksheet will be used to plan for a couple's future retirement needs.

You are going to estimate their retirement income using the following assumptions:

- Both people living in the household will receive a company pension.
- One will also receive a social security benefit.
- They will receive interest on their savings account and certificates.
- Both will receive income from 401k and IRA investment accounts.

First, make an outline for the retirement income budget by entering the row and column labels prior to entering specific numbers into the worksheet. Use the point and click method, via the mouse, to select the cells in which you will type the labels. Remember, with point and click, you place the mouse in the correct location on the worksheet and click the left mouse button. Once the cell has been selected, you can type in the cell data. For example, move your mouse pointer over cell A2, and click your left mouse button. Notice, cell A2 will have the thick black box surrounding the cell. The computer is ready for you to enter data, so type the row label "Pension 1." To leave the cell in which you are currently typing, use the mouse to select another cell.

Continue using the point and click method to select the cells and type the row labels shown in the following table. Remember, if you not sure what cell is currently selected, look at the Name Box located at the top of the screen.

Chapter 9: Practice Entering & Formatting Data!

Cell	Data		Cell	Data
A3	Pension 2		A8	401k 2
A4	Social Security		A9	IRA
A5	Savings		*Skip row A10.*	
A6	Certificate			
A7	401k 1		A11	Total Income

Entering Data into a Cell: Step by Step Instructions

1. Select the cell where you desire to type. The selected cell will then have a bold black border.
2. Type in the cell data.
3. Repeat steps 1 and 2 to add additional data to the spreadsheet.

Entering Data into a Cell: Visual Guide

Step 1:
Select the cell where you desire to type.

Step 2:
Type in the cell data.

Step 3:
Repeat steps 1 & 2 to add additional data to the spreadsheet.

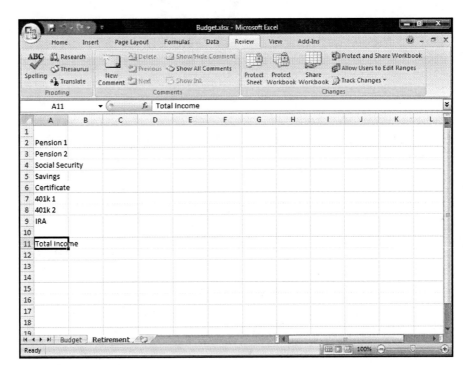

Continue using the point and click method to select the cells and enter the values as listed in the following table. Do not worry about formatting the numbers. You will do all the formatting at one time.

Chapter 9: Practice Entering & Formatting Data!

Cell	Data
B2	1400
B3	650
B4	1200
B5	5000

Cell	Data
B6	20000
B7	50000
B8	10000
B9	10000

Values entered into the retirement worksheet.

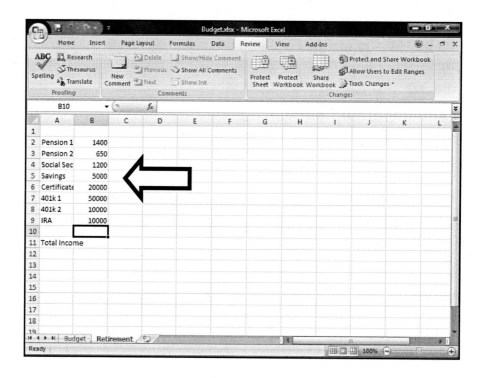

Continue using the point and click method to select the cells and enter the percentages shown in the following table. Type in the percent symbol % to ensure the computer understands these are to be used in percent format in future calculations.

Cell	Data
C5	3%
C6	6%
C7	8%

Cell	Data
C8	8%
C9	6%

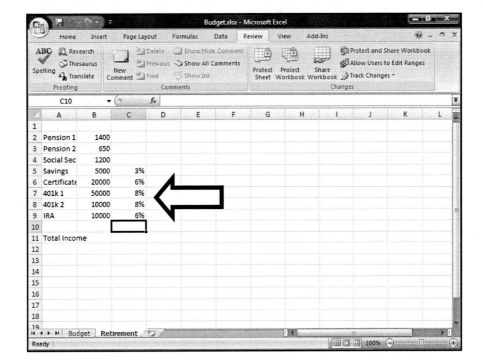

Annual interest percentages entered into the retirement worksheet.

Now you can use Excel to calculate the annual income for each row. To create the formulas, you will use the point and click method to select cells. Move the mouse pointer to cell D2 and click the left mouse button to select the cell. In this example cell, you are going to compute the yearly income for Pension 1. To tell the computer you are going to perform a calculation, type in an equal = sign. Instead of typing the value, move the mouse to cell B2 and press your left mouse button. The cell reference will now appear in the formula. However, to complete the calculation, you must multiply the value in cell B2 by 12 to compute the yearly income. Remember, the asterisk symbol (*) means multiply. Type the asterisk followed by the number 12. When you are finished, the formula bar should display the equation =B2*12. When you are finished entering the formula, press the Enter key on the keyboard. The annual income for Pension 1 (16,800) will be displayed in cell D. Please repeat the process to calculate the annual income for Pension 2 and Social Security.

Chapter 9: Practice Entering & Formatting Data!

Creating a Formula by Selecting Cells: Step by Step Instructions

1. Click on the cell in which you want to place a calculation.
2. Type an "equal sign" (=) to indicate you are entering a formula.
3. Select a cell with your mouse or type in a value.
4. Type a mathematical operator (+,-,*, /).
5. Type the value to complete the formula. You can also select other cells to complete formulas.
6. Press the Enter key on the keyboard and the computer will calculate the answer.

Creating a Formula by Selecting Cells: Visual Guide

Step 1:
Click on the cell in which you want to place a formula.

Step 2:
Type an "equal sign" (=).

Step 3:
Select a cell with your mouse or type in a value.

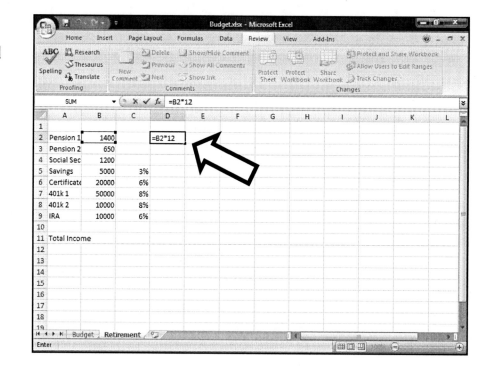

Chapter 9: Practice Entering & Formatting Data!

Step 4:
Type a the math operator (+,-,*, /).

Step 5:
Type the value or select a cell to complete the formula.

Step 6:
Press the Enter key.

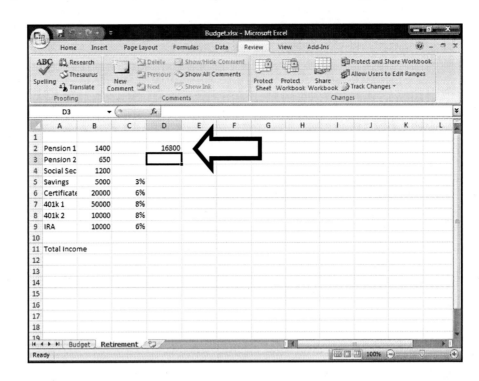

Formulas for the calculations.

Cell	Calculation
D2	=B2*12
D3	=B3*12
D4	=B4*12

Repeat the process for rows 2 and 3.

Calculations completed for cells D2, D3, and D4.

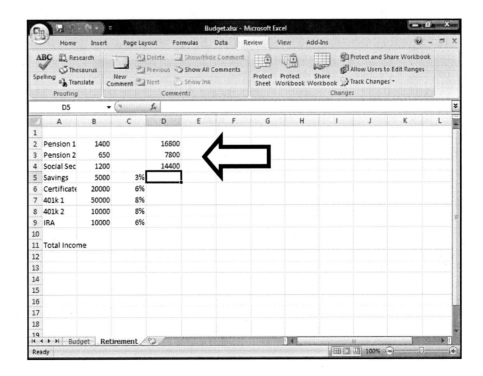

Chapter 9: Practice Entering & Formatting Data!

After you have calculated the annual income for Pension 1, Pension 2, and Social Security, you can calculate the annual interest from the Savings, Certificate, the 401k accounts, and the IRA. For these formulas you will multiple the values located in column B by the percentages entered in column C. Each of the steps for calculating the annual interest on the investment accounts is detailed below.

First, select cell D5 with the mouse. Tell the computer you are entering a formula by typing in an equal sign (=). Using the mouse, click on cell B5. Type a mathematical operator; in this case you are using * for multiplication. After entering the multiplication sign, use the mouse to select cell C5. The formula displayed in cell D5 should read =B5*C5. You have finished creating the formula, so press the Enter key to calculate the answer, 150.

Creating a Formula by Selecting Cells: Visual Guide

Step 1:
Click on the cell in which you want to place a formula.

Step 2:
Type an "equal sign" (=).

Step 3:
Select a cell with your mouse or type in a value.

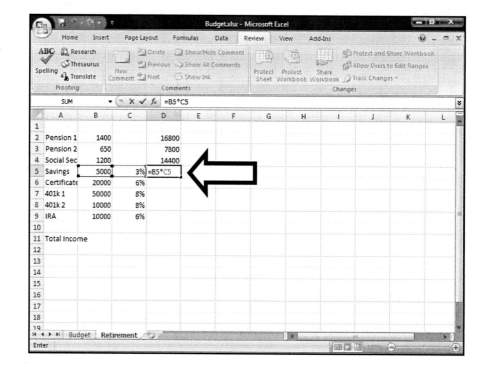

Step 4:
Type the math operator (+,-,*, /).

Step 5:
Repeat step 3 to add an additional cell to the calculation.

Step 6:
Press the Enter key.

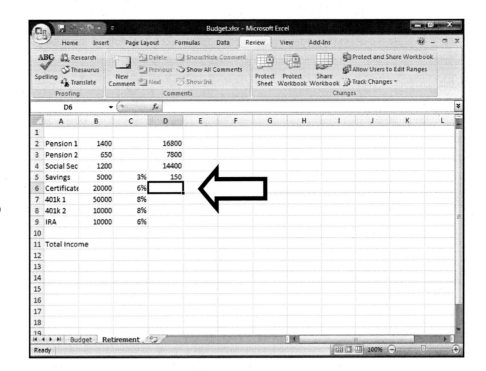

Because the formula you will use in D6, D7, D8, and D9 is the same as the formula you used to calculate the Savings income, you can copy and paste the formula in the corresponding cells to save time and effort.

Remember, the copy and paste option allows you to select a cell containing a formula, copy the formula into the computer's memory, and then paste the copied formula into another cell on the spreadsheet. Since you used cell references in the calculation, the computer will automatically adjust the cell references for the cells in the new column as you paste the formula into the new cells.

To complete the process, select cell D5 with the mouse. Then click the COPY button located on the ribbon. If you don't see the copy option, you will have to click the HOME Tab located at the top of the ribbon to view the copy and paste options. The copy button looks like two pieces of paper. Then highlight cells D6 through D9 using the mouse. When the cells are highlighted, click the PASTE button located on the ribbon. The calculation will be completed and the annual interest values will be displayed in the highlighted cells.

Chapter 9: Practice Entering & Formatting Data!

NOTE: If you are not sure what a picture (icon) on the ribbon represents, simply move your mouse pointer over the button, and words will appear in a box identifying the button.

Copying and Pasting: Step by Step Instructions

1. Select the cell containing the formula you want to copy.
2. If you don't see the copy option, you will have to click the HOME Tab located at the top of the ribbon.
3. Click the COPY button on the ribbon.
4. Highlight the cells where you want the copied formula to be placed.
5. Click the PASTE button on the ribbon.

Copying and Pasting: A Visual Guide

Step 1:
Select the cell containing the formula you want to copy.

Step 2:
If you don't see the copy option, you will have to click the HOME Tab located at the top of the ribbon.

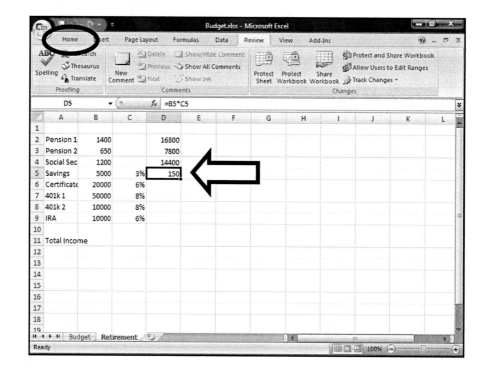

Chapter 9: Practice Entering & Formatting Data!

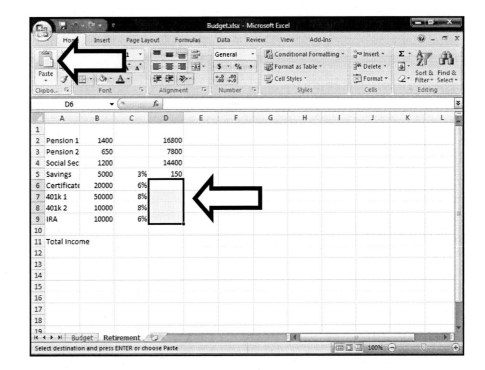

Step 3:
Click the COPY button.

Step 4:
Highlight the cells where you want the copied formula to be placed.

Step 5:
Click the PASTE button.

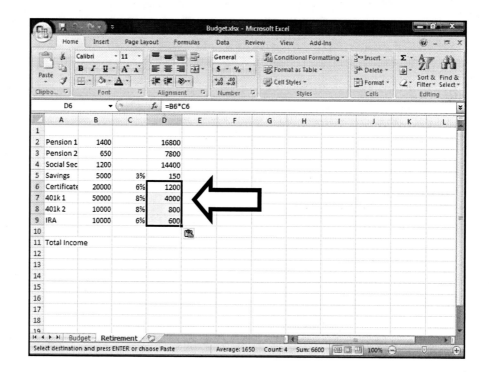

The copied formula will be pasted into the selected cells.

If you prefer to type in the formulas manually, use the table below for reference.

Formulas for the calculations.

Cell	Calculation
D5	=B5*C5
D6	=B6*C6
D7	=B7*C7
D8	=B8*C8
D9	=B9*C9

The last calculation you need is the Total Annual Income (the sum of all the values in column D). To perform this calculation, click on cell D11 to select it and then click the AUTOSUM button located on the ribbon. The AutoSum button looks like a large uppercase E. The AutoSum button will automatically put a dotted line around the cells in Column D indicating these cells will be used in the calculation. Press the Enter key on the keyboard and the Total Annual Income will be calculated, 45750.

Chapter 9: Practice Entering & Formatting Data!

Using the AutoSum Button in a Formula: Step by Step Instructions

1. Select the cell in which you want to place the formula.
2. Click the AUTOSUM Button on the toolbar.
   - Note the dotted line around the cells that will be used in the calculation.
3. Click the Enter key.

Using the AutoSum Button in a Formula: Visual Guide

Step 1:
Click on the cell in which you want to place a formula.

Step 2:
Click the AUTOSUM button located on the toolbar.

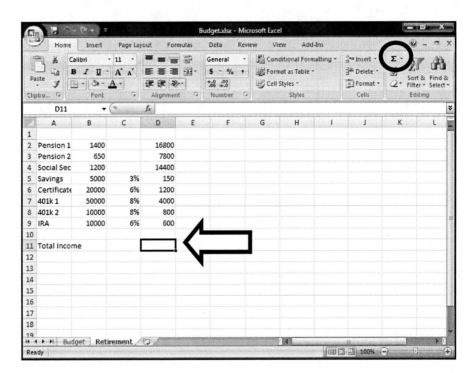

Chapter 9: Practice Entering & Formatting Data!

Note the dotted line around the cells that will be used in the calculation.

Step 3:
Press the Enter Key on the keyboard.

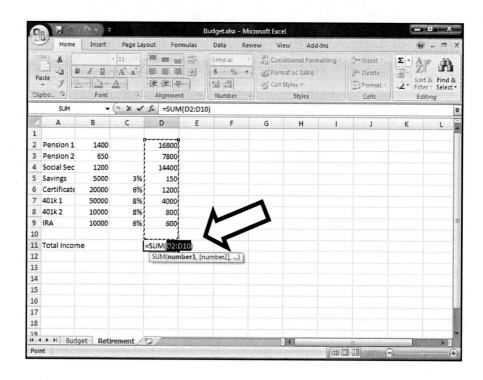

Calculated Total Annual Income.

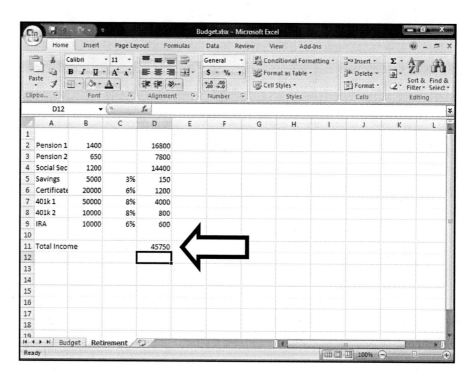

NOTE: Although the AutoSum feature is the quickest method to add a list of numbers, it is important to note that if there is a break in the sequence of numbers (in other words, if one of the cells is blank) the AutoSum will only total the numbers after the break or blank cell. If you choose to use this feature, be certain to pay attention to the numbers shown in the highlighted box after you have chosen the AutoSum feature, and before you press Enter. If it does not include the entire column, highlight the entire range of numbers you want totaled before pressing the Enter key.

Before you begin the formatting, Save your work by clicking on the SAVE button located just to the right of the Office button to save the changes you've made on the spreadsheet to the computer's main memory.

Section 39: Practice Formatting

Now that you have entered the labels and values, you can focus on formatting the worksheet. Remember the first step is to highlight the cells to which you would like to apply the new formatting. The last time you made formatting changes, you used the Format Cells Window (dialog box); this time you will use the format options located on the ribbon.

For the example, you want to bold all the row labels located in column A. To highlight the entire the column, click the column heading. Once the column is highlighted, locate the Bold button on the Font section of the ribbon. Click the BOLD button, represented by the black **B,** and the labels will be bolded. Move your mouse pointer to an unused cell on your worksheet, and click your left mouse button to unhighlight the cells you just bolded.

B

Formatting Text and Numbers: Step by Step Instructions
1. **Highlight the desired cells using the mouse.**
2. **Click on the desired format button located on the ribbon.**
3. **Click the left mouse button when the mouse pointer is positioned in an open area of the worksheet to unhighlight the cells.**

Chapter 9: Practice Entering & Formatting Data!

Formatting Text and Numbers: Visual Guide

Step 1:
Highlight the desired cells using the mouse.

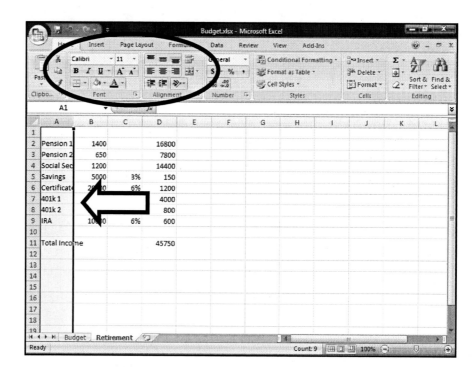

Step 2:
Click on the desired format button located on the toolbar.

Apply the Comma Style formatting to the numbers in column B. Use the COMMA STYLE button located on the NUMBER section of the ribbon to change the number format.

Chapter 9: Practice Entering & Formatting Data!

Step 1:
Highlight the desired cells using the mouse.

Step 2:
Click on the desired format button located on the ribbon.

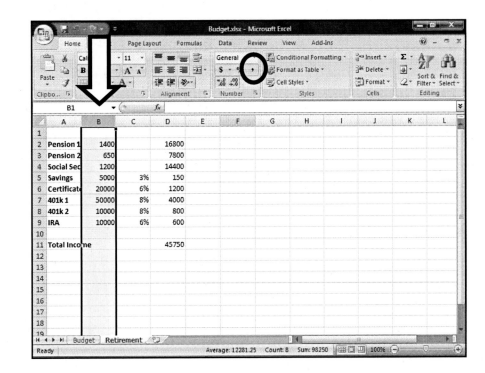

Apply the Comma Style formatting to the numbers in column D. Use the COMMA STYLE button located on the NUMBER section of the ribbon to change the number format.

Step 1:
Highlight the desired cells using the mouse.

Step 2:
Click on the desired format button located on the ribbon.

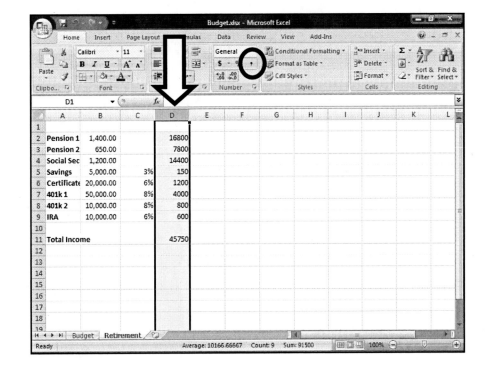

Chapter 9: Practice Entering & Formatting Data!

Apply the Currency Style formatting to the Total Annual Income located in cell D11. Use the CURRENCY STYLE button located on the NUMBER section of the ribbon to change the number format.

Step 1:
Highlight the desired cell using the mouse.

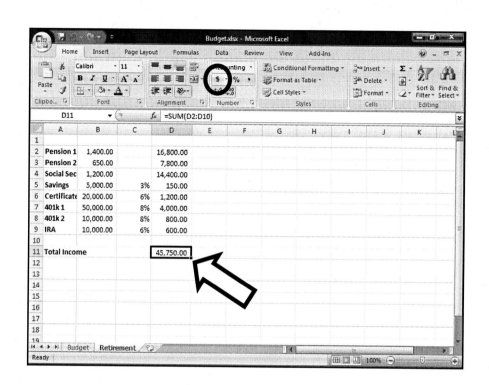

Step 2:
Click on the desired format button located on the Ribbon.

Applied Formatting.

	Formatting	Toolbar Button
Column A	Bold	B
Column B	Comma Style	,
Column D	Comma Style	,
Cell D11	Currency Style	$

You have just finished formatting the labels and numbers on the worksheet. The last formatting option you will use will apply a line to separate the Total Annual Income from the other values on the worksheet. You have the option of adding a single line, a bold line, double lines, or even complete borders to cells depending on your formatting preference. On the Retirement worksheet

Chapter 9: Practice Entering & Formatting Data!

you will add a single line above the Total Annual Income and a double line on the bottom of the cell.

To place the dividing line, first select cell D11 using the mouse. Once the cell is selected, locate the BORDER button on the ribbon located in the FONT section. Just to the right of the border button, you will see a small black arrow pointing down. If you click on the small black arrow, a list of border options will appear. From the list, click the border option displaying a single line at the top and a double line at the bottom of the cell. The lines will be applied to cell D11.

Adding Lines: Step by Step Instructions
1. **Highlight the desired cells using the mouse.**
2. **Click on the desired format button located on the ribbon.**
3. **Click the left mouse button when the mouse pointer is positioned in an open area of the worksheet to unhighlight the cells.**

Adding Lines: Visual Guide

Step 1: Highlight the desired cell using the mouse.

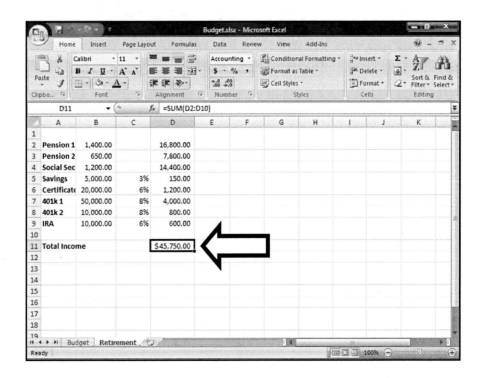

Chapter 9: Practice Entering & Formatting Data!

Step 2:
Click on the desired format button located on the toolbar.

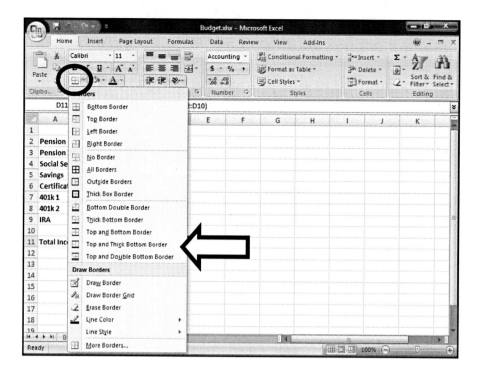

Step 3:
Click the left mouse button when the mouse pointer is positioned in an open area of the worksheet to unhighlight the newly formatted cell.

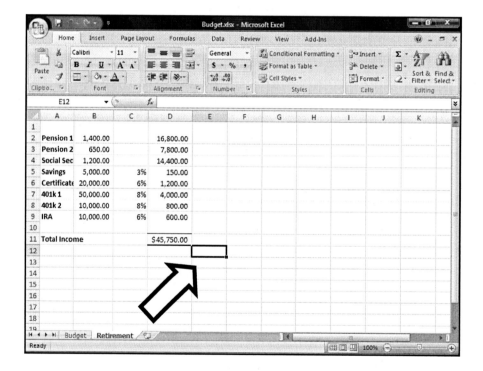

		Formatting	
Applied Formatting.	Row 11	Single Line top, double line bottom	

NOTE: Practice makes perfect. When you format your worksheets, you have the option of using either the menus or the toolbars.

Chapter 9: Practice Entering & Formatting Data!

Chapter 10

Filling In and Repeating Data!

What You Will Learn in this Chapter

✓ Automatically Fill In Repeating Data
✓ Using a Shortcut to Resize Columns
✓ Filling a Specific Sequence of Data
✓ The Options Available for Filling a Series of Data
✓ Using the Fill Handle
✓ Absolute Cell Reference
✓ Relative Cell Reference
✓ Changing Cell References

Chapter 10: Filling In and Repeating Data!

Section 40: Repeating Data

For the next example, you will use the original budget (which is located on Sheet1, which you renamed Budget.) To view the Budget worksheet, click once on the BUDGET worksheet tab located near the bottom left side of the Excel window. The Budget worksheet will display on the screen.

Look at the Salary1 row on the budget and notice how the numbers keep repeating without changing in value month after month. If you decided to expand the budget for the remainder of the year, you would have to type in the monthly values manually or use the copy and paste method. Another method to repeat data that does not change is to use Excel's Fill feature. The Fill feature enables you to duplicate cell data into adjacent cells quickly and easily.

You want to expand the budget through December. Before you start working with the monthly values, take a moment to label the columns for each consecutive month. After the columns have been labeled, you can expand the actual numbers using the Fill feature. Remember you must select a cell with the mouse before you begin typing. Add the month labels May through December to cells F1 through M1 respectively.

Chapter 10: Filling In and Repeating Data!

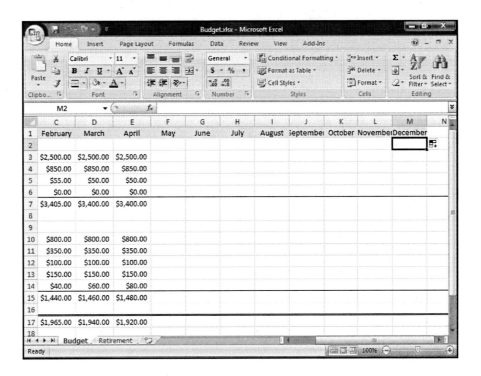

Now that the columns are labeled, you can use the Fill feature to repeat the monthly cell data which does not change for the remaining months of the year.

To Fill in repeating data, you need to highlight the cells containing the data you want repeated as well as the adjacent cells you want filled with the selected data. When you have highlighted the desired cells, the cells will have a dark black border around them. After you have highlighted the cells, click on the Fill button located on the Editing section of the ribbon. The FILL button is represented with a blue arrow pointing down on a white square.

Once you have selected the Fill button, a list will appear providing the fill options – UP, DOWN, RIGHT, or LEFT. If you wanted to fill the cells to the right of your selected data, you would choose RIGHT. If you wanted to fill the cells below your information, you would choose DOWN. The cells will be Filled with the desired data and formatting.

Using the example budget, you will fill the values for Salary 1 using the fill feature. First, highlight cell E3 which contains the value you are going to repeat. While holding down the left mouse button, highlight cells F3 through M3. When cells E3 through M3 are highlighted, release the left mouse button. Click the FILL button located on the ribbon. Since the cells you desire to fill

Chapter 10: Filling In and Repeating Data!

in are to the right of cell E3, select the option RIGHT from the list provided. Cells F3 through M3 will display the value of 2500.

Filling in Repeated Data: Step by Step Instructions

1. **Select the cell containing the data you want to repeat, as well as, the adjacent cells in which you want the data displayed by clicking and holding down the left mouse button.**
   - **The selected cells will have a dark black outline.**
2. **Click the FILL button located on the ribbon in the editing section.**
   - **A list will appear providing the possible fill options.**
3. **Choose the desired Fill option.**

Filling in Repeated Data: Visual Guide

Budget Worksheet.

Chapter 10: Filling In and Repeating Data!

Step 1:
Select the cell containing the data you want to repeat and the adjacent cells by clicking and holding down the left mouse button.

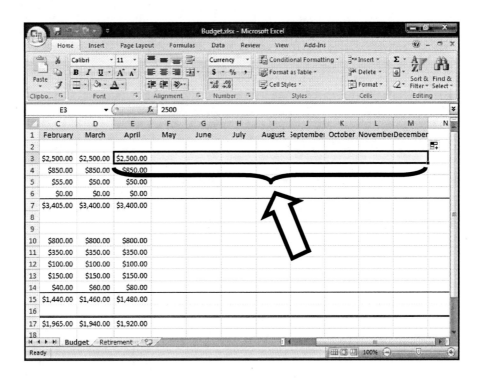

Step 2:
Click the FILL button located on the ribbon in the editing section.

Step 3:
Choose the desired Fill option (RIGHT).

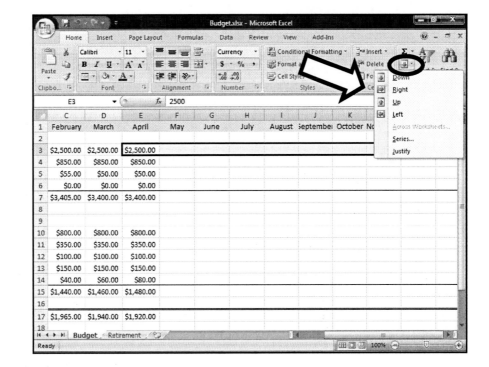

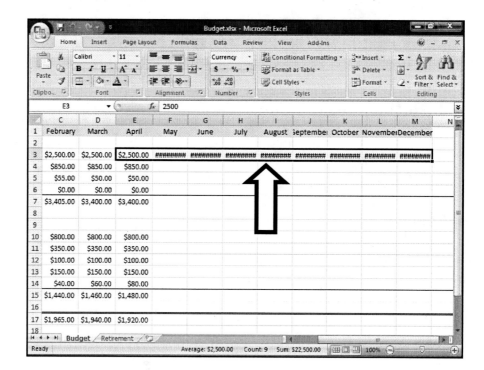

Data will be repeated and placed in the highlighted cells.

You may notice the new values are being displayed as number signs (#######) instead of as actual values. Multiple number signs indicate the data is too large to fit in the desired column. The column must be expanded to view the actual numbers. As you learned in Chapter 7, there is more than one way to change the size of a row or column. Use the mouse to increase the column width.

You want to increase the width of columns F through M. First highlight the columns using the column headings. Then notice the vertical lines between the heading letters. These lines can be used to increase or decrease the width of the column using the mouse. The mouse pointer will change from a white plus sign into a black line with two arrows pointing out the sides when it is positioned over the one of the vertical lines. You can either increase the width manually by using the click and drag method (click and hold down your mouse button while you move the line symbol) or you can double-click on the line symbol. Double clicking on the line symbol will automatically widen the columns to fit the data.

Resizing the Columns: Step by Step Instructions
1. **Highlight the desired columns using the column headings.**
2. **Double click one of the vertical lines between the highlighted column headings.**

Resizing the Columns: Visual Guide

Step 1:
Highlight the desired columns using the column headings.

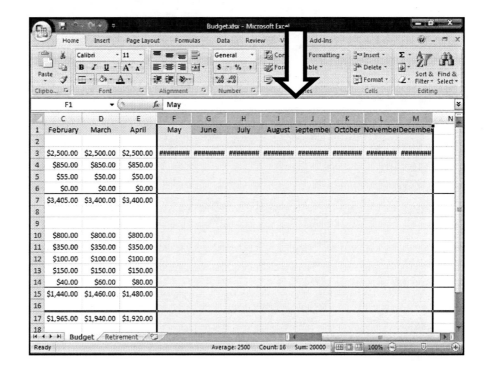

Step 2:
Double click one of the vertical lines between the highlighted column headings.

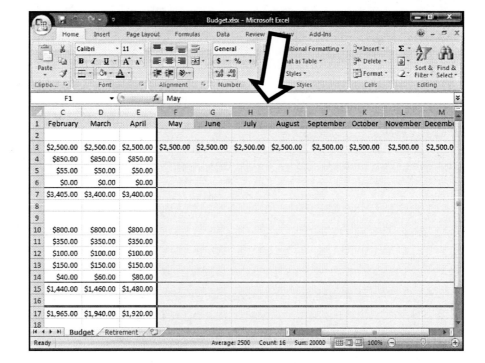

Chapter 10: Filling In and Repeating Data!

Click anywhere on the worksheet to release the highlighted area.

NOTE: You could have used the FORMAT button on the ribbon to resize the columns. The example merely illustrated a shortcut to the resizing process.

On the budget, you want to fill in the remaining income and expenses. You will use the same process as you did for repeating the data in Salary 1. The only difference in the process is highlighting multiple rows before accessing the Fill feature. On the example budget, highlight cells starting at E4 down to E17 and then over to M17. The entire block of cells from E4 through M17 should be highlighted. Then click on the FILL button located on the ribbon. From the fill list, choose the RIGHT fill option. The data from cells E4 through E17 will be filled in columns F through M.

Filling in Repeated Data: Step by Step Instructions
1. Select the data you want to repeat and the adjacent cells by clicking and holding down the left mouse button.
2. Click the FILL button located on the ribbon in the editing section.
   - A list will appear providing the possible fill options.
3. Choose the desired Fill option.

Chapter 10: Filling In and Repeating Data!

Filling in Repeated Data: Visual Guide

Step 1:
Select the data you want to repeat and the adjacent cells by clicking and holding down the left mouse button.

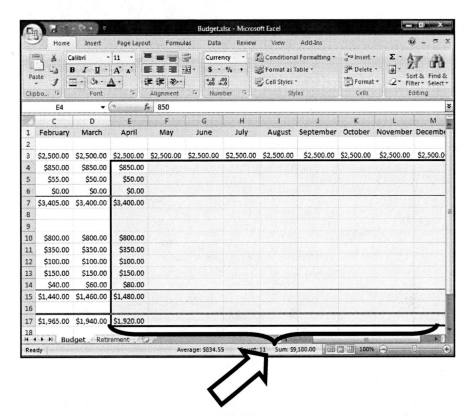

Step 2:
Click the FILL button located on the.

Step 3:
Choose the appropriate Fill option (RIGHT).

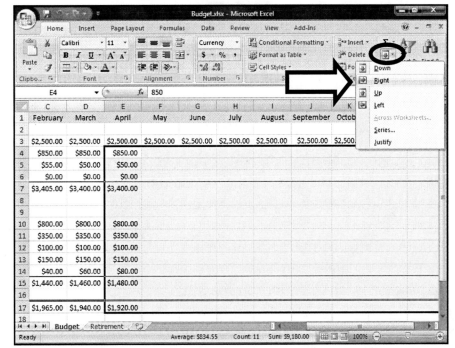

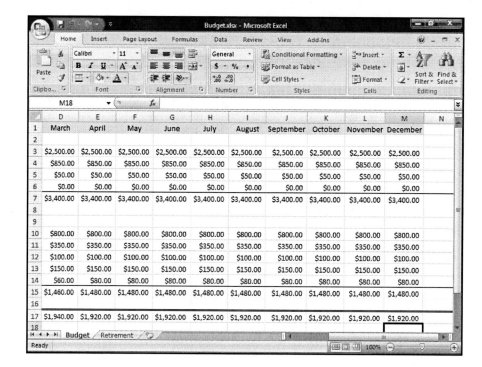

Data will be repeated and placed in the highlighted cells.

	D	E	F	G	H	I	J	K	L	M	N
	March	April	May	June	July	August	September	October	November	December	
1											
2											
3	$2,500.00	$2,500.00	$2,500.00	$2,500.00	$2,500.00	$2,500.00	$2,500.00	$2,500.00	$2,500.00	$2,500.00	
4	$850.00	$850.00	$850.00	$850.00	$850.00	$850.00	$850.00	$850.00	$850.00	$850.00	
5	$50.00	$50.00	$50.00	$50.00	$50.00	$50.00	$50.00	$50.00	$50.00	$50.00	
6	$0.00	$0.00	$0.00	$0.00	$0.00	$0.00	$0.00	$0.00	$0.00	$0.00	
7	$3,400.00	$3,400.00	$3,400.00	$3,400.00	$3,400.00	$3,400.00	$3,400.00	$3,400.00	$3,400.00	$3,400.00	
8											
9											
10	$800.00	$800.00	$800.00	$800.00	$800.00	$800.00	$800.00	$800.00	$800.00	$800.00	
11	$350.00	$350.00	$350.00	$350.00	$350.00	$350.00	$350.00	$350.00	$350.00	$350.00	
12	$100.00	$100.00	$100.00	$100.00	$100.00	$100.00	$100.00	$100.00	$100.00	$100.00	
13	$150.00	$150.00	$150.00	$150.00	$150.00	$150.00	$150.00	$150.00	$150.00	$150.00	
14	$60.00	$80.00	$80.00	$80.00	$80.00	$80.00	$80.00	$80.00	$80.00	$80.00	
15	$1,460.00	$1,480.00	$1,480.00	$1,480.00	$1,480.00	$1,480.00	$1,480.00	$1,480.00	$1,480.00	$1,480.00	
16											
17	$1,940.00	$1,920.00	$1,920.00	$1,920.00	$1,920.00	$1,920.00	$1,920.00	$1,920.00	$1,920.00	$1,920.00	
18											

Section 41: Filling a Sequence

Look closely at the expenses you just finished filling into the remaining eight months of the budget. Notice that the values for the entertainment expense didn't continue to increase by the allotted $20 per month. When repeating data, the computer takes the data located in the selected cell and only repeats the selected data, rather than entering a specific sequence of values.

If you want the computer to fill in a sequence of values from a starting point, the process is very similar to repeating data. The major difference is that you select a different fill option from the fill list. If you need to set up a sequence, choose the option SERIES. Excel will display a window offering additional

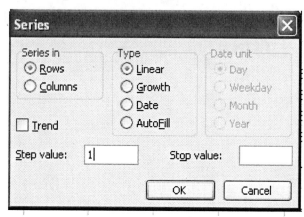

Chapter 10: Filling In and Repeating Data!

options from which to choose. The Series window displayed on the right allows you to select the type of series and to designate the value by which the series should increase, referred to as the Step Value. The Step Value for the Entertainment expense is 20.

To change the Entertainment expense, first select the last cell which contains the correct data for the series. Highlight this starting cell as well as all the adjacent cells in which you want the Entertainment expense data inserted. Then click on the FILL button. Click the SERIES option located in the fill list.

The Series window will open, allowing you to specify the details of the series. In the left corner is an option that lets you choose whether the series will appear in columns or rows. "Rows" is already selected; there is a black dot in the circle. Since you highlighted three cells in a row, Excel recognized that you intended to finish the sequence in the row and automatically chose "Rows." However, you must tell the computer what "Type" of sequence to use. You want a linear sequence because each box is going to increase by 20. Again "Linear" is already selected, confirmed by a black dot in the circle in front of "Linear."   At the bottom of the Series window is an input box labeled "Step Value" in which you enter the number you want used to increase each cell in the series. You want each column to be increased by 20, so place your mouse pointer in the Step Value box and click. When the cursor is blinking inside the box, type the number 20. Click the OK button at the bottom of the window with your left mouse button. Look at your budget. You will see that Excel filled in the series of numbers from May through December.

Filling a Sequence: Step by Step Instructions
1. **Highlight the cells containing the data you want to sequence.**
2. **Click the FILL button.**
3. **Choose the SERIES option.**
4. **Choose LINEAR under the Type heading.**
5. **Enter the Step Value.**
6. **Click on the OK button at the bottom of the Series option window.**

197

Filling a Sequence: Visual Guide

Step 1:
Select the data you want to sequence and the adjacent cells by clicking and holding down the left mouse button.

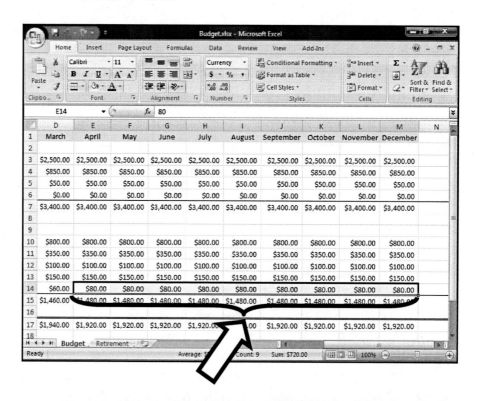

Step 2:
Click the FILL button.

Step 3:
Choose the SERIES option.

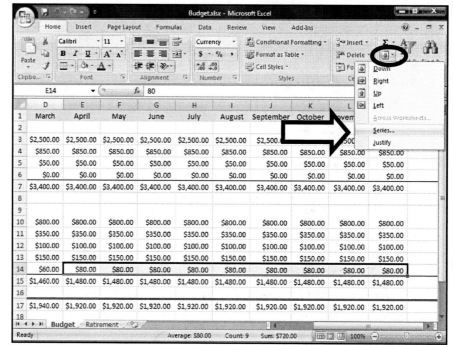

Step 4:
Choose
LINEAR under
the Type
heading.

Step 5:
Enter the Step
Value.

Step 6:
Click on the OK
button.

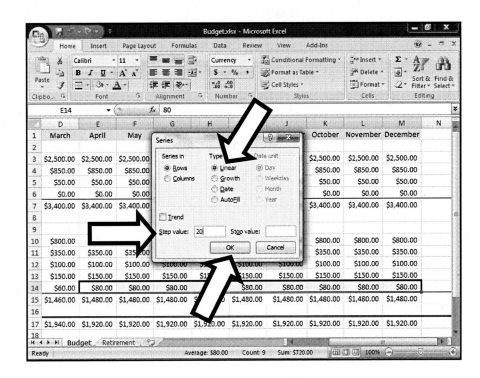

Updated Series.

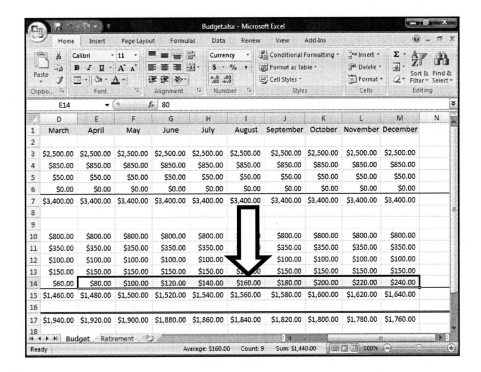

Chapter 10: Filling In and Repeating Data!

Filling in a Series can be used to complete the Retirement worksheet. Activate the Retirement worksheet by clicking on the Retirement tab in the lower left corner of the Excel Window. The Retirement worksheet will display on the screen.

Since you calculated the annual total for each income source, you can divide the annual amount by 12 to determine the average monthly income. However, before calculating the monthly income, take a moment to add month labels to cells E1 through J1. Labeling each month will keep the worksheet organized and increase its readability.

Previously, you added labels by typing them in one cell at a time. If you have a series, like consecutive months, you can type in the first month and have the computer fill in the remaining cells for you. The process of using Excel to fill in the adjacent cells is called filling a series.

To begin, select cell E1 using the mouse. When the cell is selected, type in the label January. Using the mouse, highlight cell E1 which now contains the label January, and then highlight the cells to the right through cell J1. When the cells are highlighted, release the left mouse button. Click on the FILL button. When the Fill list appears, click on the SERIES option. A new window will appear displaying a list of fill options for a series of data. Click the mouse in the dot next to the option AutoFill, and then click on the OK button. The computer will now insert the month labels from February to June in cells F1 through J1.

Filling a Series: Step by Step Instructions
1. Type the first value in the series.
2. Select the cell containing the first value in the series and the adjacent cells by clicking and holding down the left mouse button.
   - The selected cells will have a dark black outline
3. Click the FILL button.
   - A list will appear below the fill button.
4. Choose the SERIES option.
5. Click the AUTOFILL option.
6. Click on the OK button at the bottom of the Series window.

Filling a Series: Visual Guide

Step 1:
Type the first value in the series.

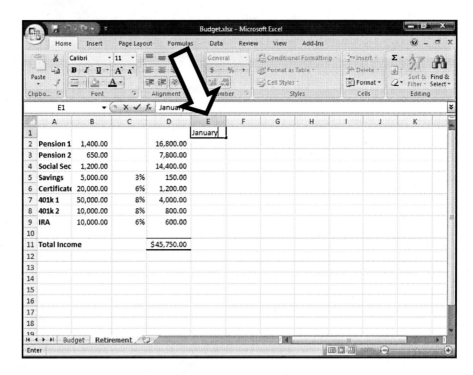

Step 2:
Select the cell containing the first value and the adjacent cells by clicking and holding down the left mouse button.

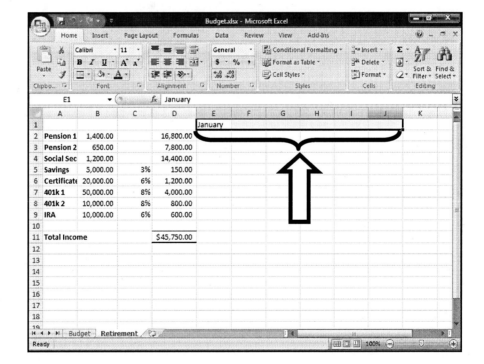

Step 3:
Click the FILL
button.

Step 4:
Choose the
SERIES
option.

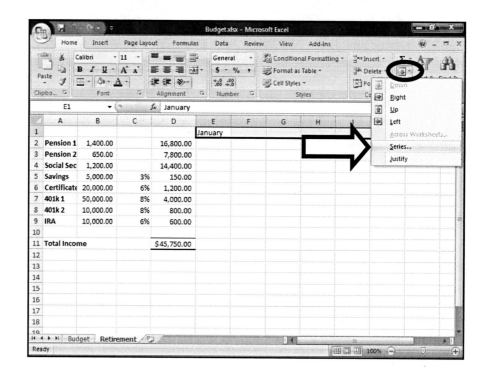

Step 5:
Click the
AUTOFILL
option.

Step 6:
Click the OK
button.

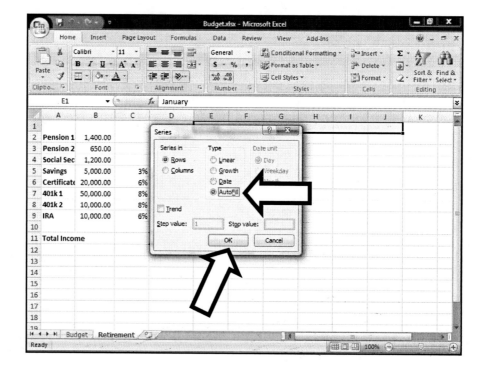

Chapter 10: Filling In and Repeating Data!

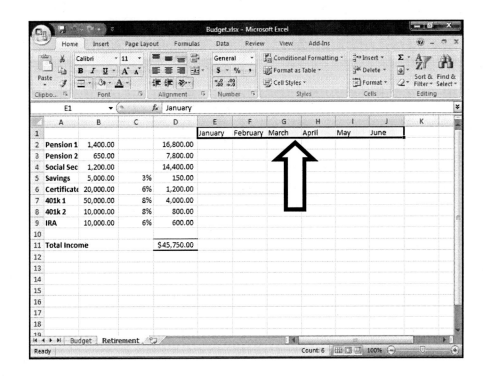

Series filled in, completing month labels for January through June.

NOTE: A <u>Linear</u> series is calculated by adding the value in the Step Value box to each cell. A <u>Growth</u> series is calculated by multiplying the value in the Step Value box by each cell value. A <u>Date</u> series fills date values incrementally by the value in the Step value box, dependent on the unit specified under Date unit. The Date option could be helpful if you used a number date (example 01/01) instead of a text date (January). An <u>Auto Fill</u> series fills in values incrementally based on the computer's best assumption using the beginning value.

Section 42: Fill Handle

After you have added the column labels, you can calculate the monthly income for each of the income sources by dividing the annual income by 12. First, select the cell where the answer to the calculation will appear. Second, type in an equal sign indicating the cell will contain a formula. Third, select the cells and type in mathematical operators for the formula. When you finish entering the formula, press the Enter key on the keyboard and the answer will be calculated.

For the example, select cell E2 using the mouse. Type an equal sign to start the formula. You will divide the annual income located in cell D2 by 12 to compute the average monthly income. The formula in cell E2 should read: =D2/12. The monthly income for Pension 1 is 1,400.

Creating a Formula by Selecting Cells: Step by Step Instructions

1. Click on the cell in which you want to place a formula.
2. Type an "equal sign" (=) to indicate you are entering a formula.
3. Select a cell with your mouse.
4. Type a mathematical operator (+,-,*, /).
5. Repeat Step 3 to add the remaining cell to the formula.
6. Press the Enter key on the keyboard. Excel will calculate the answer.

Creating a Formula by Selecting Cells: Visual Guide

Step 1:
Click on the cell in which you want to place a formula.

Step 2:
Type an equal sign (=).

Step 3:
Select a cell with your mouse.

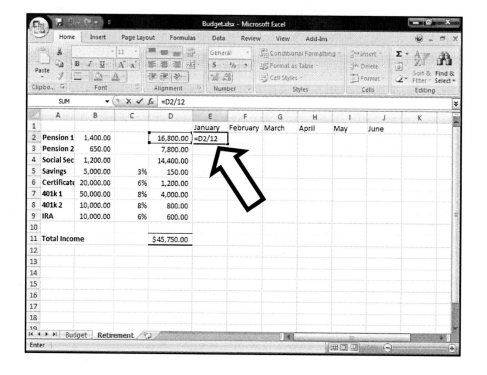

Chapter 10: Filling In and Repeating Data!

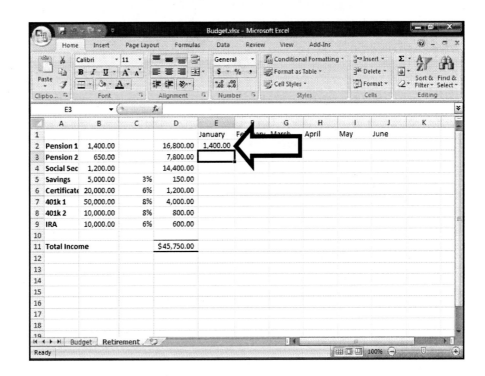

Step 4:
Type a mathematical operator.

Step 5:
Repeat Step 3 to add the remaining cell to the formula.

Step 6:
Press the Enter key.

Now that you have finished calculating the monthly income for Pension 1, you can apply the same formula to the remainder of the retirement income lines. The Fill Handle, which allows you to pull the data or formula from one cell into adjacent cells, can be used to complete the process. If the formula in a cell uses cell references, instead of numbers, the formula will change appropriately as it is filled into adjacent cells.

The Fill Handle is just a quick method of repeating data or a sequence. To copy the formula, first select the cell containing the data or formula you want entered into adjacent cells. For the example, click on cell E2 using the mouse. The cell will have a dark outline, and in the lower right corner of the outline will be a small black square. The small black square is the Fill Handle. Position the mouse pointer on the Fill Handle, and the mouse pointer will change into a narrow plus + symbol. Click and hold down the left mouse button to grab hold of the Fill Handle. While holding the Fill Handle, move the mouse over the cells you want filled in with the data/formula. In the example, move the mouse to cell E9. The cells between E2 and E9 should be outlined by a light gray line. Release the mouse button and the data/formula will be filled into the selected cells. Notice the formulas update in each cell because you used cell references while creating the formula. The computer automatically updates the cell references when placing the formula into new cells.

Chapter 10: Filling In and Repeating Data!

Using the Fill Handle: Step by Step Instructions

1. Click your mouse in the cell containing the data/formula you want to repeat.
   - The selected cell will have a dark black outline.
2. Click and hold down the left mouse button on the Fill Handle.
   - The Fill Handle is the small black square in the lower-right corner of the selected cell outline.
3. Move the mouse over the cells you want filled with the selected data.
   - The selected cell will have a light gray outline.
4. Release the left mouse button.

Using the Fill Handle: Visual Guide

Step 1:
Click your mouse in the cell containing the data/formula you want to repeat.

Step 2:
Click and hold down the left mouse button on the Fill Handle.

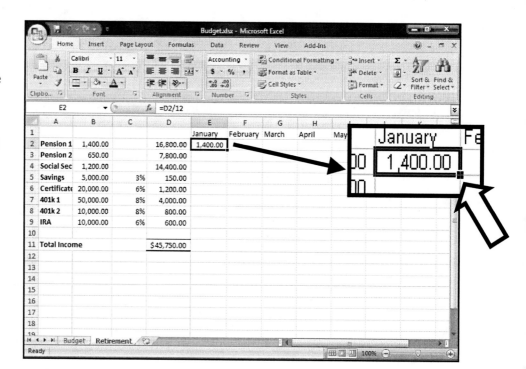

Step 3:
Move the mouse over the cells you want filled with the selected data.

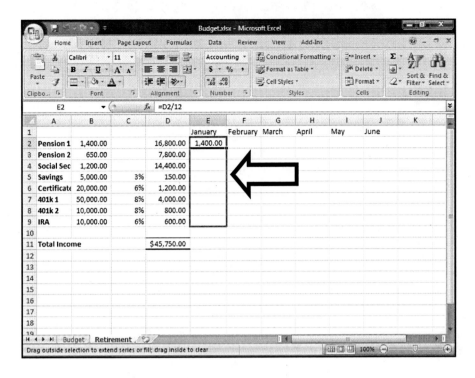

Step 4:
Release the left mouse button.

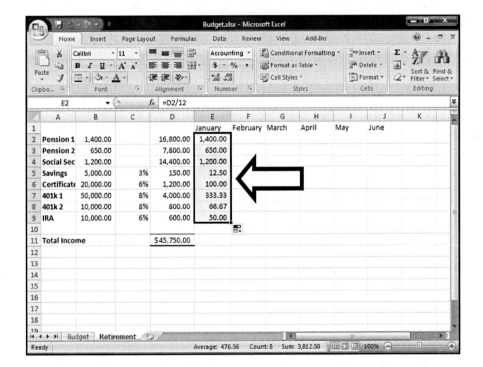

NOTE: If you find that using Fill Handle option is too difficult because the placing of the cursor must be so exact, don't use it. Use the FILL button in the ribbon, or the copy and paste method -- whichever is the easiest for you.

Section 43: Absolute & Relative Cell References

When you use Copy and Paste or the Fill option, either from the menu or via the Fill Handle, it is important to understand how the formulas change in the process. In the last example, you took the formula created in cell E2 and placed it into cells E3 through E7. After the process was completed, you looked at the filled cells and noticed the formula updated the cell references in the new cells. This process works well if you want the cell reference to update, but what if you don't want the cell reference to change. The next example will illustrate this dilemma and present a solution. You will use the data in column E to fill in the cells for the months of February through June (columns F through J) on the Retirement worksheet.

To make the value of a cell fixed, make the cell reference an absolute reference instead of a relative reference. "Absolute Cell Reference" means that a specified cell reference in a formula will not change regardless of the new location for the formula. "Relative Cell Reference" means that a specified cell reference in a formula will change when the formula is placed in a new location. The computer places a $ in front of the Column Letter, Row Number, or both to show the reference is Absolute. The absence of the $ indicates the reference is Relative. Typically all cell references, unless otherwise specified, are relative references.

Chapter 10: Filling In and Repeating Data!

To change a cell reference in a formula from Relative to Absolute, use the F4 key on the keyboard to toggle through the combinations. Pressing the F4 key once changes the cell column and row reference to Absolute. Pressing the F4 key a second time will make the row Absolute and the column Relative. Pressing the F4 key a third time will make the column Absolute and the row Relative. Pressing the F4 key a fourth time will return the entire cell reference to Relative.

Cell Reference	Press F4	Cell Reference Changes to
Absolute Cell Reference – (Absolute column and Absolute row)	Once	$A$1
Relative column and Absolute row	Twice	A$1
Absolute column and Relative row	Three	$A1
Typical Cell Reference– (Relative column and Relative row)	Four	A1

Don't let the cell reference names confuse you. The main point to remember is, when you copy a formula from one cell to another, you have to determine if you want the cell references to update in the new location. If the answer is yes, don't change anything in the calculation. If the answer is no, use the F4 key on the keyboard to change the cell reference to Absolute so that it doesn't change.

Using the Retirement worksheet, you will fill in the monthly income for each line. You can use either the Fill Handle or the Fill button on the ribbon to update the worksheet. Since the Fill Handle is typically easier, the example will use this method.

Using the Fill Handle: Step by Step Instructions
1. Click your mouse in the cell containing the data/formula you want to repeat.
2. Click and hold down the left mouse button on the Fill Handle.
3. Move the mouse over the cells you want filled with the selected data.
4. Release the left mouse button.

Chapter 10: Filling In and Repeating Data!

Using the Fill Handle: Visual Guide

Step 1:
Click the mouse in the cell containing the data/formula you want to repeat.

Step 2:
Click and hold down the left mouse button on the Fill Handle.

Step 3:
Move the mouse over the cells you want filled with the selected data.

Step 4:
Release the left mouse button.

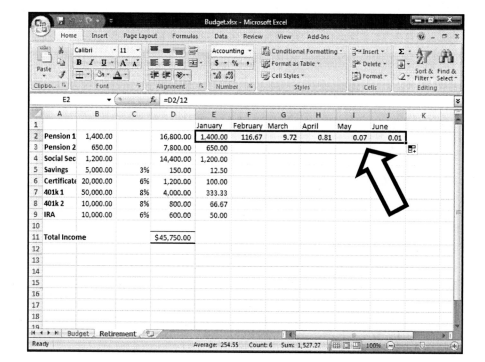

Chapter 10: Filling In and Repeating Data!

Notice the monthly value decreased even though the monthly income should have remained constant each month. To locate the problem, click on the cell F2 to view the formula for February. Click on cell E2 to view the formula for January. Compare the two formulas. In the formula bar, you can see the cell reference which was originally cell D2 (in January) is now E2 (in February). This change occurred because the calculation used a relative cell reference. The relative cell reference updated automatically when the formula was placed in the new cells. To fix the problem, you must change the formula in cell E2 to make the cell reference to cell D2 "Absolute," and then Fill the adjacent cells again. The incorrect fill data will be replaced with the new correct formula.

Click on the cell where you think the error first occurred, and look at the formula bar to view the formula.

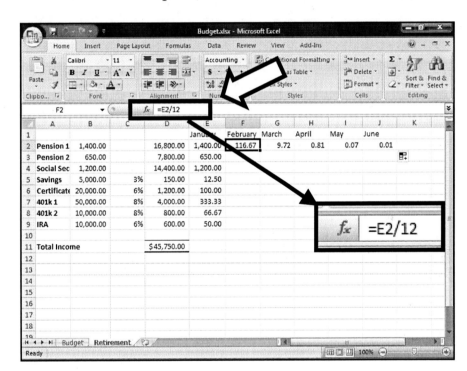

Changing a Cell Reference to Absolute: Step by Step Instructions

1. **Click your mouse in the cell containing the data/formula you want to repeat in other cells to select it.**
2. **Click your mouse in the Formula Bar.**
3. **Press the F4 key on the keyboard to change the cell reference to Absolute.**
   - **The cell reference will display a $ (dollar sign) in front of both the column and row identifier.**
4. **Press the Enter key on the keyboard to finish changing the formula.**

Changing a Cell Reference to Absolute: Visual Guide

Step 1:
Click your mouse in the cell containing the formula you want to change to Absolute.

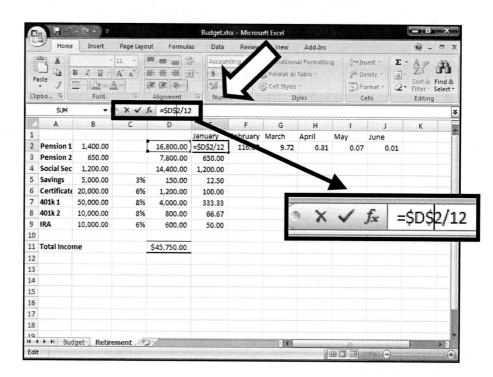

Step 2:
Click your mouse in the Formula Bar.

Step 3:
Press the F4 key on the keyboard.

Step 4:
Press the Enter key on the keyboard.

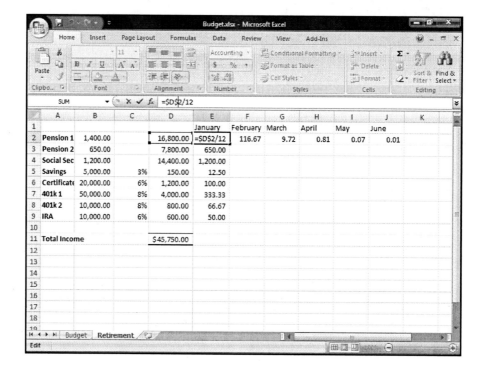

Use the Fill Handle to fill in the monthly income from January to February through June, thus replacing the incorrect data.

Chapter 10: Filling In and Repeating Data!

Using the Fill Handle: Step by Step Instructions

1. Click your mouse in the cell containing the data/calculation you want to repeat.
2. Click and hold down the left mouse button on the Fill Handle.
3. Move the mouse over the cells you want filled with the selected data.
4. Release the left mouse button.

Using the Fill Handle: Visual Guide

Step 1: Click your mouse in the cell containing the data/formula you want to repeat.

Step 2: Click and hold down the left mouse button on the Fill Handle.

Step 3:
Move the mouse over the cells you want filled with the selected data.

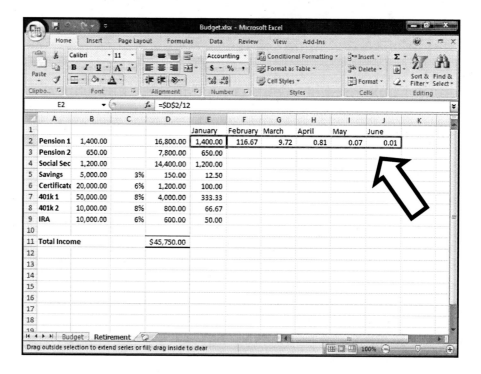

Step 4:
Release the left mouse button.

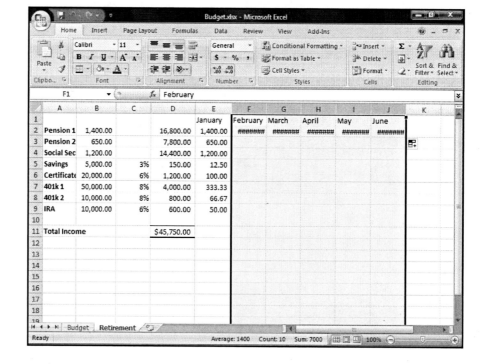

If the numbers do not fit in the columns (######) you will have to resize the columns.

Highlight the columns and then double click on the vertical line in between the column headings.

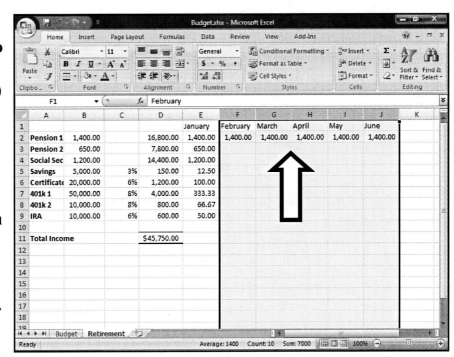

Click on a cell which was just filled and look at the formula bar to verify that the formula is now correct.

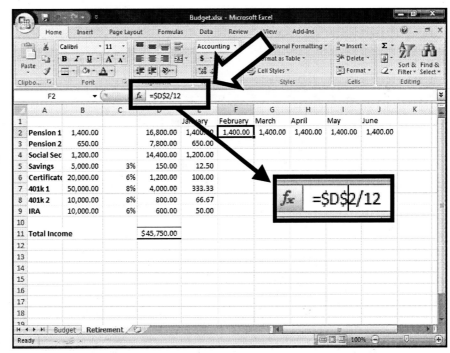

Change the cell reference used to calculate the monthly income for January in each of the remaining income rows. The calculations for each income line for January should be exactly as displayed in the following table. The cell containing the annual income should have an absolute cell reference.

Chapter 10: Filling In and Repeating Data!

Cell	Formula	Cell	Formula
E2	=$D$2/12	E6	=$D$6/12
E3	=$D$3/12	E7	=$D$7/12
E4	=$D$4/12	E8	=$D$8/12
E5	=$D$5/12	E9	=$D$9/12

Changing a Cell Reference to Absolute: Step by Step Instructions

1. Click your mouse in the cell containing the data/formula you want to change.
2. Click the mouse in the Formula Bar.
3. Press the F4 key on the keyboard.
4. Press the Enter key on the keyboard to recalculate the answer.

After changing the formulas, fill in the monthly income for each income line for February through June.

Using the Fill Handle: Step by Step Instructions

1. Highlight the cell containing the data/formula you want to repeat.
2. Click and hold down the left mouse button on the Fill Handle.
3. Move the mouse over the cells you want to fill with the selected data.
4. Release the left mouse button.

Chapter 10: Filling In and Repeating Data!

Using the Fill Handle: Visual Guide

Step 1:
Highlight the cell containing the data/formula you want to repeat.

Step 2:
Click and hold down the left mouse button on the Fill Handle.

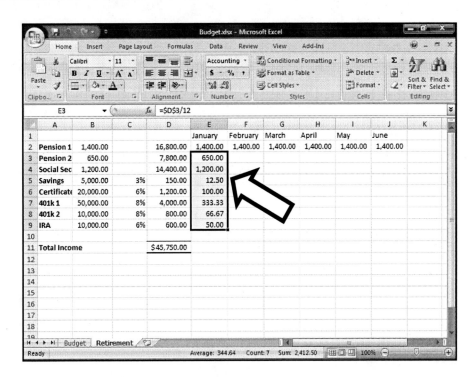

Step 3:
Move the mouse over the cells you want filled with the selected data.

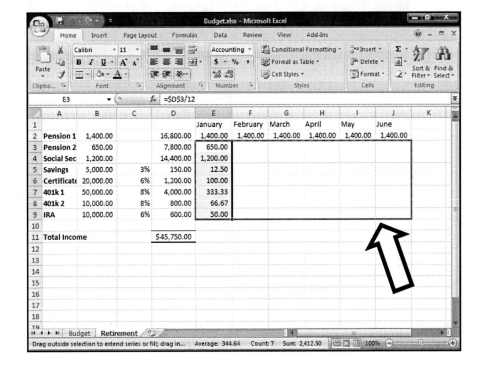

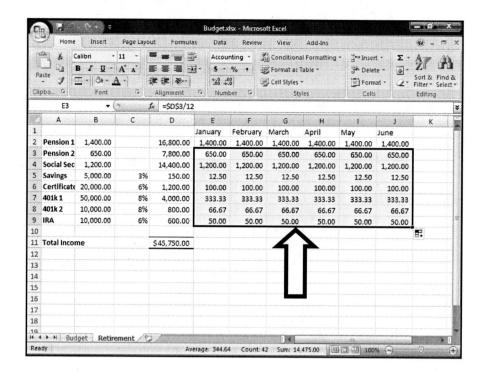

Step 4:
Release the left
mouse button.

Section 44: Practice Using the Fill Handle

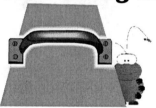

The only way to gain a full understanding of the Fill Handle and Cell References is through practice. The more often you use these features, the easier they will become. As you prepare more complex spreadsheets, you will find these features incredibly valuable.

Using the Retirement worksheet, you want to calculate the total income for each month. The easiest way to complete the task is to calculate the total for one month using cell references and then use the Excel's Fill feature to repeat the calculation for the remaining months.

Calculate the total income for the month of January. You can add each cell manually by typing, or pointing to and selecting, each cell you want in the total (example: =E2+E3+E4+E5+E6+E7+E8+E9). Or you can use the AutoSum feature you used earlier in this book. The AUTOSUM button is located on the ribbon and looks like a large uppercase E.   To perform this calculation, click cell E11. Once the cell is selected, click the AUTOSUM button located on the Standard toolbar. AutoSum will automatically put a dotted line around the cells in Column E indicating these cells will be used in the calculation. Press the Enter key on the keyboard and the Total Monthly Income will be calculated, 3812.50.

Step 1:
Click on the cell in which you want to place a calculation.

Step 2:
Click the AUTOSUM button located on the ribbon.

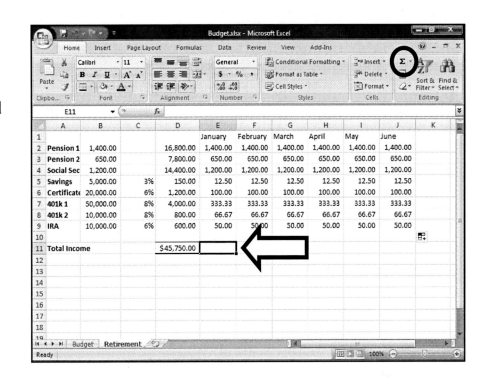

Step 3:
Press the Enter
key on the
keyboard.

Calculated
Total Annual
Income.

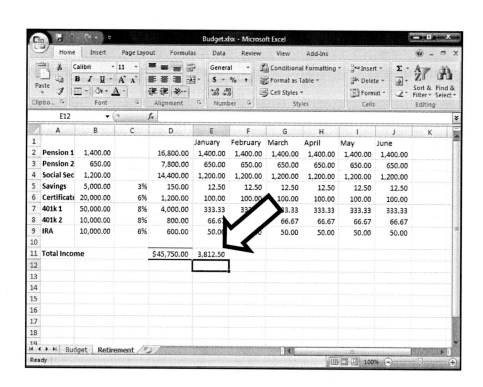

Chapter 10: Filling In and Repeating Data!

The last step is to fill in the total monthly income for the remaining months. Select cell E11. Then use the Fill Handle to repeat the calculation for February through June. You don't have to worry about the cell references because you want them to update as the calculation is placed in the new cells. The updated cell references ensure the calculation was conducted correctly for each column (that each column is totaled separately).

Using the Fill Handle: Step by Step Instructions
1. **Highlight the cell containing the data/formula you want to repeat.**
2. **Click and hold down the left mouse button on the Fill Handle.**
3. **Move the mouse over the cells you want filled with the selected data.**
4. **Release the left mouse button.**

Using the Fill Handle: Visual Guide

Step 1:
Highlight the cell containing the data/formula you want to repeat.

Step 2:
Click and hold down the left mouse button on the Fill Handle.

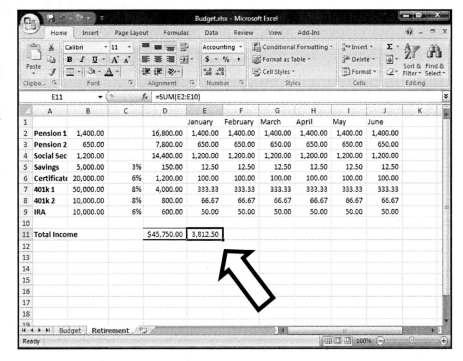

Step 3:
Move the
mouse over the
cells you desire
to fill with the
selected data.

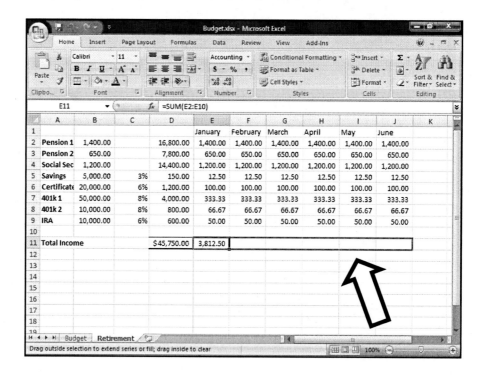

Step 4:
Release the left
mouse button.

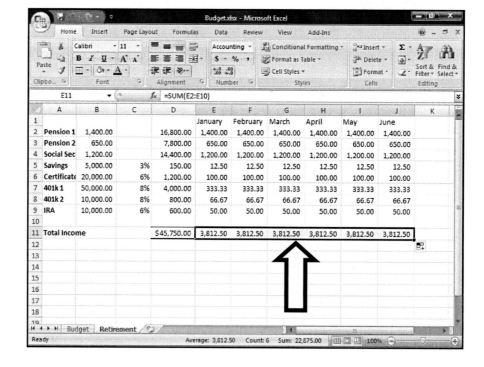

Chapter 10: Filling In and Repeating Data!

NOTE: You can fill any type of sequence. You can fill a sequence of numbers going up by ones, twos, fours, etc. You can also fill a sequence of dates. If you want the computer to put in a series of numbers, for example one to one hundred, going up by ones, you could instruct the computer to start at 1, put in a step value of 1, and input a stopping value of 100. Excel would put 1, 2, 3, 4, 5, …, all the way to 100.

WARNING: You cannot use the "Fill" option when your data changes in an unusual manner. In the budget, the Entertainment expense increases monthly. For irregular lines, you either have to use the Series option or input the values manually. The data or formulas must either be entered or copied into the cells.

REMINDER: When you reference (link) to a cell with a formula, if you change the formula, the linked cell will also change.

Chapter 10: Filling In and Repeating Data!

Chapter 11

Linking Worksheets!

What You Will Learn in this Chapter
- ✓ Linking Data on Multiple Worksheets
- ✓ Identifying Linked Cells
- ✓ Using the Fill Handle

Section 45: Linking Data Contained on Different Worksheets

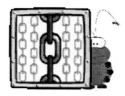

One of the most useful features of Microsoft Excel is its ability to link data contained in different worksheets, either in the same Excel file or between different Excel workbooks. However, you must understand exactly how the linking process works to avoid problems. Linking data from one cell to another is similar to having a one-sided conversation – the data or information flows in only one direction.

At least two cells are involved. The first cell, the one that contains the information, is often called the "source" or "reference" cell. The second cell, the one that links itself to the first cell, may be referred to as the "receiving" or "linked" cell. Information flows in only one direction – from the source cell to the linked cell.

You have already linked cells. Every time you referred to another cell in a formula, you linked to it. When you totaled cells by entering a formula, e.g. +B1+B2+B3, you linked to those cells. The total of the data in the source cells was displayed in the linked cell. You can expand on that fundamental linking process to link cells on different worksheets.

Important things to remember about linking are:
- A link is established by entering a formula in a cell which refers to the source cell.
- Whenever a change is made to a source cell, Excel automatically makes the same change in the linked cell.
- Changes made in the linked cell will **not** be made to the source cell. You can add additional data or formulas to the linked cell that will not be reflected in the source cell. You can also link to multiple source cells in one formula.
- The source cells can contain text, dates, numbers, formulas, etc. which will be copied to the linked cell. However, the formatting in the source cell does not copy over.

Chapter 11: Linking Worksheets!

A quick example will make this concept easier to understand. Suppose you are working with two cells, B1 and C1. C1 is the source cell and B1 is the cell which is linked to the source cell:

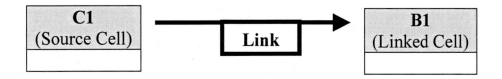

- If Cell C1 contains the number 20 and you left click on cell B1 and enter the formula =C1, the number 20 will immediately appear in B1.
- If you change the number in C1 to 500, 500 will automatically appear in B1.
- If you put in a formula in C1 (+400/2) the result (200) will appear in both C1 and B1.
- The data in B1 changes every time the data in C1 changes.
- If you change the formatting in C1 to bold, the formatting in B1 will not change.
- If C1 contains the number 20 and you enter the formula =C1*10 in B1, a total of 200 (20*10) will appear in B1. However, C1 will still display the number 20. Due to the one-way line of communication in the linking process, the number in the source cell does not change when the formula in the linked cell does.

Using the worksheets you have already created, you will determine whether your retirement income will cover your current expenses. Transfer the expenses you entered in the Budget worksheet to the Retirement worksheet. You have two options to transfer the data. You can re-enter the data manually on the Retirement worksheet, or you can link the Budget worksheet expenses to the Retirement worksheet. Retyping can lead to errors and is very time consuming, so let's link the worksheets together.

Before you begin to link cells, you must decide on exactly what data you want to include on the Retirement worksheet. In the example budget, first add the labels for the expenses and then add the monthly expenses for January through June to the Retirement worksheet. The process of linking cells is similar to the process you used to reference cells in your formulas. First, select the cell in which to display the result. Then type in an equal sign to begin creating a link in the cell. Third, locate and click on the cell which contains the data to which you want to link (the source cell). When you are done, press the Enter key on the keyboard to complete the process. The data in the referenced/linked cell will be displayed in the selected cell.

Using the Retirement worksheet, click on cell A13. This is the cell in which you are going to place the label Expenses. Instead of typing in the label you can link to the label located on the Budget worksheet. Type in an equal sign (=) to indicate you intend to add a cell reference. Then activate the Budget worksheet by clicking on the worksheet tab at the bottom of the screen. On the Budget worksheet, locate cell A9 which contains the label Expenses, and click on the cell (you may have to use the horizontal scroll bar to see column A.) The computer will display the cell reference in the Formula Bar. Press the Enter key on the keyboard. The computer will automatically return you to the Retirement worksheet, and cell A13 will be linked to cell A9 on the Budget worksheet.

NOTE: The cell reference will display the name of the worksheet followed by an exclamation mark, followed by the cell name, to indicate the cell is referenced to a different worksheet. The example cell reference is: =Budget!A9.

Linking Cells: Step by Step Instructions
1. **Click on the cell in which you want to place the linked data.**
2. **Type in an "equal sign" (=) to indicate that you are entering a cell reference.**
3. **Open the desired worksheet.**
4. **Select a cell with your mouse.**
5. **Press the Enter Key on the keyboard. The computer will display the result.**

Chapter 11: Linking Worksheets!

Linking Cells: Visual Guide

Step 1:
Click on the cell in which you want to place the linked data.

Step 2:
Type an "equal sign" (=).

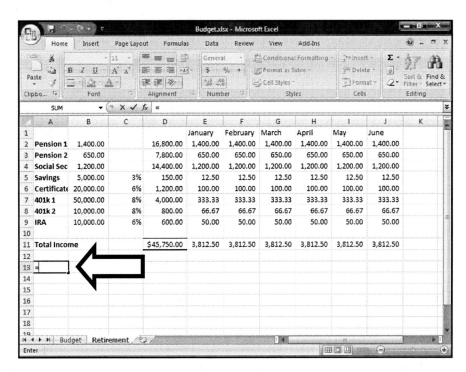

Step 3:
Open the desired worksheet.

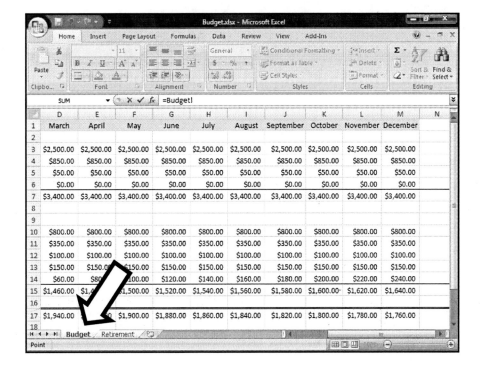

Step 4:
Select a cell with your mouse.

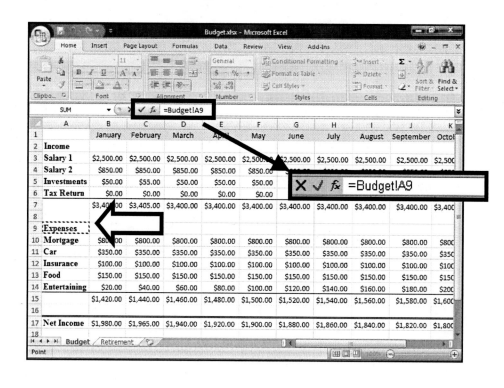

Step 5:
Press the Enter Key on the keyboard.

Selected cell is linked to source cell.

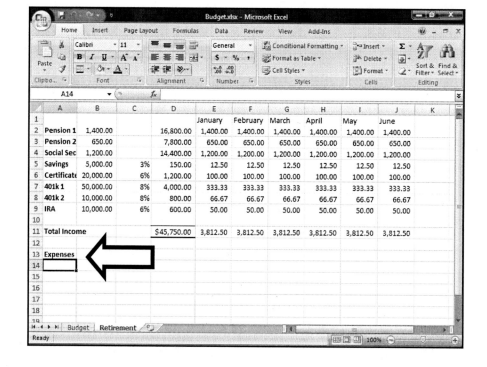

Follow the same steps to add all the expense labels to the Retirement worksheet.

Chapter 11: Linking Worksheets!

Linking Cells: *Step by Step Instructions*

1. Click on the cell in which you want to place the linked data.
2. Type an "equal sign" (=) to indicate that you are entering a cell reference.
3. Open the desired worksheet.
4. Select a cell with your mouse.
5. Press the Enter key on the keyboard. The computer will display the result.

Linking Cells: *Visual Guide*

Step 1:
Click on the cell in which you want to place the linked data.

Step 2:
Type an "equal sign" (=).

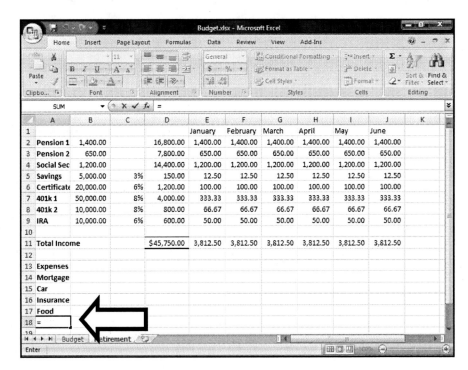

Chapter 11: Linking Worksheets!

Step 3:
Open the
desired
worksheet.

Step 4:
Select a cell
with your
mouse.

Step 5:
Press the Enter
Key on the
keyboard.

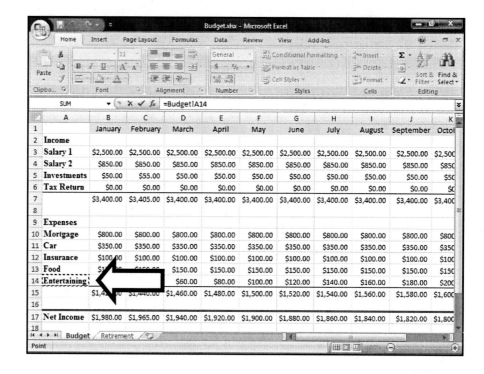

Expense
Labels
Finished.

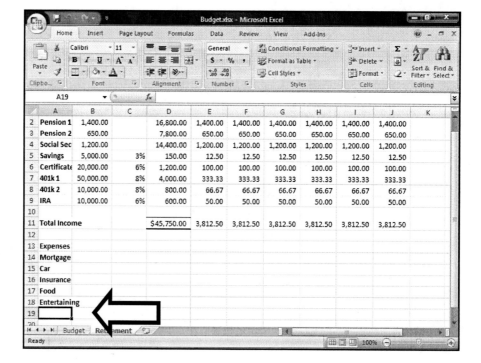

Chapter 11: Linking Worksheets!

Once the expense labels have been added, you will add the individual monthly expense values to the Retirement worksheet. After adding the first expense, the mortgage for January, use the fill process to insert the remaining values. Pay particular attention to the cell you are selecting; if you accidentally choose the wrong cell, your expenses will be incorrect.

On the Retirement worksheet, select cell E14. Make certain you are adding the expenses under the correct column. Column E has the income for January.

Linking Cells: Step by Step Instructions
1. **Click on the cell in which you want to place the linked data.**
2. **Type an "equal sign" (=) to indicate that you are entering a cell reference.**
3. **Open the desired worksheet.**
4. **Select a cell with your mouse.**
5. **Press the Enter Key on the keyboard. The computer will display the result.**

Linking Cells: Visual Guide

Step 1: Click on the cell in which you want to place the linked data.

Step 2: Type an "equal sign" (=).

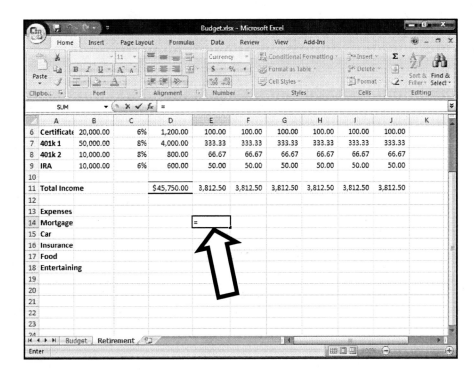

Chapter 11: Linking Worksheets!

Step 3:
Open the
desired
worksheet.

Step 4:
Select a cell
with your
mouse.

Step 5:
Press the Enter
Key on the
keyboard.

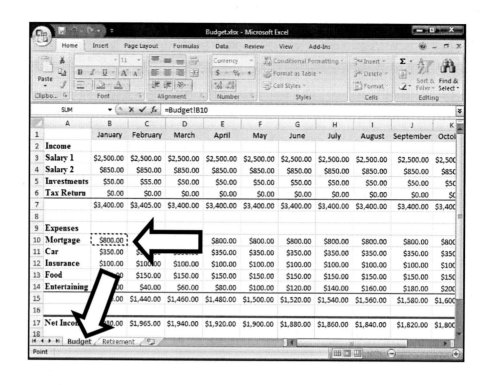

January
mortgage
expense added
to the
Retirement
worksheet.

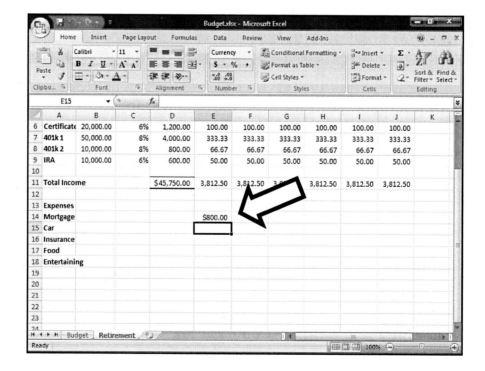

Chapter 11: Linking Worksheets!

Since the expense cells are lined up in the same way as the ones you are adding to the Retirement worksheet, you can use the Fill option to link the remainder of the expenses to the correct cells on the retirement worksheet. First, fill in the cells vertically, E15 through E18.

Using the Fill Handle: Step by Step Instructions
1. **Highlight the cell containing the data/formula you want to repeat.**
2. **Click and hold down the left mouse button on the Fill Handle.**
3. **Move the mouse over the cells you want filled with the selected data.**
4. **Release the left mouse button.**

Using the Fill Handle: Visual Guide

Step 1: Highlight the cell containing the data/formula you want to repeat.

Step 2: Click and hold down the left mouse button on the Fill Handle.

Step 3:
Move the mouse over the cells you want filled with the selected data.

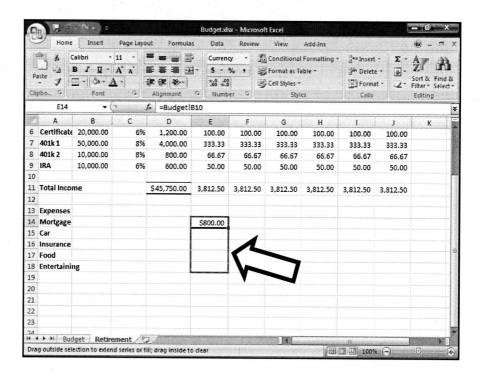

Step 4:
Release the left mouse button.

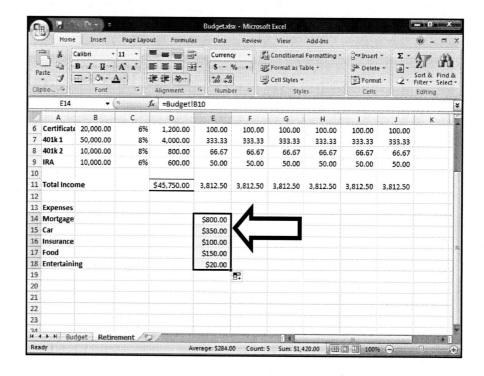

Repeat the process and fill in the cells horizontally, columns F through J. Depending upon your version of Excel, it may not allow you to fill in both vertically and horizontally when using cell references to link cells.

Chapter 11: Linking Worksheets!

Step 1:
Highlight the cell containing the data/formula you want to repeat.

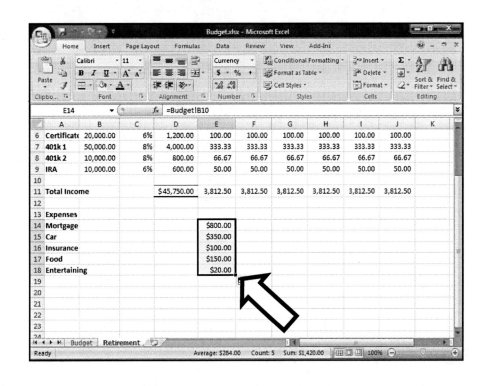

Step 2:
Click and hold down the left mouse button on the Fill Handle.

Step 3:
Move the mouse over the cells you want filled with the selected data.

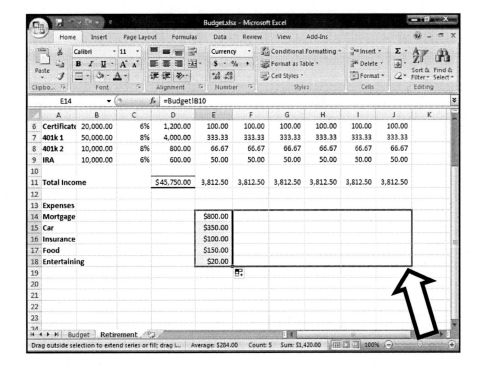

Step 4:
Release the left
mouse button.

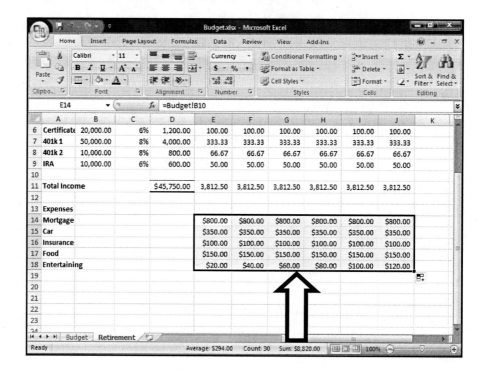

WARNING: You cannot link cells containing text to cells containing numbers.

NOTE: If you link cells on different worksheets, it is a good idea to place a note in the linked cell so that when you open the worksheet at a future date you will be reminded of the link.

Section 46: Practice Adding Calculations

To finish the Retirement worksheet, you will calculate the total Monthly Expenses and the Net Income. To calculate the total expenses for the month of January, you will add up all the expense rows. You can add each cell manually by typing in, or pointing to and selecting, each cell you want in the total. Or you can use the AutoSum feature you used earlier in the book. The AUTOSUM button is located on the ribbon and looks like a large uppercase E. To perform this calculation, click on cell E20. When the cell is selected, click AUTOSUM. The AUTOSUM button will automatically place a dotted line around the expense cells in Column E indicating these cells will be used in the calculation. Notice the AutoSum feature ignores the income lines because it is designed to stop at blank rows or columns. Press the Enter key on the keyboard and the Total Monthly Expenses will be calculated, 1420.00.

Step 1:
Click on the cell in which you want to place a formula.

Step 2:
Click the AUTOSUM button.

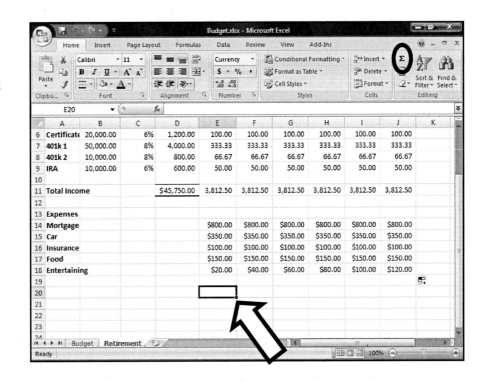

Step 3:
Press the Enter
Key on the
keyboard.

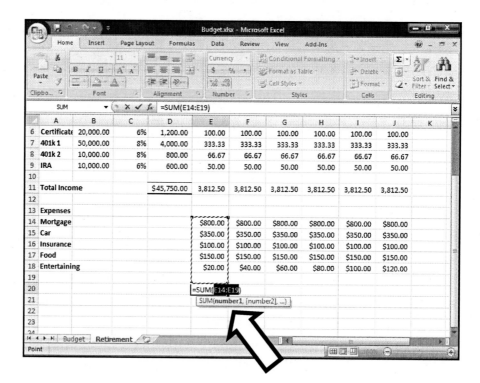

Calculated
Total Monthly
Expenses.

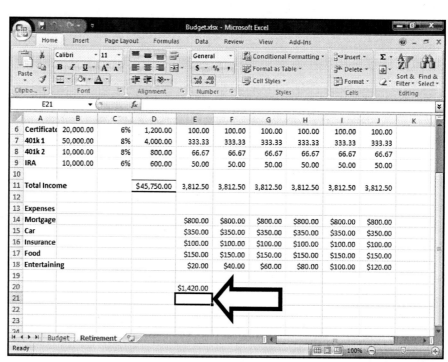

Chapter 11: Linking Worksheets!

To calculate the Net Income for the month of January, you will subtract the total monthly income from the total monthly expenses. To perform this calculation, first click cell E22. Once the cell is selected, type an equal sign (=). Select the Total Income cell for January, E11. Then type a minus sign (-). Finally, select the Total Expense cell for January, E20. When you have finished the formula, press the Enter key on the keyboard to calculate the answer. The Net Income for January is 2392.50.

Creating a Formula by Selecting Cells: Step by Step Instructions

1. **Click on the cell in which you want to place a calculation.**
2. **Type an "equal sign" (=) to indicate that you are entering a calculation.**
3. **Select a cell with your mouse.**
4. **Type the mathematical operator (+,-,*, /).**
5. **Repeat Step 3 to add the remaining cell to the formula.**
6. **Press the Enter Key on the keyboard. Excel will calculate the answer.**

Creating a Formula by Selecting Cells: Visual Guide

Step 1:
Click on the cell in which you want to place a formula.

Step 2:
Type an "equal sign" (=).

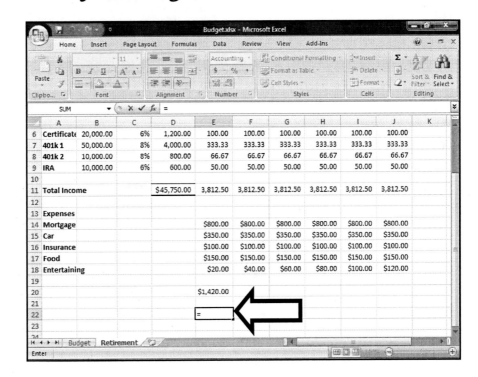

Chapter 11: Linking Worksheets!

Step 3:
Select a cell
with your
mouse.

Step 4:
Type a
mathematical
operator
(+,-,*, /).

Step 5:
Repeat Step 3
to add the
remaining cell
to the formula.

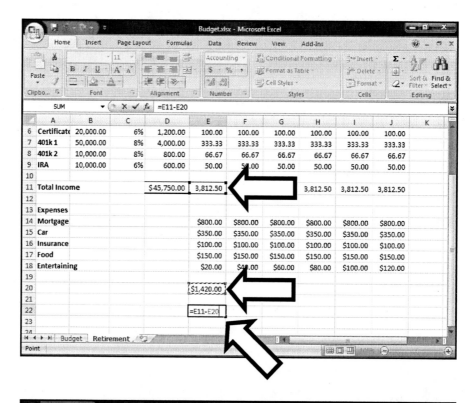

Step 6:
Press the Enter
Key.

**Finished
Calculation.**

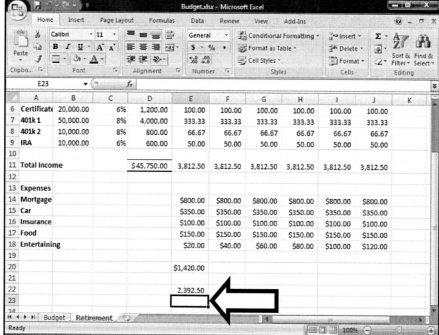

Chapter 11: Linking Worksheets!

The last step is to fill in the Total Monthly Expenses and Net Income for the remaining months. Select cells E20 through E22, and use the Fill handle to repeat the calculation in columns February through June.

Using the Fill Handle: Step by Step Instructions

1. Highlight the cells containing the data/formula you want to repeat.
2. Click and hold down the left mouse button on the Fill Handle.
3. Move the mouse over the cells you want filled with the selected data.
4. Release the left mouse button.

Using the Fill Handle: Visual Guide

Step 1: Highlight the cell containing the data/formula you want to repeat.

Step 2: Click and hold down the left mouse button on the Fill Handle.

Step 3:
Move the mouse over the cells you want filled with the selected data.

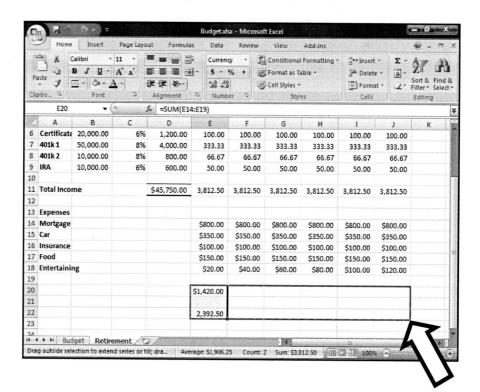

Step 4:
Release the left mouse button.

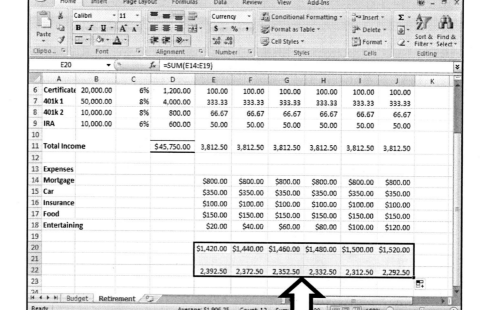

Chapter 11: Linking Worksheets!

You have completed linking the Retirement worksheet to the Budget expenses and calculating the Total Expenses and Net Income for January through June. Just for formality, add the label Total Expenses to cell A20 and Net Income to cell A22. After the labels are entered, resize column A so the labels fit entirely in the column. Then save your work.

Data labels have been added.

Resize column A to fit the data.

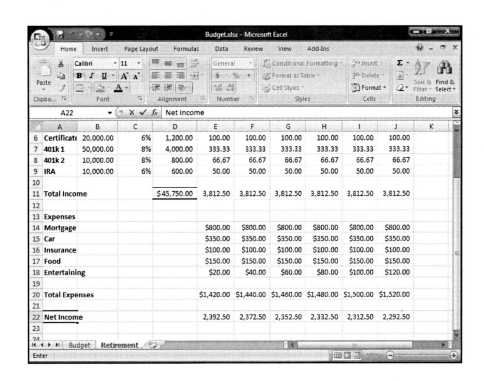

Chapter 11: Linking Worksheets!

Chapter 12

Inserting and Deleting Rows and Columns!

What You Will Learn in this Chapter
- ✓ Inserting Rows and Columns
- ✓ Deleting Rows and Columns

Chapter 12: Inserting & Deleting Rows and Columns!

Section 47: Inserting Rows and Columns

One of the advantages of Excel is the ease with which columns and rows can be added. When you add a row or column to a worksheet, the data in the other rows or columns will be moved but will not be changed. Adding rows or columns allows you to continuously add data to your existing spreadsheet without having to recreate the whole thing.

To add a row or column to a worksheet, you first have to decide where you would like the new row or column to be placed. Once you decide on a location, you have to select the location using the row or column headings. The new row or column will be inserted in the selected location and the existing data will be moved (down if you add a row or to the right if you add a column). In this example, assume you anticipate a family member will be moving in and will be paying rent. You can add a new income line for Rent.

Move the cursor to the left edge of the worksheet. Left click on row heading 4. The entire fourth row will be highlighted. Click on the INSERT button located on the CELLS section of the ribbon. A list of options will appear. Click the INSERT SHEET ROWS option. A blank row will be inserted in row 4. The data previously in row 4, as well as all of the data below it, will be moved down one row on the worksheet. Notice none of the values in the existing rows were altered because of inserting the row. However, if any of the cells in the existing rows were linked to other cells, the cell references would have changed automatically.

Inserting Rows or Columns: Step by Step Instructions
1. **Highlight the rows or columns, using the row or column headings, at the location where you want the new row or column to be placed.**
2. **Click the INSERT button located on the CELLS section of the ribbon.**
3. **Click the INSERT SHEET ROWS option.**

Chapter 12: Inserting & Deleting Rows and Columns!

Inserting Rows or Columns: Visual Guide

Step 1: Highlight the row, using the row or column heading, at the location where you want the new row to be placed.

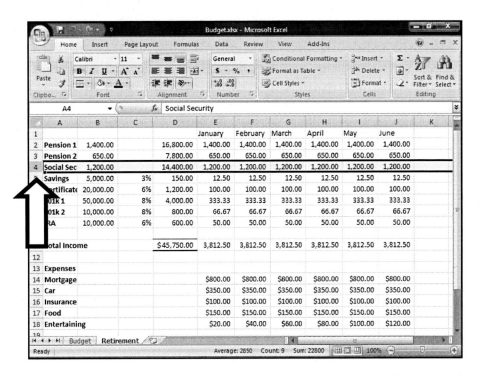

Step 2: Click the INSERT button.

Step 3: Click the INSERT SHEET ROWS option.

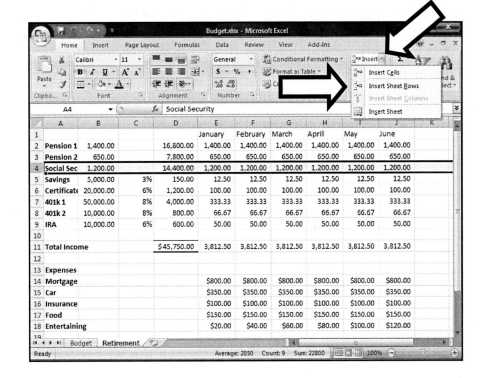

A new blank row has been inserted into the worksheet.

Follow the same process to add an additional row. The new row will be used to hold the Income label similar to the Expenses heading currently located in row 14. Move the cursor to the left edge of the worksheet and left click on row heading 2. The entire second row will be highlighted. Click on the INSERT button located on the ribbon. Then, select the INSERT SHEET ROWS option from the list. A blank row will be inserted in row 2.

Chapter 12: Inserting & Deleting Rows and Columns!

Step 1:
Highlight the row where you want the new row to be placed.

Step 2:
Click the INSERT button.

Step 3:
Click the INSERT SHEET ROWS option.

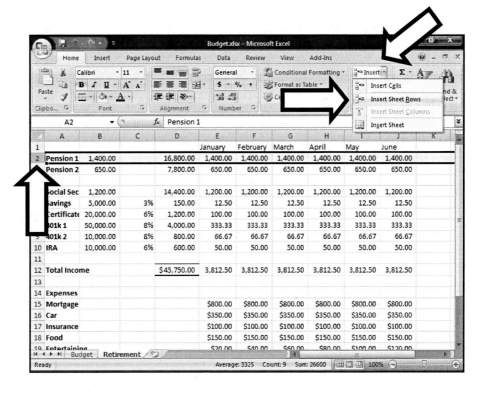

A new blank row was inserted into the worksheet.

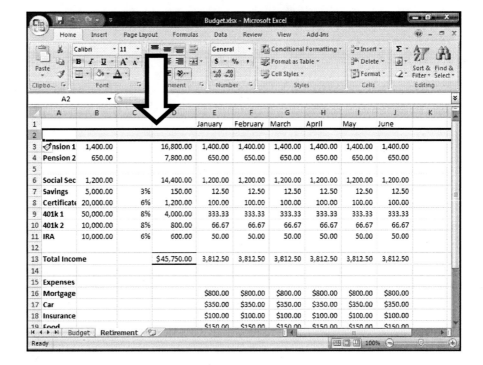

Chapter 12: Inserting & Deleting Rows and Columns!

To keep in tune with the rest of the Retirement budget, you need to add the amount of monthly rental income you are planning to receive. Select cell E5 with your mouse and type a value of 200.

Step 1:
Select a cell using the mouse.

Step 2:
Type the desired cell data.

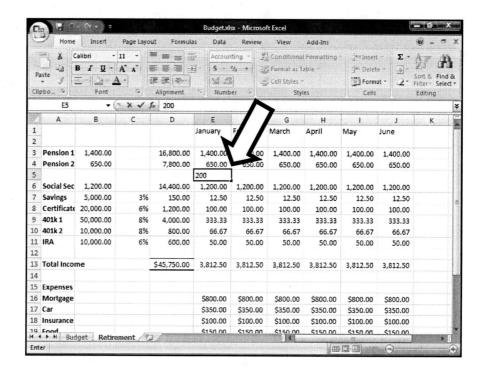

You can then use the Fill Handle to fill/repeat the 200 value in February through June. If you have any difficulty using the Fill Handle or inputting data, refer to the early chapters of this book for guidance and practice.

Step 1:
Highlight the cell containing the data/formula you want to repeat.

Step 2:
Click and hold down the left mouse button on the Fill Handle.

Step 3:
Move the mouse over the cells you want filled with the selected data.

Step 4:
Release the left mouse button.

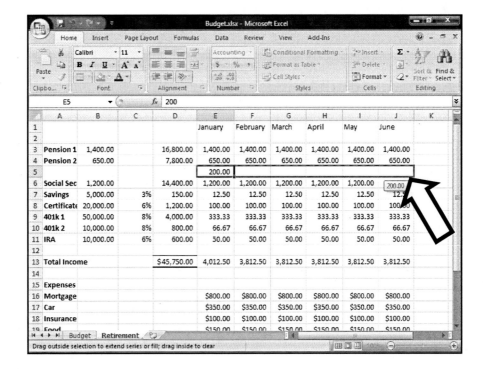

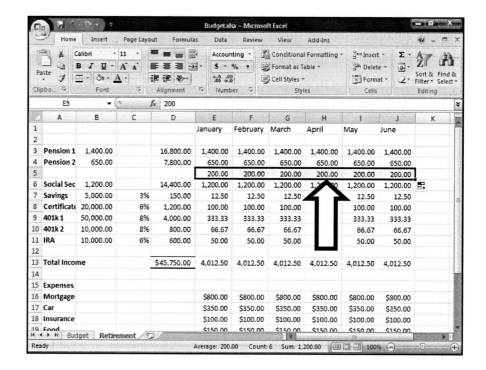

Cell data has been repeated in selected cells.

Note, after you filled in the monthly rental data, the Total Income was recalculated. This happened because you previously used the AutoSum option to add the column values between row 3 and row 12. Excel remembers the formula and adjusts the total whenever a new row is inserted between the rows specified in the calculation.

Section 48: Deleting Rows and Columns

If you decide you want to delete an entire row, you will follow almost the same steps used to insert a row except you will select the DELETE button from the ribbon. When you delete a row or column from a worksheet, the data in the other rows and columns will move to fill the deleted space. If any of the cells

Chapter 12: Inserting & Deleting Rows and Columns!

were used in a calculation which is still being displayed, the calculation will automatically update. However, if any of the deleted cells were linked to other cells, the remaining linked cells will display the error notation #REF. To remove this error message, correct the formula in the cell.

To delete a row or column from a worksheet, first select the desired row or column using the row or column heading. Second click the DELETE button located on the CELLS section of the ribbon. Then from the list which appears, click the DELETE SHEET ROWS option. The row or column will be deleted, and the remaining data will be moved up or to the left to fill the blank space. In this example, you will remove the blank row located between the last individual income line and the Total Income line. Then you will repeat the steps to delete the row separating the expenses from the Total Expense line.

Move the mouse arrow over the row heading for row 12, and click the left mouse button. The entire row 12 will be highlighted. Click the DELETE button located on the CELLS section of the ribbon. Then from the list which appears, click the DELETE SHEET ROWS option. The selected row will be removed from the worksheet. The data previously in row 5, as well as all of the data below it, will be moved up one row on the worksheet.

Deleting Rows or Columns: Step by Step Instructions
1. Highlight the row or column you want to delete, by using the row or column heading.
2. Click the DELETE button located on the ribbon.
3. Click the DELETE SHEET ROWS option.

Chapter 12: Inserting & Deleting Rows and Columns!

Deleting Rows or Columns: Visual Guide

Step 1:
Highlight the rows or columns you want to delete, by using the row or column headings.

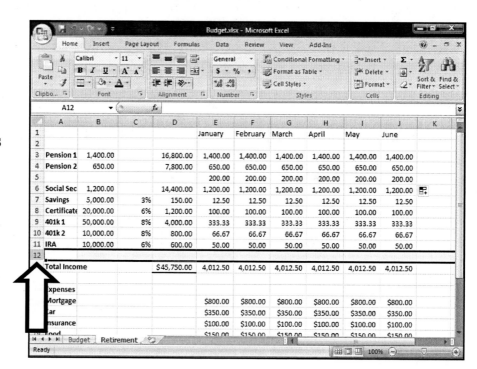

Step 2:
Click the DELETE button.

Step 3:
Click the DELETE SHEET ROWS option.

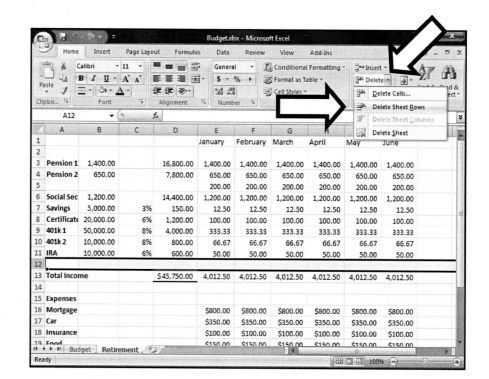

The selected row was successfully deleted.

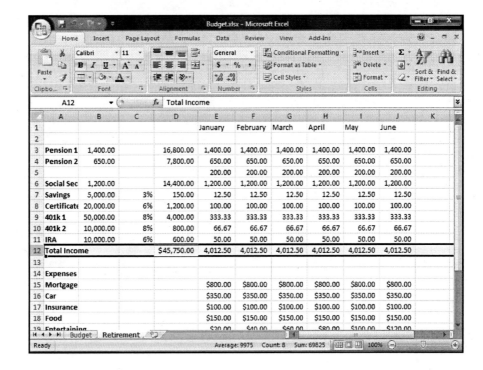

Repeat the steps to delete the row separating the expenses from the Total Expense line. Delete row 20.

Step 1: Highlight the row you want to delete.

Step 2: Click the DELETE button.

Step 3: Click the DELETE SHEET ROWS option.

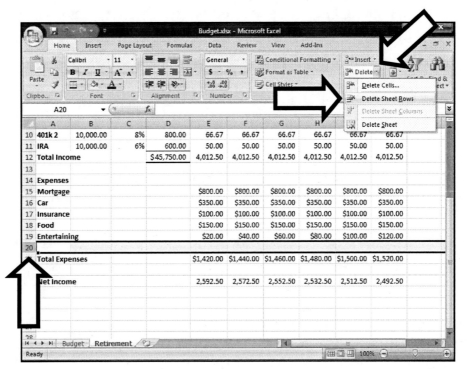

Chapter 12: Inserting & Deleting Rows and Columns!

The selected row was successfully deleted.

	A	B	C	D	E	F	G	H	I	J	K
10	401k 2	10,000.00	8%	800.00	66.67	66.67	66.67	66.67	66.67	66.67	
11	IRA	10,000.00	6%	600.00	50.00	50.00	50.00	50.00	50.00	50.00	
12	Total Income			$45,750.00	4,012.50	4,012.50	4,012.50	4,012.50	4,012.50	4,012.50	
13											
14	Expenses										
15	Mortgage				$800.00	$800.00	$800.00	$800.00	$800.00	$800.00	
16	Car				$350.00	$350.00	$350.00	$350.00	$350.00	$350.00	
17	Insurance				$100.00	$100.00	$100.00	$100.00	$100.00	$100.00	
18	Food				$150.00	$150.00	$150.00	$150.00	$150.00	$150.00	
19	Entertaining				$20.00	$40.00	$60.00	$80.00	$100.00	$120.00	
20	Total Expenses				$1,420.00	$1,440.00	$1,460.00	$1,480.00	$1,500.00	$1,520.00	
21											
22	Net Income				2,592.50	2,572.50	2,552.50	2,532.50	2,512.50	2,492.50	
23											
24											
25											
26											
27											

You can delete columns in the same fashion. Place your mouse pointer on the column heading, and click the left mouse button to highlight the entire column. Click the DELETE button located on the CELLS section of the ribbon. Then from the list which appears, click the DELETE SHEET COLUMNS option. The selected column will be deleted from the worksheet.

NOTE: If you realize that you needed the information in the row or column you just deleted, you can use the UNDO option (a circular arrow pointing left) located in the toolbar found above the ribbon and to the right of the OFFICE button. The deleted data will reappear. Each time you click the undo button, Excel reverses one action you performed. If you change your mind, and want to restore the action, you can click the REDO button (a circular arrow pointing right). You will find that Undo can become your best friend when working in Excel.

However, once you close your worksheet, you cannot Undo any action made prior to closing the file. If you close your worksheet and reopen it, the Undo option will be a light gray indicating the command is not available.

Chapter 13

Hiding Data!

What You Will Learn in this Chapter
- ✓ Hiding Data
- ✓ Hiding Rows and Columns
- ✓ Unhiding Rows and Columns

Chapter 13: Hiding Data!

Section 49: Hiding Data

As you begin working with Excel more frequently, you may occasionally work with data that is confidential – data that you do not want to share with anyone else. Perhaps you want others to see the results of your analysis, but not the detail leading to those results. Or perhaps you have detailed data which you used to calculate results, but the details are not important to display on a printed report. If you find yourself in any of these situations, you can use the Hide function of Excel.

The HIDE function allows you to select rows or columns and remove them from view. The hidden data will continue to play a role in the calculations, but will not be displayed on the screen or on a printed report. When rows or columns are hidden, the row or column headings do not display on the screen. The example below illustrates the effect hiding columns has on the sequence of the column headings. The example displayed below is the result of hiding columns B, C, and D.

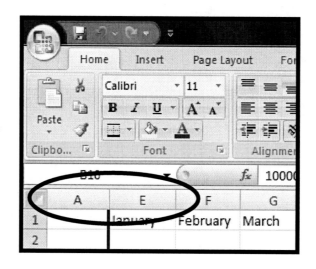

Chapter 13: Hiding Data!

You can unhide the hidden rows or columns at any time, and the worksheet will return to its normal display. If you look at a spreadsheet and the row or column headings do not increase sequentially, you can be fairly certain the spreadsheet has some data hidden from view.

Working through an example will make the concept of hiding columns and rows clearer. Suppose you wanted to discuss your retirement budget with a friend. Instead of printing the worksheet as is, with both the annual income and monthly income detailed, you decide to make the worksheet less confusing by hiding the unnecessary data.

To hide columns, first select the desired columns by highlighting the columns using the column headings. Then click on the FORMAT button located in the CELLS section of the ribbon. Highlight the HIDE & UNHIDE option from the list. A submenu will appear. From the submenu select the HIDE COLUMNS option. The selected columns will be hidden from view.

Assume you want to hide all the annual details contained in columns B, C, and D. Position your mouse pointer over the column B heading. Click and hold down the left mouse button. While holding down the left mouse button, move your mouse pointer over to the column D heading. Release the mouse button and columns B, C, and D will remain highlighted. Click the FORMAT button from the ribbon. When the list appears, highlight the HIDE & UNHIDE option. When the submenu opens choose the option HIDE COLUMNS. Columns B, C, and D will disappear from your viewing screen. The information is still there; it simply cannot be seen at this point.

Hiding Rows or Columns: Step by Step Instructions

1. **Using the row or column heading, highlight the rows or columns you want to hide.**
2. **Click the FORMAT button from the ribbon.**
3. **Highlight the HIDE & UNHIDE option.**
4. **Click the HIDE COLUMNS option.**

Chapter 13: Hiding Data!

Hiding Rows or Columns: Visual Guide

Step 1:
Highlight the rows or columns you want to hide, using the row or column headings.

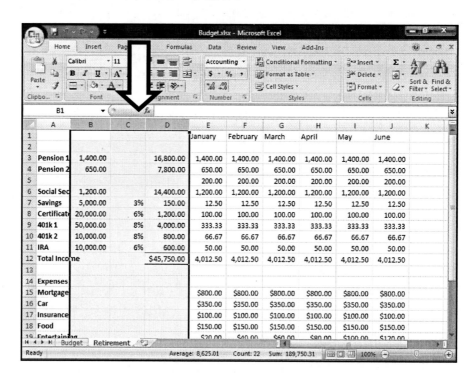

Step 2:
Click the FORMAT button from the ribbon.

Step 3:
Highlight the HIDE & UNHIDE option.

Step 4:
Click the HIDE COLUMNS option.

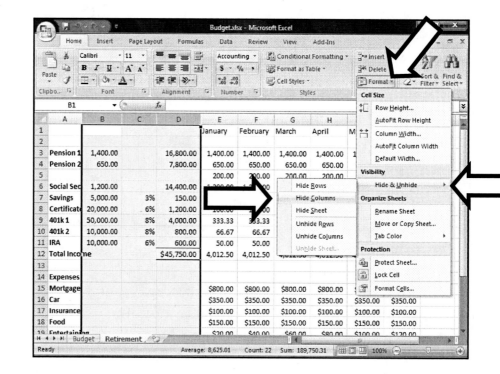

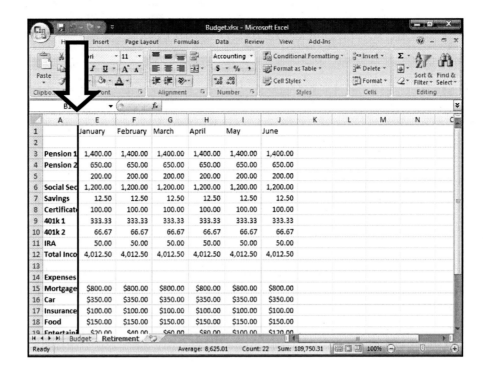

The selected columns have been successfully hidden.

Now, when you show your friend the worksheet on the computer or in printed format, the unnecessary details will not be displayed.

NOTE: Look at the column headings. The column headings jump from A to E. When you see a gap in column letters or row numbers in the headings, you can assume there are hidden columns or rows on the spreadsheet. If you had deleted the columns or rows, rather than hidden them, Excel would have updated the letters or numbers so that they would once again be in sequence.

Chapter 13: Hiding Data!

Section 50: Unhiding Data

It is always important to learn how to reverse the process you have just completed. If you needed to update the Retirement budget and use some of the hidden data, you would have to unhide the columns or rows before you could make the changes.

To unhide the columns, highlight/select the columns on either side of the hidden columns, using the column headings. The two columns will be highlighted. Then click the FORMAT button in the CELLS section of the ribbon and highlight the HIDE & UNHIDE option. From the submenu which appears, click the option UNHIDE COLUMNS. The selected columns will reappear in your viewing area.

Assume you want to unhide all the annual details contained in columns B, C, and D. Position your mouse pointer over the column A heading. Click and hold down the left mouse button. While holding down the left mouse button, move your mouse pointer over to the column E heading. Release the mouse button and columns A and E will remain highlighted.   Click the FORMAT button and highlight the HIDE & UNHIDE option. A submenu will appear. From the submenu, click the option UNHIDE COLUMNS. Columns B, C, and D will reappear on your viewing screen.

Unhiding Rows or Columns: Step by Step Instructions
1. **Using the row or column headings, highlight the rows or columns on either side of the rows or columns you want to unhide.**
2. **Click the FORMAT button from the ribbon.**
3. **Highlight the HIDE & UNHIDE option.**
4. **Click the UNHIDE COLUMNS option.**

Unhiding Rows or Columns: Visual Guide

Step 1:
Highlight the rows or columns on either side of the rows or columns you want to unhide, using the row or column headings.

Step 2:
Click the FORMAT button.

Step 3:
Highlight the HIDE & UNHIDE option.

Step 4:
Click the UNHIDE COLUMNS option.

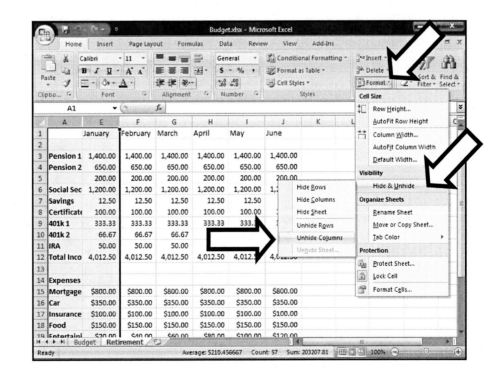

Chapter 13: Hiding Data!

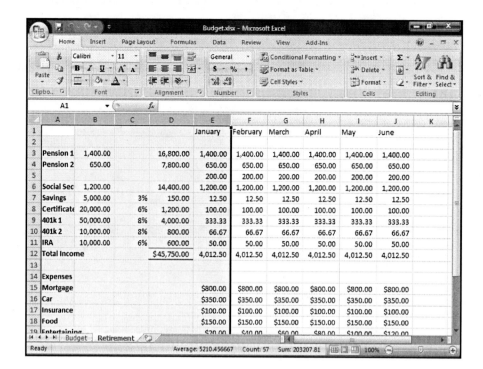

The selected columns have reappeared.

![Caution icon]

Caution: What you learn here can help you keep your data hidden from the average computer user. However, a skilled user or hacker will be able to access hidden data unless you've gone through great lengths to protect the worksheet from intrusion.

The next chapter is going to discuss printing the worksheets, so take a moment to re-hide columns B, C, and D.

Hiding Rows or Columns: Step by Step Instructions
1. Using the row or column headings, highlight the rows or columns, you want to hide.
2. Click the FORMAT button from the ribbon.
3. Highlight the HIDE & UNHIDE option.
4. Click the HIDE COLUMNS option.

The selected columns have been successfully hidden.

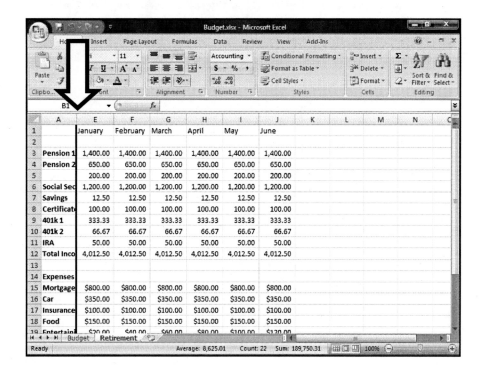

You are now ready to learn how to print the worksheet.

Chapter 13: Hiding Data!

Chapter 14

Printing!

What You Will Learn in this Chapter
- ✓ Previewing your Spreadsheet Prior to Printing
- ✓ Recognizing Page Breaks
- ✓ Manually Inserting and Remove Page Breaks
- ✓ Changing Page Settings to Print Worksheets
- ✓ Inserting Headers and Footers
- ✓ Printing Spreadsheets

Chapter 14: Printing!

Section 51: Print Preview

Once you have created and saved your spreadsheet, you probably want to print it on a piece of paper. Unfortunately, depending upon the length and width of your worksheet, what you see on your computer screen may not be what prints on the paper. It is always a good idea to preview how your spreadsheet will appear in print, using the Print Preview option located in the Office Menu. Open the Office Menu by clicking the OFFICE button located in the upper left corner of the window. Highlight the PRINT option and then move into the submenu and click on the PRINT PREVIEW option. A new screen will appear, showing you what your spreadsheet will look like if you printed it immediately.

Print Preview: Step by Step Instructions
1. **Click the OFFICE Button.**
2. **Highlight the PRINT option.**
3. **Click the PRINT PREVIEW option.**
4. **After previewing the worksheet, click the CLOSE PRINT PREVIEW button to return to the original screen (edit mode).**

Chapter 14: Printing!

Print Preview: Visual Guide

Step 1:
Click the OFFICE Button.

Step 2:
Highlight the PRINT option.

Step 3:
Click the PRINT PREVIEW option.

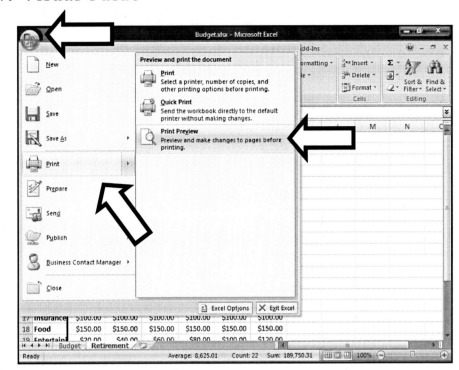

Worksheet in Print View.

Step 4:
After previewing the worksheet, click the CLOSE PRINT PREVIEW button to return to the original screen.

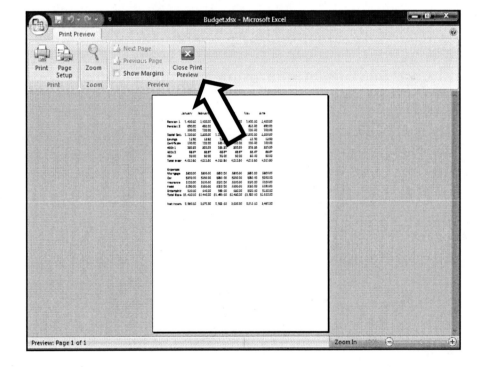

Chapter 14: Printing!

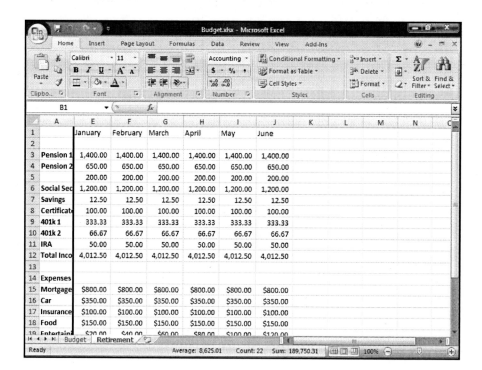

Worksheet in Normal View.

The Print Preview screen will display only the data located on the active worksheet. If you desire to see how the regular Budget will print, activate the Budget worksheet using the worksheet tabs. Once the correct worksheet is displayed on the screen, select the PRINT PREVIEW option.

The Print Preview screen will show you the first page of your worksheet. If the worksheet will require additional pages when printed, a NEXT PAGE button will become available on the ribbon. Clicking the NEXT PAGE button will display a preview of the next printed page of your worksheet. To go back and see the first page, click the PREVIOUS PAGE button directly below the NEXT PAGE button. Clicking on the "Previous" button takes you to the page directly before the one you are currently viewing.

To see which page you are currently viewing, look at the bottom left corner of the Print Preview screen. In the gray status bar the computer will indicate which page you are currently viewing. The page notation is displayed as page x of y pages. If the notation displays page 1 of 2, you are currently looking at the first page of two total pages to be printed.

To practice, activate the Budget worksheet using the worksheet tabs. Once the Budget worksheet is active, open the Print Preview screen.

Chapter 14: Printing!

Print Preview: Step by Step Instructions

1. Click the OFFICE Button.
2. Highlight the PRINT option.
3. Click the PRINT PREVIEW option.
4. If the blue status bar at the bottom of the screen indicates there are additional pages which will be printed, click the NEXT PAGE button to view the second page of the worksheet.
5. After previewing the worksheet, click the CLOSE PRINT PREVIEW button to return to the original screen (edit mode).

Print Preview: Visual Guide

Activate the Budget worksheet.

Step 1:
Click the OFFICE Button.

Step 2:
Highlight the PRINT option.

Step 3:
Click the PRINT PREVIEW option.

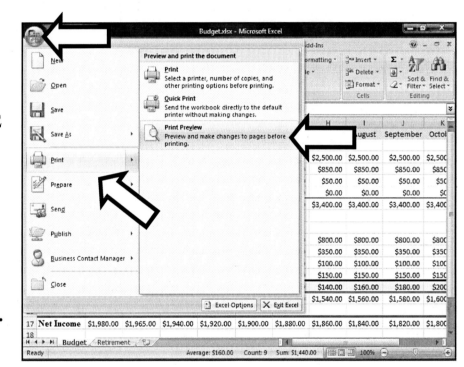

Chapter 14: Printing!

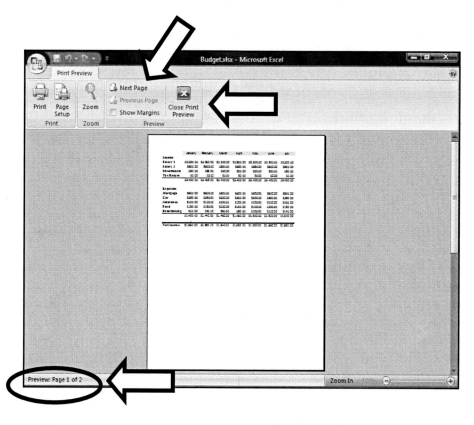

Note the Page number notation at the bottom left of the screen.

Step 4:
Click the NEXT PAGE button to view the second page.

Step 5:
Click the CLOSE PRINT PREVIEW button to return to normal view.

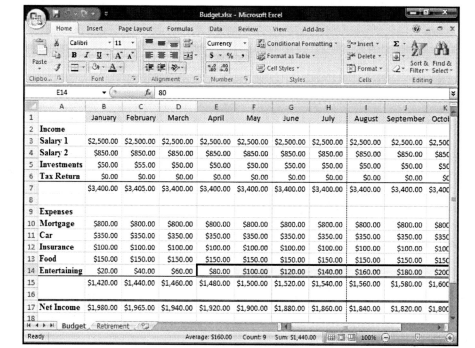

Worksheet in Normal View.

If you see an error on your worksheet while you are on the Print Preview screen, you must return to normal (edit) view to correct the error. You cannot make changes on the Print Preview screen. To change the spreadsheet, close the Print Preview screen by clicking on the CLOSE PRINT PREVIEW button located on the ribbon at the top of the screen. The spreadsheet will reappear on the normal view screen where you can make changes. The Print Preview screen is only for viewing the worksheet.

Section 52: Inserting Page Breaks

Once you return to normal view, from the Print Preview screen, you will notice a slight change within your worksheet. Since you have indicated that you are thinking of printing the worksheet, Excel will display a dotted line showing the individual printed page borders. The dotted lines can be used to reference how many columns and rows will fit on a printed piece of paper. On your Budget worksheet, you will see this dotted line between columns H and I. Each time you run out of space on your paper, a dotted line will show the break between one page and the next. This dotted line is called the Page Break.

The dotted line, displayed between rows H and I, is called a Page Break.

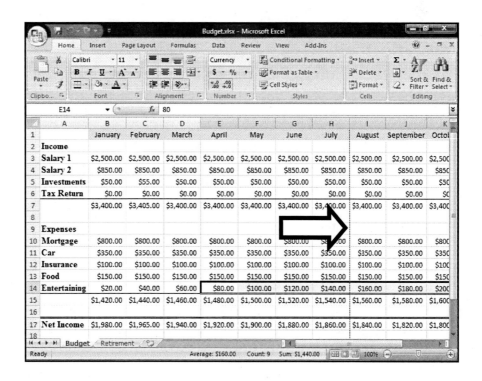

The computer will automatically insert a page break where one printed page ends and the next begins. However, page breaks are often placed in less than ideal locations, especially when working with large spreadsheets. A page break may occur between two lines of data which need to be displayed together for readability. If this happens, you can manually insert a page break.

The printer can only fit so much data on one piece of paper, so you may need to insert your manual page break before the computer's automatic break. On the Budget you created, notice that the page breaks appears between July and August. Instead of having the page break occur between the seventh and eighth month, it is better suited to occur after June. Ideally a page break just after June would provide six months of data on one printed page and the remaining six months on the second printed page.

To insert a manual page break, place your mouse pointer in the first cell in the column, in this case cell H1, and click your left mouse button. You have selected the cell immediately to the right of where you want the page to break to be inserted. Click on the PAGE LAYOUT tab to change the options displayed on the ribbon. Then click the BREAKS button to view the list of available break options. From the list click the INSERT PAGE BREAK option. The dotted page break line will be located between columns G and H.

Inserting a Vertical Page Break: Step by Step Instructions
1. **Click the column heading, or the first cell beneath the column heading, at the location you desire to insert the page break.**
2. **Click the PAGE LAYOUT tab to change the options displayed on the ribbon.**
3. **Click the BREAKS button.**
4. **Click the INSERT PAGE BREAK option.**
   - **A dotted line will appear on the screen representing the Page Break.**

Chapter 14: Printing!

Inserting a Vertical Page Break: Visual Guide

Step 1: Click either the column heading or the first cell beneath the column heading at the location you desire to insert the page break.

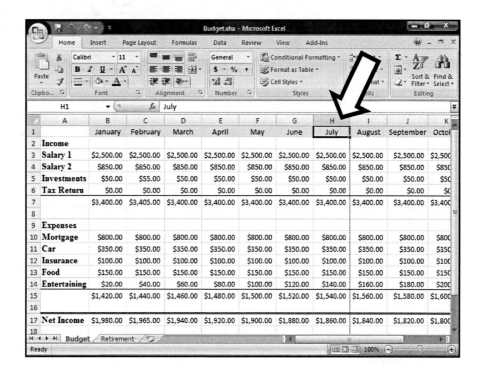

Step 2: Click the PAGE LAYOUT tab to change the options displayed on the ribbon.

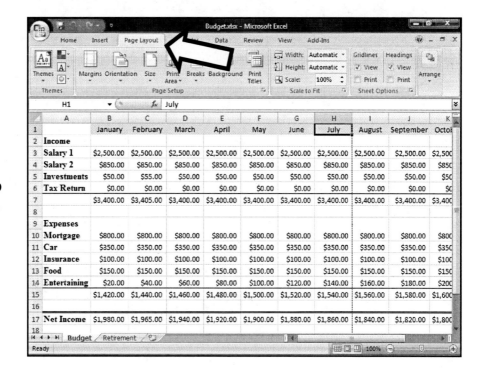

Step 3: Click the BREAKS button.

Step 4: Click the INSERT PAGE BREAK option.

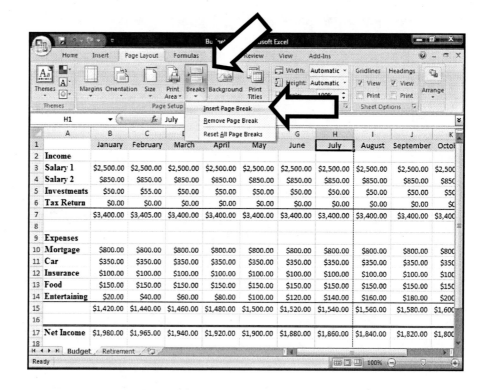

A dotted line will appear on the screen representing the Page Break.

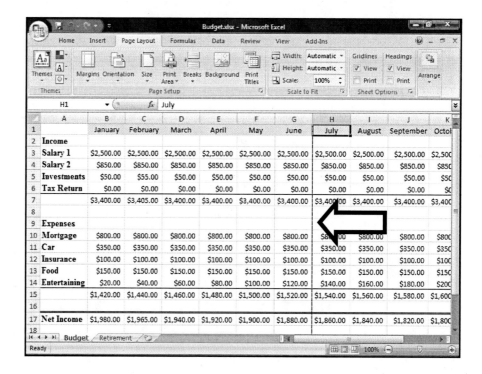

In the last example you created a vertical page break. You can also insert horizontal page breaks. If your data on a worksheet doesn't fit horizontally on the printed page, a horizontal page break can be inserted. Imagine if the worksheet contained data on rows 1 through 100. All 100 rows will not fit on one printed page. A horizontal page break could be used to designate how many rows of data will print on each printed page.

To insert a horizontal page break, select either the row heading or a cell in the first column (furthest to the left) immediately below the row where you want to place the page break. Click on the PAGE LAYOUT tab to change the options displayed on the ribbon. Then click the BREAKS button to view the list of available break options. From the list click the INSERT PAGE BREAK option. The menu will disappear, and the dotted page break line will appear immediately above the selected cell.

In the example, place your mouse pointer in cell A9 and click your left mouse button. You have selected the cell immediately below where you want to insert the page to break. Click the PAGE LAYOUT tab to change the options displayed on the ribbon. Then click the BREAKS button to view the list of available break options. From the list click the INSERT PAGE BREAK option. The dotted page break line will be displayed between rows 8 and 9. The rows containing the monthly income will appear on the first page; the rows containing the monthly expenses will appear on the second page.

Inserting a Horizontal Page Break: Step by Step Instructions
1. **Click the row heading, or the cell immediately to the right of the row heading, at the location you desire to insert the page break.**
2. **Click the PAGE LAYOUT tab to change the options displayed on the ribbon.**
3. **Click the BREAKS button.**
4. **Click the INSERT PAGE BREAK option.**

Chapter 14: Printing!

Inserting a Horizontal Page Break: Visual Guide

Step 1:
Click either the row heading, or the cell immediately to the right of the row heading, at the location you desire to insert the page break.

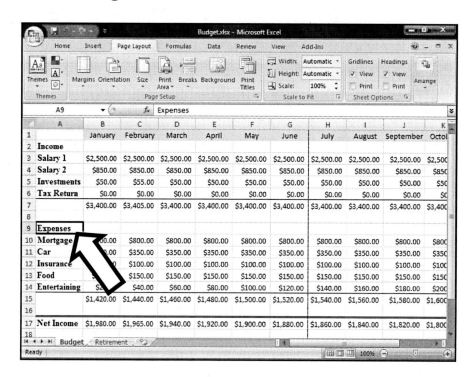

Step 2:
Click the PAGE LAYOUT tab.

Step 3:
Click the BREAKS button.

Step 4:
Click the INSERT PAGE BREAK option.

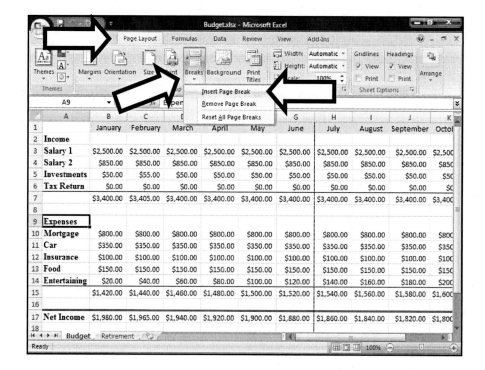

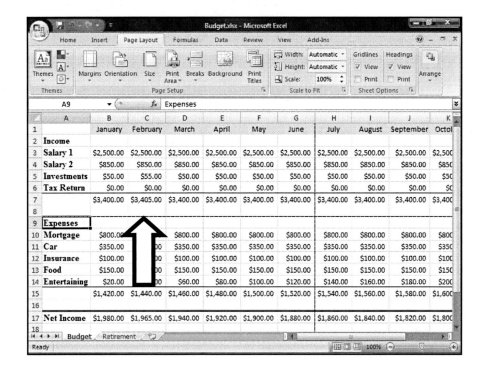

A dotted line will appear on the screen representing the Page Break.

To see how the worksheet will print, use the Print Preview option. Remember, Print Preview can be found in the OFFICE Menu. You can now see the effects of adding page breaks to the worksheet. Notice the vertical page break limits the data on the first page – it now ends with June. The horizontal page break limits the data on the first page to the income rows only.

Print Preview: Step by Step Instructions
1. Click the Office Button.
2. Highlight the PRINT option.
3. Click the PRINT PREVIEW option.
4. If the blue status bar at the bottom of the screen indicates there are additional pages which will be printed, click the NEXT PAGE button to view the second page of the worksheet.
5. After previewing the worksheet, click the CLOSE PRINT PREVIEW button to return to the original screen (edit mode).

Print Preview: Visual Guide

**Step 1:
Click the
OFFICE
Button.**

**Step 2:
Highlight the
PRINT option.**

**Step 3:
Click the
PRINT
PREVIEW
option.**

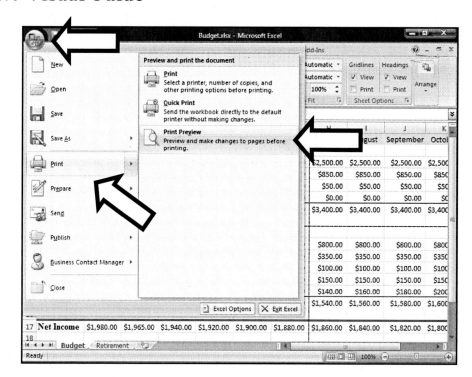

**Step 4:
Click the NEXT
PAGE button.**

**Step 5:
Click the
CLOSE PRINT
PREVIEW
button to return
to normal view.**

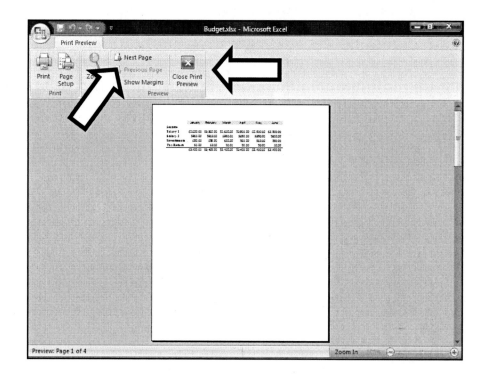

If you like the way the worksheet looks, you can leave the page breaks in place. In the next section you will learn how to remove a page break.

NOTE: You can insert page breaks both vertically and horizontally at the same time. To insert both a vertical and horizontal page break at once, select the cell immediately below and to the right of the area you want to include in the printed page. Click on the PAGE LAYOUT tab to change the options displayed on the ribbon. Then click the BREAKS button to view the list of available break options. From the list click the INSERT PAGE BREAK option. Two dotted page break lines will appear. One will appear vertically to the left of your selected cell, and the other will appear horizontally above the selected cell.

NOTE: Inserting Page Breaks:
- **Horizontal Page Break** - Click the row heading, or the cell furthest to the left, immediately below the row you desire to place the page break.
- **Vertical Page Break** - Click the column heading, or the top cell, immediately to the right of the area you desire to place the page break.
- **Horizontal & Vertical Page Break** - Click a cell immediately below and to the right of the area you want to include in the printed page.

Section 53: Removing a Page Break

Page breaks which have been manually added to a worksheet can be removed, but the page breaks which have been automatically added by the computer cannot be removed. If you have not manually added page breaks, the computer will insert the page breaks automatically when you print the worksheet. The page breaks which are added by the computer are inserted at the edges of each printed piece of paper.

If you would like to remove the page break added in the last example, you can complete the task using the BREAKS option found on the ribbon. To remove a horizontal page break, select a cell below the dotted page break line. On the example budget, select cell A9. Click the PAGE LAYOUT tab to change the options displayed on the ribbon if you are not already viewing the Page Layout options. Then click the BREAKS button to view the list of available break options. From the list click the REMOVE PAGE BREAK option. The horizontal page break will be removed from the worksheet. Now the income lines and expense lines will be printed on the same page.

Removing a Page Break: Step by Step Instructions
1. **Select a cell that is touching the Page Break (dotted) line.**
2. **Click the PAGE LAYOUT tab to change the options displayed on the ribbon.**
3. **Click the BREAKS button.**
4. **Click the REMOVE PAGE BREAK option.**

Removing a Page Break: Visual Guide

Step 1:
Select a cell that is touching the Page Break (dotted) line.

Step 2:
Click the PAGE LAYOUT tab to change the options displayed on the ribbon.

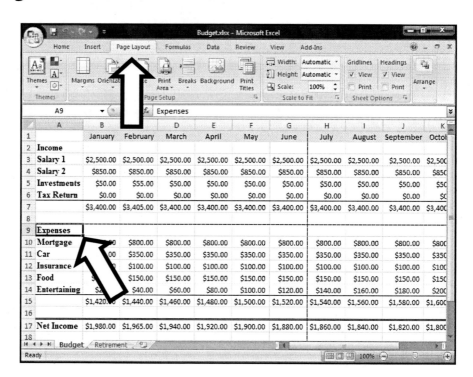

Step 3:
Click the
BREAKS
button.

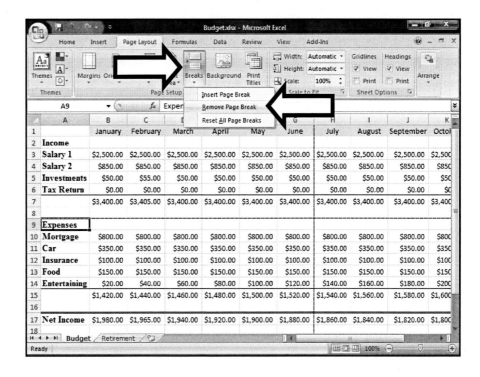

Step 4:
Click the
REMOVE
PAGE BREAK
option.

The horizontal
page break has
successfully
been removed
from the
worksheet.

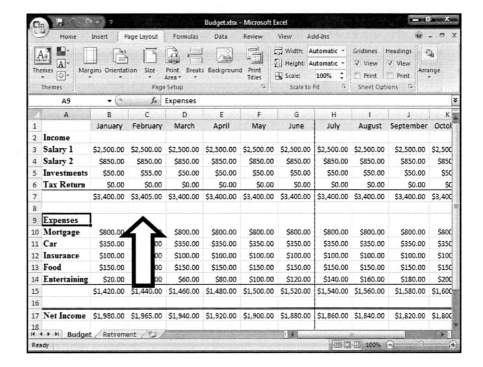

NOTE: To remove Page Break:
- **Horizontal Page Break** - select the cell below the dotted Page Break line.
- **Vertical Page Break** - select the cell to the right of the dotted Page Break line.
- **Horizontal & Vertical Page Break** - select the cell immediately below and to the right of the intersection of the Page Break line.

Section 54: Page Setup

Page Setup provides options to change the page layout, page margins, and other various features of the printed page. The Page Setup is frequently altered just before printing the worksheet. Excel users typically change the page setup options while in Print Preview so they can see the effects of their changes on the preview page.

To display the page setup options, open the Print Preview Screen. To open the Print Preview screen, click the OFFICE button, highlight PRINT, and then click the PRINT PREVIEW option. Located near the top of the screen is the PAGE SETUP button. Click the PAGE SETUP button using your mouse. The Page Setup window will appear.

Located at the top of the Page Setup screen are a number of tabs. Each tab provides different options which can change the overall layout of the page. The Page tab allows you to change the way the page looks. If the PAGE tab is not currently selected, click on the tab using the mouse.

The Page tab will display options to adjust the overall layout of the printed page and the scaling of the data placed on the page. Look at the options located under the ORIENTATION heading. There are two options -- PORTRAIT and LANDSCAPE. These options change the way the data will print on the paper. Most documents print in Portrait. Portrait is the way a book, handout, or letter is normally printed. Landscape, on the other hand, is often used for financial documents like spreadsheets. Landscape takes the 8½x11 sheet of paper and turns it on its side. With Landscape, you can fit more columns across the top of the page. However, fewer rows will fit down the page.

To change the page orientation, click your mouse on the small dot located next to the option you want to select. A dot will appear in the circle, indicating the option has been selected. Then click the OK button located at the bottom of the window to close the Page Setup window and view the changes on the Print Preview screen. To return to the Page setup screen, click the PAGE SETUP button located at the top of the window. Take a moment to change the page orientation and view the difference on the Print Preview screen.

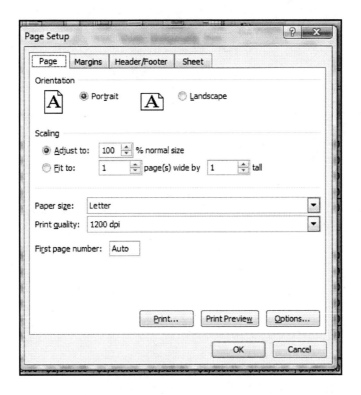

The Page tab also provides options to "Scale" the data to determine how much information will print on each page. Decreasing the scaling decreases the size of the data (makes the print smaller) allowing you to fit more data on each page. Increasing the scaling increases the size of the data (makes the print larger) resulting in less data fitting on one printed page.

Excel also includes a "Fit to:" setup option to fit one page of a worksheet onto one piece of paper. This scaling option is useful when your worksheet is just a little too large to fit on one printed page. Using "Fit to:" scaling allows you to get the entire spreadsheet on one page, but the text will be smaller.

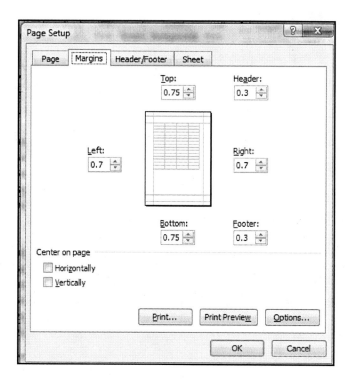

NOTE: If you have inserted manual page breaks on the worksheet, the page breaks will override changes to the page scaling. As a result, the printed page will not contain any more data than specified by the page break no matter how much you decrease the scaling (size of the printed data).

The Margins tab on the Page Setup window provides the means to change the margins on the printed page. To view the margin options, click once on the MARGINS tab. Note the margins. These are the typical margins for a standard piece of paper. Each margin (top, bottom, left, and right) has a box below it displaying the margin number in inches or fractions of an inch. If you want to change a margin, place your mouse pointer on the arrows next to the number in that margin's box. Click your mouse button on the UP arrow to increase the margin. Click your mouse button on the DOWN arrow to decrease the margin.

Chapter 14: Printing!

In the center of the Page Setup screen is a preview box, showing you what the spreadsheet will look like with different margin settings. At the bottom of the window is an area which allows you to center your worksheet on the page. If you want your data to be in the middle of the page, click your left mouse button in the squares in front of HORIZONTALLY and again in front of VERTICALLY. This will center your information in the middle of the piece of paper.

The Sheet tab allows you to change the page order and also provides options to print features found on the worksheet, including gridlines and column and row headers. Click once on the SHEET tab to display the available options.

In the middle of the Page Setup screen is the heading "Print." The Print options let you choose the features you want to print. For example, Excel does not automatically print the gridlines you see on the spreadsheet. If you want gridlines to print, click the mouse on the square box in front of the GRIDLINES option. A checkmark will appear in the box, confirming your selection to print gridlines. Excel does not automatically print the Column (A-N) and Row (1-54) Headers. If you want the column and row headers to appear on the printed page, place your mouse pointer in the box in front of ROW AND COLUMN HEADINGS and click your left mouse button. A checkmark will appear in the box, confirming your selection to print the headers.

Below the Print Order Heading are two options used to determine how the computer will select the order of the pages to be printed. The computer is setup to first look down the worksheet and then across when it is printing the pages. You can change the setup to have the computer look across the entire spreadsheet and then down by clicking the mouse in the circle in front of the desired print order option. Most often, users use the default setting.

After you have made all of your changes to the Page Setup, click the OK button located at the bottom of the window. You will be returned to the Print Preview screen where you can view all of your changes.

Changing the Page Setup: Step by Step Instructions

1. **Click the OFFICE button.**
2. **Highlight the PRINT option.**
3. **Click the PRINT PREVIEW option.**
4. **Click the PAGE SETUP button.**
5. **Make changes using the options located under the Page Setup tabs:**
    - **Page tab – Options to change the page layout (Portrait or Landscape) paper type and paper size.**
    - **Margins tab – Options to change the page margins.**
    - **Header/Footer tab – Options to insert page headers/footers.**
    - **Sheet tab – Options to keep the gridlines and/or Column and Row Headings are found here.**
6. **Click the OK button.**

Changing the Page Setup: Visual Guide

Step 1:
Click the
OFFICE
button.

Step 2:
Highlight the
PRINT option.

Step 3:
Click the
PRINT
PREVIEW
option.

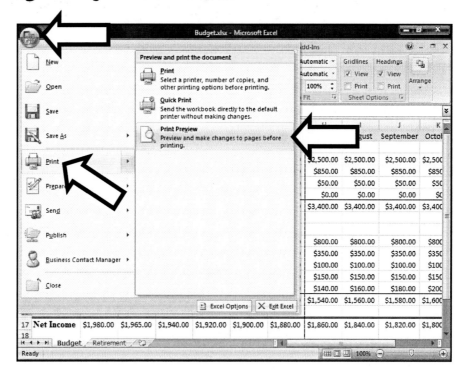

Step 4:
Click the PAGE
SETUP button.

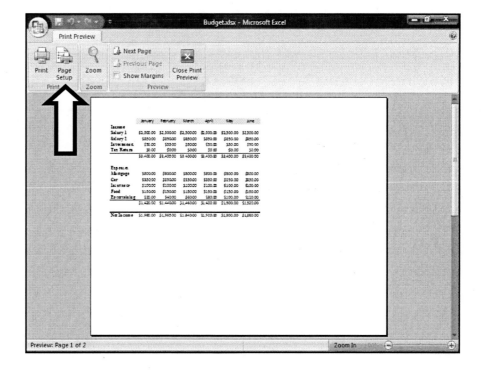

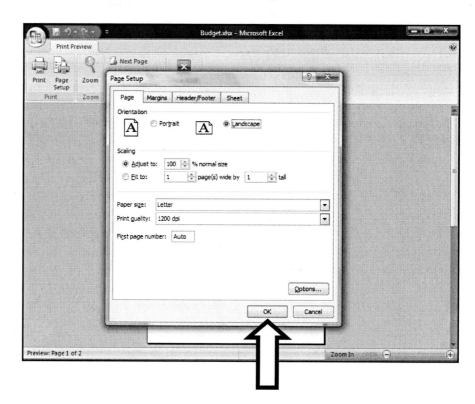

Step 5:
Make changes using the options located under the Page Setup tabs.

Step 6:
Click the OK button.

Section 55: Headers and Footers

Another thing you can do with an Excel spreadsheet is to insert custom Headers and Footers. A Header is placed at the top of a spreadsheet and often contains titles, author names, and/or dates. The Footer, placed at the bottom of a sheet, usually contains page numbers. You do not have to worry about making space for your headers and footers, because they appear in the area set aside for the margins at the top and bottom of each page. Once you have set up a header or footer, it will appear on each page of your spreadsheet.

The Page Setup window has the Header and Footer options. When you are inserting a Header or Footer, it is usually best to complete the process in the Print Preview screen. The Print Preview screen allows you to view the header and footer just as it will appear on the printed page. If you have closed the Print Preview screen, open it now by clicking on the Office button, highlighting the PRINT option, and clicking the PRINT PREVIEW option.

Once the Print Preview screen is open, click the PAGE SETUP button located at the top of the screen. When the Page Setup window is displayed, click the HEADER/FOOTER tab.

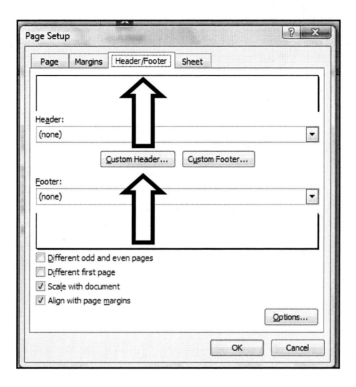

If you try to click in the Header or Footer box to type in information, nothing happens. You need to tell the computer what you are doing. Since this is the first time you will try to create a header, you need to click on the CUSTOM HEADER button located in the middle of the window. A new window will appear allowing you to enter the header information.

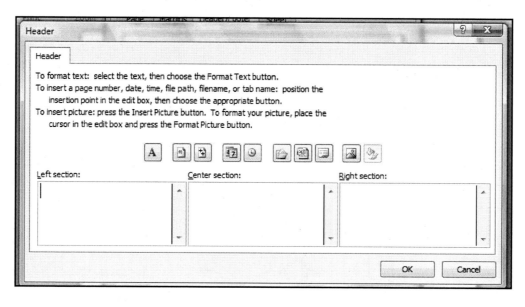

The Custom Header window is divided into three smaller input boxes. Each input box illustrates where in the margin the header information will be displayed. If you want the information to appear to the top right of your page, type in the input box labeled "Right Section." If you want the information in the center, type in the input box labeled "Center Section." If you want it on the left side of the paper, type in the input box labeled "Left Section." Type the information you want displayed in the top margin of the printed document.

For the example, you will add a title to your paper and will center it on the top of the page. Click your mouse in the "Center Section" box and type in the Heading: Monthly Budget. When you are finished typing, click the OK button. The custom header will appear in the header preview box located Page Setup window.

Inserting a Custom Header: Step by Step Instructions
1. **Click the OFFICE button.**
2. **Highlight the PRINT option.**
3. **Click the PRINT PREVIEW option.**
4. **Click the PAGE SETUP button.**
5. **Click the HEADER/FOOTER tab.**
6. **Click the CUSTOM HEADER button.**
7. **Click in the desired input box and type the information you want displayed in the header.**
8. **Click the OK button.**

Chapter 14: Printing!

Inserting a Custom Header: Visual Guide

Step 1:
Click the
OFFICE button.

Step 2:
Highlight the
PRINT option.

Step 3:
Click the PRINT
PREVIEW
option

Step 4:
Click the PAGE
SETUP button.

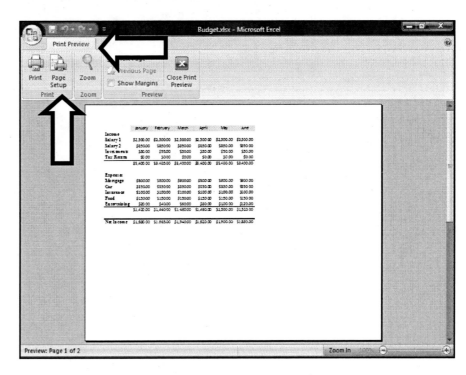

Step 5:
Click the
HEADER/
FOOTER tab.

Step 6:
Click the
CUSTOM
HEADER
button.

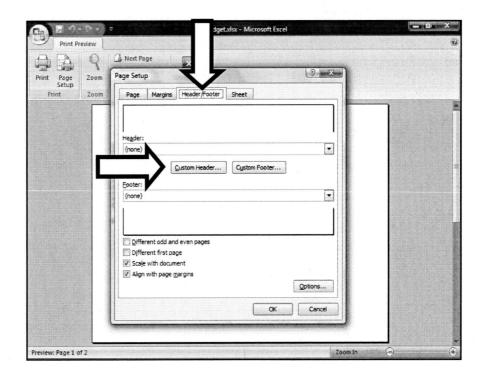

Step 7:
Click in the desired input box and type in the information you want displayed in the header.

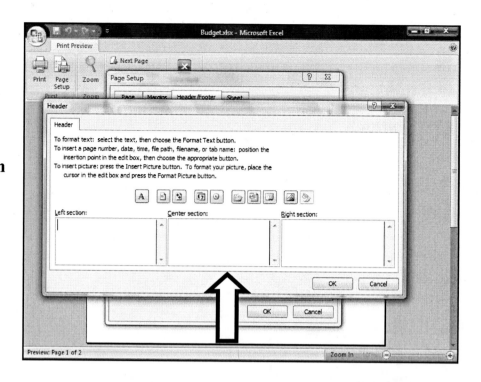

Step 8:
Click the OK button.

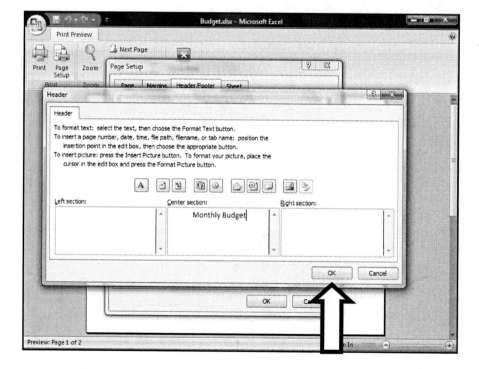

Chapter 14: Printing!

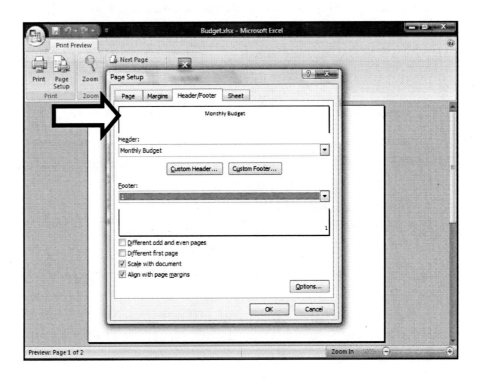

Custom Header will be displayed in the header preview area.

To add a footer to the page, click the CUSTOM FOOTER button. The Customer Footer window will open, with three separate sections just like the Customer Header window. You will add the page number to the bottom right corner of the page. Click the mouse in the "Right Section" input box.

If you look above the section input boxes, you will see a number of pictures/buttons. The buttons make up the Header/Footer Toolbar. Each button automatically inputs specific data.

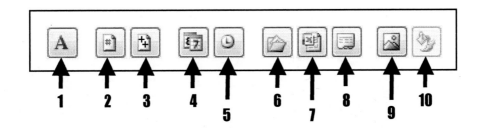

1. Font
2. Insert Page Number
3. Insert # of Total Pages
4. Insert Date
5. Insert Time

6. Insert File Path and Name
7. Insert File Name
8. Insert Worksheet Name
9. Insert Picture
10. Format Object

Chapter 14: Printing!

Instead of typing a page number, click the INSERT PAGE NUMBER button. Using the Insert Page Number button ensures that each printed page has the correct page number displayed in the footer.

Inserting a Custom Footer: Step by Step Instructions
1. **Click the OFFICE button.**
2. **Highlight the PRINT option.**
3. **Click the PRINT PREVIEW option.**
4. **Click the PAGE SETUP button.**
5. **Click the HEADER/FOOTER tab.**
6. **Click the CUSTOM FOOTER button.**
7. **Click in the desired input box, and either type in the information or use the available toolbar buttons to provide the information.**
8. **Click the OK button.**

Inserting a Custom Footer: Visual Guide

Steps 1 - 5: Completed in last example.

Step 6: Click the CUSTOM FOOTER button.

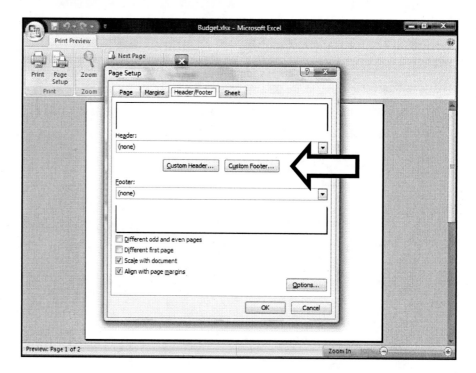

Step 7:
Click in the desired input box and type in the information you want displayed in the footer, or use the available toolbar buttons to provide the information.

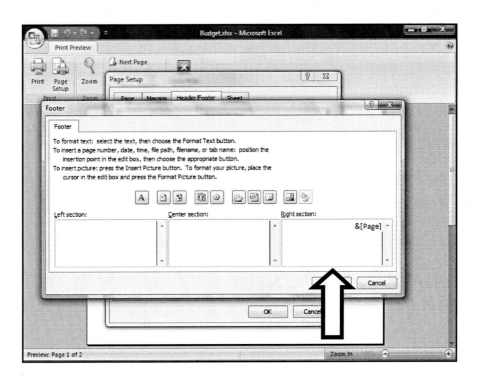

Step 8:
Click the OK button.

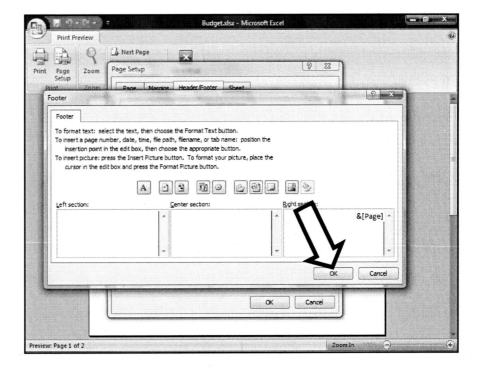

Custom Footer will be displayed in the footer preview area.

Click the OK button to close the Page Setup Window and return to the Print Preview screen.

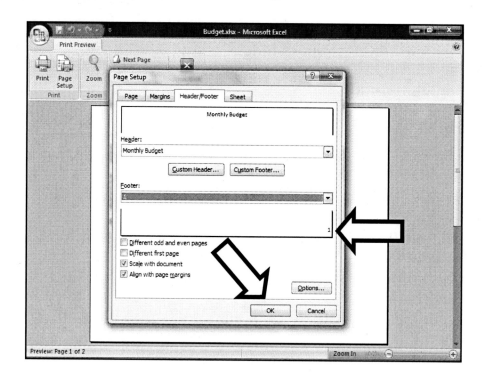

Once you are finished, click the OK button at the bottom of the Page Setup window. You will be returned to the Print Preview screen. Notice the custom header and footer are displayed on the print preview.

Print Preview screen.

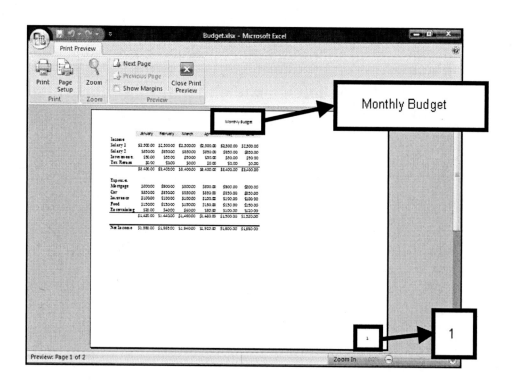

Chapter 14: Printing!

Section 56: The Printing Process

When you have completed your worksheet, you can print a paper copy if you have a printer connected to your computer. The PRINT option is located in the Office menu. The Office menu is located at the upper left side of the Microsoft Excel screen. Click your left mouse button on the OFFICE Button to open the menu. Slide your mouse arrow down the Office menu, and click on PRINT. The File menu will close and the Print screen will appear.

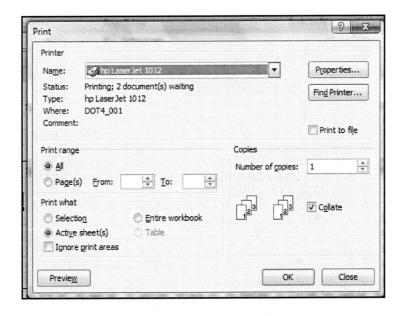

There are several important features on the print screen. At the top you should see the name of your printer. On the left hand side of the screen is the page range that will be printed. Page range refers to what pages of your document will print. For example, you can choose to print every page of your worksheet, one page, or just specific pages. The computer is set to automatically use the

Chapter 14: Printing!

ALL option, meaning it will print all of the pages in your worksheet. If you have created a 500-page worksheet, the ALL option will print all 500 pages.

If you do not want to print every page of your worksheet, you can choose another option by clicking on the little white circle next to the desired option. A successful click will place a small black dot in the white circle. The ACTIVE SHEET option prints only the worksheet on which your cursor (blinking line) is currently located. The print SELECTION option is ONLY available if you have highlighted a section of your worksheet. If you highlight a section and choose print SELECTION, only the highlighted text will print. This option is very handy when you want to conserve ink and only print specific sections of your worksheet. The ENTIRE WORKBOOK option prints all the contents of each worksheet which makes up the spreadsheet. The PAGES option lets you print specific page numbers. For example, if you want to print a few pages which are not in consecutive order, you can type in each page number separated by a comma (1,4,6,10). If you want to print a series of consecutive pages, type in the first page number followed by a dash and then the ending page number for the series (5-8). In this example, the computer would print pages 5,6,7, and 8.

The right side of the print screen contains the option NUMBER OF COPIES where you may select the number of times you want to print the selected pages. Excel's default is one copy. If you need more than one copy, you must change this option by clicking on the tiny UP and DOWN arrows located to the right of the white input box located to the right of NUMBER OF COPIES. Each click on the UP arrow increases the number of copies by 1; each click on the DOWN arrow decreases the number by 1.

Located just below the NUMBER OF COPIES is the COLLATE option. The Collate option can be either checked (turned on) OR unchecked (turned off). The Collate option is only used when you print multiple copies of a worksheet. When collate is checked, the computer prints one full copy of the worksheet, then prints the next full copy, and so on, with all pages in the proper sequence. If the Collate option is unchecked (off) the computer prints all the copies of page one, then all the copies of page two, then all the copies of page three, and so on. You then have to put the copies in order manually. As you can see, making certain the Collate option is checked can save you a lot of time and effort.

Chapter 14: Printing!

After you choose the number of copies and the page range you want, click on the OK button located on the lower right side of the print screen. The print screen will close, and your printer will make a paper copy of your worksheet.

Printing a File: Step by Step Instructions

1. Click the OFFICE button.
2. Click the PRINT option.
3. (Optional): Select the PAGE RANGE and NUMBER OF COPIES
4. Click the OK button.

Printing a File: Visual Guide

Step 1:
Click the
OFFICE
button.

Step 2:
Click the
PRINT option.

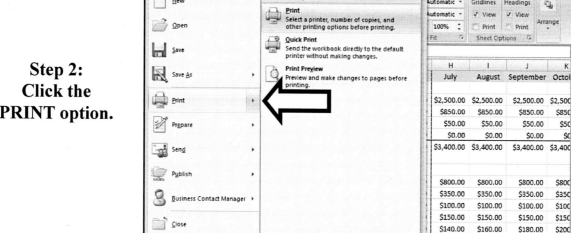

Step 3:
Optional:
Select the
PRINT
RANGE and
NUMBER of
Copies

Step 4:
Click the OK
button.

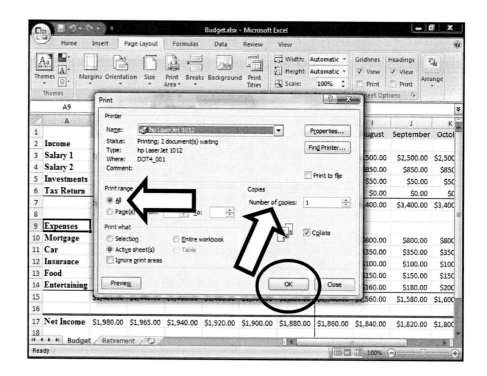

Chapter 14: Printing!

Congratulations! You have finished the course!
Save your spreadsheet. Then click the X in the upper right corner of the screen to close Microsoft Excel.

Remember that Microsoft Excel is simply a tool for you to use to record and calculate data. Like any other tool, it takes patience and practice to learn to use it proficiently. Please take time to review and practice the material. Once you are comfortable using Excel, you will realize what a great program it is and will be amazed how often you use it and how much fun it is to complete tasks quickly and easily.

We hope you enjoyed the material found in this book as much as we enjoyed writing it.

Keep on computing!

Index!

Index!

Index!

Appendix!

Thank you for using the Web Wise Seniors' Basic Excel Computer book. We hope you enjoyed learning with us. Please let us know what you think of the book. If you found it easy to use and enjoyed the learning experience, please tell your family and friends.

Feel free to send your comments and feedback
to us at the following address:

Web Wise Seniors, Inc.
305 Woodstock Rd.
Eastlake, Ohio 44095

Or E-mail us at
Larry@WebWiseSeniors.com

Thank You!

Appendix!

Web Wise Seniors is Proud to Present...
The "for Beginners" Series

	Title	Subtitle	ISBN #
Book	Basic Computers for Beginners	Windows XP	1-933404-45-0
Book	Basic Computers for Beginners	Windows Vista	1-933404-46-9
Book	Basic Internet for Beginners	Internet Explorer 7	1-933404-47-7
Book	Basic Email for Beginners		1-933404-48-5
Book	Microsoft Word 2007 for Beginners	Microsoft Word 2007	1-933404-49-3
Book	Microsoft Excel 2007 for Beginners	Microsoft Excel 2007	1-933404-50-7
Book	Microsoft Word for Beginners	Microsoft Word 2003	1-933404-51-5
Book	Microsoft Excel for Beginners	Microsoft Word 2003	1-933404-52-3
Large Print Books are $34.95 each.			

To Order Call Toll Free: 1-866-232-7032

	Title	Subtitle	ISBN #
Windows Vista Series			
DVD	Basic Computers Part 1 VISTA	Introduction for Beginners	1-933404-54-X
DVD	Basic Computers Part 2 VISTA	Essentials of the Keyboard	1-933404-55-8
DVD	Basic Computers Part 3 VISTA	Filing Fundamentals	1-933404-56-6
DVD	Basic Computers Part 4 VISTA	Customizing Your Computer	1-933404-57-4
DVD	The Internet Part 1 IE7	Searching the Internet	1-933404-58-2
DVD	The Internet Part 2 IE7	Better Searching Techniques	1-933404-59-0
DVD	E-mail Part 1 Windows Mail	The Basics	1-933404-60-4
DVD	E-mail Part 1 Windows Mail	Advanced Techniques	1-933404-61-2
Windows XP Series			
DVD	Basic Computers Part 1 XP	Introduction for Beginners	1-933404-74-4
DVD	Basic Computers Part 2 XP	Essentials of the Keyboard	1-933404-75-2
DVD	Basic Computers Part 3 XP	Filing Fundamentals	1-933404-76-0
DVD	Basic Computers Part 4 XP	Customizing Your Computer	1-933404-77-9
DVD	The Internet Part 1 IE6	Searching the Internet	1-933404-78-7
DVD	The Internet Part 2 IE6	Better Searching Techniques	1-933404-79-5
DVD	E-mail Part 1 Outlook Express	The Basics	1-933404-80-9
DVD	E-mail Part 2 Outlook Express	Advanced Techniques	1-933404-81-7

<u>Additional Titles on the Next Page</u>

Appendix!

Web Wise Seniors is Proud to Present...
The "for Beginners" Series

	Title	Subtitle	ISBN #
Microsoft Office 2007 Series			
DVD	Word 2007 Part 1	An Introduction to Word Processing	1-933404-62-0
DVD	Word 2007 Part 2	Essential Word Tools	1-933404-63-9
DVD	Excel 2007 Part 1	An Introduction to Spreadsheets	1-933404-64-7
DVD	Excel 2007 Part 2	Essential Tools	1-933404-65-5
Microsoft Office 2003 Series			
DVD	Word Part 1	An Introduction to Word Processing	1-933404-82-5
DVD	Word Part 2	Essential Word Tools	1-933404-83-3
DVD	Word Part 3	Bullets and Numbers	1-933404-84-1
DVD	Word Part 4	Mail Merge and More	1-933404-85-X
DVD	Excel Part 1	An Introduction to Spreadsheets	1-933404-86-8
DVD	Excel Part 2	Essential Tools	1-933404-87-6
DVD	PowerPoint Part 1	Creating a Presentation	1-933404-88-4
DVD	PowerPoint Part 2	Transitions and More	1-933404-89-2
DVD	Publisher Part 1	An Introduction to Publisher	1-933404-90-6
DVD	Publisher Part 2	Utilize the Power of Publisher	1-933404-91-4
DVD	Outlook Part 1	An Introduction to Outlook	1-933404-92-2
DVD	Outlook Part 2	The Tools of Outlook	1-933404-93-0
Spanish DVD Series			
DVD	Basic Computers XP Part 1	Introduction for Beginners	1-933404-67-1
DVD	Basic Computers Vista Part 1	Introduction for Beginners	1-933404-66-3
DVD	Basic Computers Vista Part 2	Essentials of the Keyboard	1-933404-70-1
DVD	Basic Computers Vista Part 3	Filing Fundamentals	1-933404-71-X
DVD	The Internet IE7 Part 1	Searching the Internet	1-933404-68-X
DVD	E-mail Windows Mail Part 1	The Basics	1-933404-69-8
DVD	Word 2007 Part 1	An Introduction to Word Processing	1-933404-72-8
DVD	Excel 2007 Part 1	An Introduction to Spreadsheets	1-933404-73-6
DVDs are $19.95 each.			
To Order Call Toll Free: 1-866-232-7032			

Appendix!

<u>Notes:</u>